THE BEATLES BOOK

THE BEATLES BOOK

Book design by Ed Caraeff
Cover design by Pearce Marchbank

Omnibus Press
London/New York/Sydney/Cologne

We greatly appreciate the generous co-operation for reprint of the following:
Paul McCartney Interview
Dedication to John Lennon
Used by permission of *Musician Player and Listener* Magazine
John Lennon Interview
Originally appeared in *Playboy* Magazine;
Copyright © 1980 by *Playboy*
What Went On: Lennon On Who Wrote What
© *Hit Parade* Magazine
A Charlton Publication
Poems by Joel, Nat and Lem Oppenheimer
originally appeared in *The Village Voice*

Photographs: Special thanks to **Dezo Hoffmann** for his major contribution, including rare early work
Also, thanks to Wide World and Pictorial Parade.
Special thanks to Sam Trust.

Exclusive distributors:
Book Sales Limited
78 Newman Street, London W1P 3LA, UK.
Music Sales Corporation
24 East 22nd Street, New York,
NY 10010, USA.
Omnibus Press
GPO Box 3304, Sydney,
NSW 2001, Australia.
To the Music Trade only:
Music Sales Limited
78 Newman Street, London W1P 3LA, UK.

ISBN 0.7119.0703.X
Order No. OP43439

Printed in Great Britain by
Scotprint Limited, Musselburgh, Scotland.

Great to have you with us

George Harrison

Ringo Starr

Paul McCartney

John Lennon

CONTENTS:

Musical History:

(1962-1970)

Once upon a time there were three little boys called John, George, and Paul, by name christened. They decided to get together because they were the getting together type. When they were together they wondered what for after all, what for? So all of a sudden they all grew guitars and formed a noise.

—"Being a Short Diversion on the Dubious Origins of Beatles, Translated from the John Lennon" *Mersey Beat* Vol 1, No 1.

According to singer-songwriter Don McLean in his hit song "American Pie," 1959 was the year "the music died." On February 2, Buddy Holly, Ritchie Valens, and J.P. Richardson a.k.a. the Big Bopper perished in a plane crash shortly after a concert performance in Clear Lake, Iowa. That same year, Chuck Berry was indicted on morals charges for which he would later be sent to jail and rock & roll wildman Jerry Lee Lewis became a pop persona non gratis for marrying his thirteen-year-old cousin the year before. And by 1959, Elvis Presley was already a year into his three-year gig with the U.S. Army.

Though no one realized it at the time, the music was busy being reborn that same year in the grimy seaport city of Liverpool, England. A few years earlier, John Lennon (born October 9, 1940) and James Paul McCartney (born June 18, 1942) first met at a Woolton Parish Church party where Lennon's band, the Quarrymen, were playing. By 1957, Lennon and McCartney were strumming their guitars and raising their adolescent voices in song as the Nurk Twins. Not long after, they were the Quarrymen again, this time with the addition of another young guitarist of Paul's acquaintance named George Harrison (born February 25, 1943) and an art school friend of John's, Stuart Sutcliffe, on bass.

1959 was the turning point. The boys all left school to pursue a full-time career in rock & roll, now billing the band as Johnny and the Moondogs and then as the Silver Beatles. By the time in 1960 that they hired Liverpool neighbor Pete Best as drummer and served their first apprenticeship on the club circuit and mean streets of Hamburg, Germany, they were simply called the Beatles.

Many people ask what are Beatles? Why? Beatles? Uh, Beatles, how did the name arrive? So we will tell you. It came in a vision—a man appeared on a flaming pie and said unto them "From this day on you are Beatles with an A." Thank you, Mister Man, they said, thanking him.

—John Lennon, *Mersey Beat* Vol 1, No 1.

Playing eight hours a night in low-rent Hamburg bistros like the Indra Club, the Kaiserkeller Club, and later the famous Star Club was good practice for a lot of young English bands in the early '60s. The Beatles were certainly no exception as proven by the 1977 double album *Live! at the Star Club*, unwittingly captured for posterity in 1962 (ironically Ringo Starr was subbing for Pete Best that night). In Hamburg, the Beatles not only toughened up their image with black leather jackets and long moppish hair, but they toughened and tightened up their sound with punch and wit.

The first Hamburg trip in 1960 was cut short when German authorities discovered young George to be underage and sent the band packing. Their '61 visit was more successful, resulting in their first recording session backing up a poor Presley imitation by the name of Tony Sheridan. But they got a chance to cut a few numbers of their own at the session, two of which became their first single. At that point, a Liverpool record store manager named Brian Epstein stepped into their lives when one Raymond Jones came into his store asking for a record called "My Bonnie" by the Beatles.

To say the rest is history is a gross understatement. Epstein groomed the Beatles for popular consumption—to the point of keeping John's marriage to Cynthia Powell in 1962 a secret—without dulling the edge of their sharp pop'n'rock sound. The group failed an audition for Decca Records in 1962, mixing early products of the Lennon-McCartney writing team like "Hello Little Girl" and "Love of the Loved" with such incongruous cover versions as Chuck Berry's "Memphis" and "Sheik of Araby." But after getting the cold shoulder from several other British record companies, the Beatles would pass a June 6 audition for producer George Martin of EMI's Parlophone label. A popular Liverpool drummer named Ringo Starr (born Richard Starkey July 7, 1940) would replace Pete Best and before the year was out they would start making a long series of hit records. Through a winning combination of musical talent, chops, and daring, Epstein's astute management, and almost impeccable timing, the Beatles would then go on to change the lives of generations of rock fans.

Oh, yeah, they would also change the course of pop music forever.

16-year-old John and 14-year-old Paul as the Quarrymen in 1956.

The first photograph ever taken of the Beatles as they were in Hamburg, Germany, 1961. From left to right: Pete Best, the original drummer; George; John; Paul; and Stu Sutcliffe, the original bass player.

The story of the Beatles, the English pop group, starts in Liverpool where school dropouts John Lennon, Paul McCartney, and George Harrison first started playing youth clubs and living room parties in 1958 as the Quarrymen.

The story of the Beatles, the world pop phenomenon, starts four years later and several hundred miles away in the bustling no-nonsense metropolis of London. After cutting their performing teeth in the seedy clubs of Hamburg, Germany's red light district, becoming a top draw at the Cavern Club back home, and being rejected by nearly every major record company in England, these four smartmouthed guitar-toting Liverpudlian punks—Lennon, McCartney, Harrison, and new drum recruit Ringo Starr—were about to turn an important corner in their young rock & roll lives.

The day was September 11, 1962. The place was the Spartan seclusion of EMI Studios where the Beatles were playing for a severely critical audience of one, producer George Martin. The song was "Love Me Do," the Beatles' debut single-to-be.

At an audition for Martin the previous June, the group ran through six selections from their stage set with charter drummer Pete Best—one sappy standard from their Hamburg days called "Besame Mucho," another Hamburg leftover originally popularized by Fats Waller called "Your Feet's Too Big," and four Lennon-McCartney originals, "Hello Little Girl" (one of the first songs John ever wrote), "Ask Me Why," "P.S. I Love You," and "Love Me Do." Martin signed the band to EMI's Parlophone label on the basis of that audition, although two other EMI chiefs had already given the group thumbs down. Martin had his doubts about the commercial chances of Lennon and McCartney's originals, but decided to go with "Love Me Do" as the first single because, as he said later, it was "the best of the bunch. It was John's harmonica which gave it its appeal."

Martin did not show the same enthusiasm for Ringo's drumming. In the time between the Parlophone audition and their first session, the group had fired Pete Best and hired Ringo away from Rory Storm's Hurricanes. Unwilling to take a chance on an unfamiliar drummer, Martin brought in veteran sessioneer Andy White to keep the beat on "Love Me Do," much to the band's chagrin. As a compromise, Martin agreed to record two versions of the song, one with Ringo and one with White on which Ringo would merely bang a tambourine. For the flip side "P.S. I Love You," White again played drums with Ringo demoted to shaking maracas.

It took the Beatles twenty takes to get "Love Me Do" down right and even then Parlophone could not make up its corporate mind which version to release. The Parlophone single issued October 5, 1962 featured Ringo. The version later heard on the *Please Please Me* album and on subsequent U.S. releases was the Andy White take (the Ringo version finally surfaced Stateside in 1980 on the *Rarities* LP). All that confusion and for such a simple song …

"You can't have anything simpler, yet more meaningful than 'love, love me do,'" Paul once said. "I think I slagged off school to write that one with John when we first started."

"Love Me Do," later described by McCartney as "our greatest philosophical song," peaked on the British charts at number 17. Not great, but not bad either.

The next single, "Please Please Me," coupled with "Ask Me Why," did much better, becoming their first number one record on March 2, 1963. Ironically, "Please Please Me" nearly didn't become a Beatles record at all. Still harboring reservations about the saleability of the band's own songs, George Martin lobbied for a song called "How Do You Do It," penned by British hit composer Mitch Murray, as their next single. Determined to stand by their originals, the group petulantly dragged their heels through take after take of "How Do You Do It" until Martin relented and suggested giving "Please Please Me" a go. Paul claims the tune was originally conceived as "a Roy Orbison-type thing," but admitted that it sounded like a hit after Martin suggested speeding up the tempo.

Barely three weeks after they topped the singles charts with "Please Please Me," the Beatles were also well on their way up the album charts with their first album, wisely titled after their recent hit. In addition to the four previously released singles sides, *Please Please Me* (issued by Parlophone on March 22) included ten tracks recorded in one day—the previous February 11—at a cost of less than $2000. Four of the songs were originals—"Misery," "I Saw Her Standing There," "There's a Place," and George Harrison's lead singing debut "Do You Wanna Know a Secret," which John claimed was inspired by a song in the Walt Disney movie *Snow White and the Seven Dwarfs* called "Wishing Well" (*Do you wanna know a secret?/Promise not to tell/You are standing by a wishing well*).

The other six tunes came from the four corners of popdom. Ringo got his first recorded vocal workout on the hot rock raver "Boys." "Anna" came from the soulful pen of R&B tunesmith Arthur Alexander and "Twist and Shout" was originally a hit for the Isley Brothers. The prolific team of Gerry Goffin and Carole King contributed "Chains," buoyed here by the band's effervescent harmonies, while the schmaltz quotient came at two with "A Taste of Honey" (another Hamburg leftover) and the Bacharach-David weeper "Baby It's You." In all, patchy but promising. And when it was hot, this record was hot. It hit number one May 4, the same day the Beatles' next single "From Me to You" topped the singles chart.

Released in Britain on April 12 and picked up in the States by Vee Jay Records for their first Yankee single, "From Me to You" was an "instant" classic in the literal sense of the word, inspired by a newspaper column titled "From Us to You" and knocked off in a few spare minutes by John and Paul while the band was on its first nationwide tour, playing second banana to British vocalist Helen Shapiro. Feeling it was too bluesy to be a hit, they hesitated recording the song until George Martin suggested adding a harmonica. The B-side "Thank You Girl" provided ebullient teen pop contrast, jacked up by brash group harmonies and the resonant clang of electric guitars.

With the release July 1 of "She Loves You" backed with "I'll Get You," the Beatles took one giant step to stardom. In nothing flat, they went from hometown heroes to Britain's hottest pop property since Cliff Richard started riding Elvis Presley's coattails. As befits a group with the biggest selling English single ever (an unbeaten record [pun intended] for almost fifteen years), the Beatles suddenly became concert headliners, actually dethroning top-billed Chris Montez on one tour. And before the end of 1963, the group would receive their first gold record for one million sales of "She Loves You," hold the top spot on the *Melody Maker* singles charts for seven weeks, cause a riot outside the London Palladium where they were making a live TV concert appearance, and finally receive the blessing of the stuffed shirts at a Royal Command Performance for the Queen Mother, Princess Margaret, and Lord Snowdon. Britain was in the grip of Beatle fever and records like "She Loves You" only made it worse.

Yeah, yeah, yeah, everyone knows "She Loves You" was a great, yeah, *immortal* pop song. That chorus —which was the Beatle fans' battle cry at airports, concerts, and outside hotels over the next two years—was John and Paul's idea, probably an unconscious fusion of R&B doo-wop harmonies and the Everly Brothers' twang they had perfected in their formative musical years. According to Paul, that jazzy major 6th chord at the end was George Harrison's idea. George Martin thought that last flourish was a bit corny ("Glenn Miller was doing it twenty years ago"), but he liked it and kept it in.

It's hard to believe, as Paul told *Musician Player and Listener* in a 1980 interview, that in its first week "She Loves You" was slammed in some quarters as "the worst song the Beatles had ever thought of doing." In fact, more than any Beatle recording up to that point, "She Loves You" was and remains the original Beatle sound in three-minute microcosm, a perfect miniaturization of the sound soon to shake the world.

In addition to the "o-o-o-h"'s and "yeah"'s, "She Loves You" captured in raw rock & roll fidelity Ringo's hydraulic drumming (stopping on a dime for those flashy fills), George's Duane Eddy-cum-Chuck Berry riffing, John's emphatic strum, and Paul's pumping bass—all boosted in a hot volcanic mix that would be often imitated but rarely duplicated. With "She Loves You," the Beatles dug up American rock roots, cultured them with distinctly British class, and harvested hit after hit.

With Beatlemania at fever pitch, Parlophone kept their ball rolling with the November 23 release in Britain of *With The Beatles*, a new album of fourteen songs recorded in a single day, the previous July 15. The album was later dissected for U.S. release as *Meet the Beatles* and *The Beatles' Second Album*. And only a week after that, the company released with plenty of fanfare a new single "I Want to Hold Your Hand" backed with "This Boy", subtitled "Ringo's Theme" although John and Paul did the crooning.

1963 had already been a banner year for the Beatles and even the intelligentsia began to sit up and take notice. In the *London Times*, critic William Mann cited Lennon and McCartney as "the outstanding English composers" of the year, saying lots of flattering things about their "chains of pandiatonic clusters," "flat submediant key switches," and the "Aeolian cadence" of "Not a Second Time" which Mann likened to the chord progression that ends Mahler's *Songs of the Earth*. The Beatles were no longer just cutting rock & roll corn for the kiddies. With "Please Please Me," "From Me to You," and "She Loves You," they had fired pop music shots that were heard all over England.

The next shot, "I Want to Hold Your Hand," would be heard 'round the world.

1964

In 1975, *Life* magazine published a list titled "The 100 Events That Shaped America." The arrival of the Beatles on U.S. Shores came in at number 96.

Looking back at wild, wonderfully wacky era ushered in by the release January 13 by Capitol of "I Want to Hold Your Hand" coupled with "I Saw Her Standing There," their appearances on *The Ed Sullivan Show* February 9 and 16, and the unprecedented radio reaction to their records, it is hard to believe the Beatles were only the 96th most important thing to ever happen to this country and its kids. In 1964, they were number one at everything else.

By New Year's Day, America was in a serious funk. The civil rights movement was opening the country's deep racial wounds, causing tempers to flare and blood to flow. A police action in Southeast Asia was quickly escalating into a war nobody would really *want* to fight.

And in a moment of what must have been cosmic irony, the Beatles released their second English album *With The Beatles* on November 22, 1963, the same day President John F. Kennedy was assassinated in Dallas, Texas. The torch, as it turned out, was passed from one youthful leader to four new ones.

If nothing else, the Beatles were good for what ailed America come 1964. Their music was full of *joie de vivre*. They were young, visually appealing, intelligent, and wickedly funny (cut to a Dublin press conference in 1964—"How do you find America?" "Turn left at Greenland."). They also brought American rock & roll out of the doldrums brought on by pop wimps PG-rated Elvis clones like Fabian and Frankie Avalon.

The Beatles ball first started rolling in America December 29, 1963 when WMCA in New York debuted their latest U.K. single "I Want to Hold Your Hand" on U.S. radio. On January 3, TV talk show host Jack Paar gave the country its first look at the Beatles in a videotape of the group performing "She Loves You" in concert, complete with delirious, screaming, crying, hysterical teenage girls. Many critics proclaimed the performance anti-climactic and one pundit at the *New York Times* sniffed that Beatlemania would never catch on. "On this side of the Atlantic, it is dated stuff."

What the press snobs were not counting on was the surprisingly articulate, unbridled adolescent joy of Beatles music. With "I Want to Hold Your Hand," John and Paul added a few new wrinkles to the rousing "She Loves You" sound with some clever time signature twists and a one-octave vocal leap on the word "hand" that sounded so wild and alive it seemed the singer was about to grab something other than her hand. But the song was written innocently enough. John and Paul polished it off while sitting in the basement den of McCartney girlfriend Jane Asher's house.

With the Ed Sullivan appearances, all hell broke loose. But it remains a testament to the five-star quality and explosive impact of their *music* that when the group first arrived in America at New York's Kennedy Airport February 7, representatives for Capitol Records were there to greet them with two gold records for "I Want to Hold Your Hand" and their debut American album *Meet The Beatles*.

And where Beatles fans went, the marketing men were sure to follow. What self-respecting Beatle fan could bear to be without the latest fan magazines so as not to miss a single shred of Fab Four news? Wearing Beatle buttons by the dozen was a sign to the world you were of the Beatle faith. Books, posters, bubblegum cards, lunchboxes, plastic guitars, even wallpaper—if there was a buck to be made, somebody made it off the Beatles. Besides, for those unlucky enough not to see John, Paul, George, and Ringo in concert (they played a total of 34 U.S. concert performances that year), Beatle souvenirs and novelties were the next best thing to being there—except for records.

For as hard as they tried, the Madison Avenue hypesters simply could not match the sheer volume of music released under the Beatles' name that year. Capitol alone issued no less than four albums *Meet The Beatles, The Beatles' Second Album, Something New, Beatles '65*, a documentary LP, seven singles, and one four-track EP. Labels like Vee-Jay, Tollie, and Swan which had licensed early Beatle waxings (MGM and Atco even dug up the old Tony Sheridan sides cut in Germany) flooded the market with their own releases, sometimes packaging and repackaging the same material with different covers. United Artists released the soundtrack to the group's first feature film *A Hard Day's Night*. Then there were the countless cover versions of Beatle tunes, orchestral recordings muzak-style, novelty records, and even interview LPs.

Still, fans could not seem to get enough of the Beatles. On April 4, the Beatles set a still unbeaten chart record by holding down the number one, two, three, four, and five spots on *Billboard*'s singles charts with "Can't Buy Me Love," "Twist and Shout," "She Loves You," "I Want to Hold Your Hand," and "Please Please Me" respectively. By then, *Meet The Beatles* and Vee-Jay's *Introducing the Beatles* (an abridged version of the U.K. *Please Please Me* LP) had already nailed down the top two slots on the album charts for six weeks running and would do so for three more.

In England, Parlophone continued to release singles and albums at a steady pace and in a rather orderly manner, as George Martin explains: "We never used to take singles off albums. We used to make them separate from each other. And we reckoned it was cheating if we put a single on an album."

Capitol in America had no compunctions about dissecting British albums like *With The Beatles* and *Beatles For Sale* for Stateside consumption, slapping on singles and B-sides, but usually only putting ten to twelve tracks per album (compared to the British fourteen-track LPs) in order to get the most albums out of the fewest songs. Fans were buying anything Beatle at the time, so no one was really counting. Yet Capitol's haphazard release program often confuses the chronology of the Beatles' nevertheless rapid maturation as songwriters, musicians, and trendsetters.

Meet The Beatles, of course, was the start of *our* beautiful friendship with the fabulous foursome. Capitol thoughtfully led off the album with "I Want to Hold Your Hand" and "I Saw Her Standing There" just in case there was someone out there who had not yet bought the single. "This Boy"—the one with the pandiatonic clusters, according to the *London Times*—was the English flip to "I Want to Hold Your Hand." The other nine numbers were all plundered from *With The Beatles*.

A variation on the "yeah yeah yeah"'s in "She Loves You" showed up in "It Won't Be Long," an early Lennon number with ricocheting "yeah"'s in the chorus. No doubt high school music majors noticed those Aeolian cadences in "Not a Second Time" while English teachers would have been surprised to hear that McCartney originally wrote the words to "All My Loving"—the first Beatles song to be extensively covered by

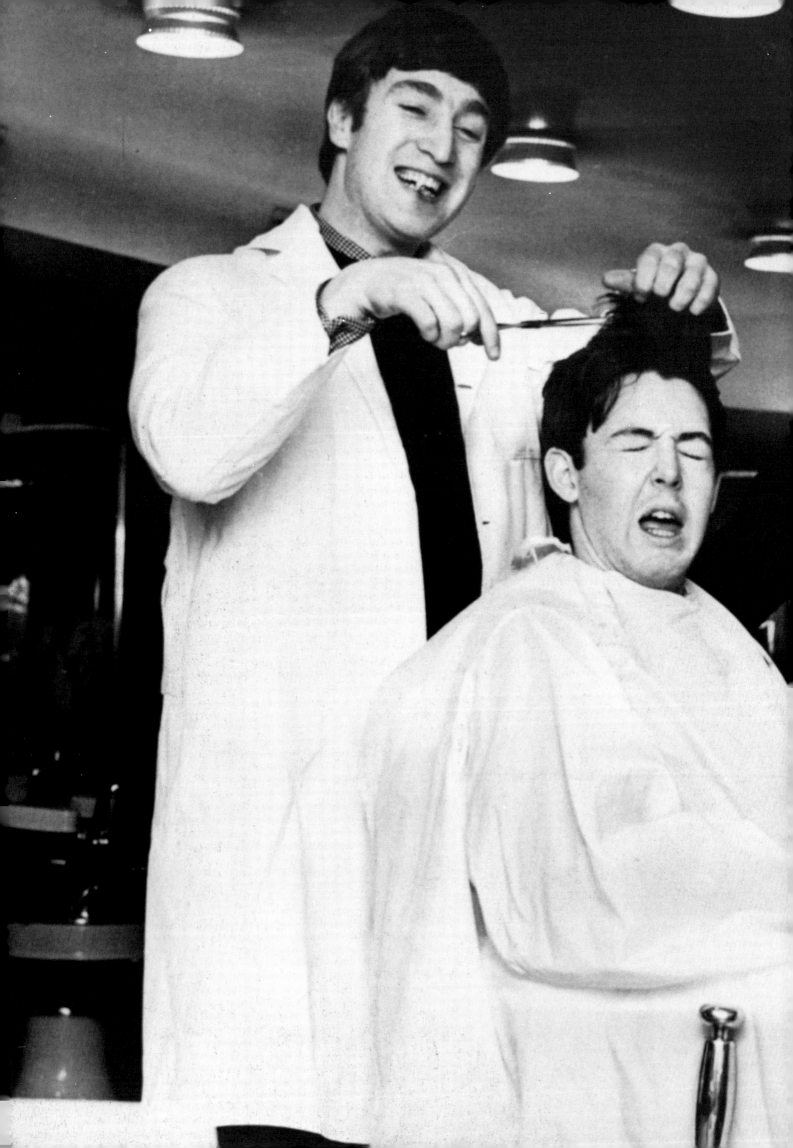

other artists—as what he called "a bit of poetry" and added the music later. Paul took a turn on piano and John blew some of his trademark wheezy harmonica on "Little Child," George made his songwriting debut with "Don't Bother Me" (also taking vocal honors while Paul played claves, John the tambourine, and Ringo the bongos), and everyone sounded a little rough on "Hold Me Tight," done in one take.

The album's one concession to the Mom-and-Pop crowd was a weepy cover of "Til There Was You" (from *The Music Man*), but the boys made up for it with a punky romp through "I Wanna Be Your Man" (Ringo on lead throat), originally written by Lennon and McCartney for the Rolling Stones. The story goes that Stones manager Andrew Loog Oldham was strolling down a London street when he was offered a ride by a passing limo with the Fab Two inside. When Oldham mentioned that the Stones were desperate for some hit tunes, Lennon said "We've a couple of spare songs we just finished that are more up their street than ours." They drove to a club where the Stones were rehearsing, ran through one tune, John and Paul stepped into a back room for ten minutes to tidy up the middle eight bars, and the Stones had their first big hit, "I Wanna Be Your Man."

And just for the record, "All I've Got to Do" checked in on Side One, song four.

"Can't Buy Me Love," the Beatles' second Capitol single, was a hit before it was even released. Written in February by John and Paul in Miami on their way to tape an Ed Sullivan appearance, the record (backed with "You Can't Do That") had advance orders of over 1.5 million and when it finally was released March 16, "Can't Buy Me Love" took only two weeks to make number one (it stayed there until May 2).

George Martin has noted that "Can't Buy Me Love" was a significant departure in arranging for the group, an indication of their growing sophistication as songwriters despite their lack of musical training and inability to actually read music. Most of Lennon and McCartney's songs had been written verse-chorus-verse-chorus-break-verse-chorus. Martin did some fine tuning here and there. But with "Can't Buy Me Love," he suggested that for a catchy introduction, the band start with the chorus instead of a verse. It worked like a charm, which may or may not have had something to do with the fact that it was recorded on February 25, George Harrison's birthday.

"Can't Buy Me Love" did not show up on *The Beatles' Second Album*, which hit the streets April 10. "You Can't Do That"—John Lennon's attempt "at being Wilson Pickett"—did, along with ten other odds and ends stitched together by Capitol like some kind of long-playing hi-fidelity Frankenstein. The revved-up covers of Chuck Berry's "Roll Over Beethoven," "Money," "Devil in Her Heart," and the Miracles' more sultry "You Really Got a Hold on Me" all came via *With The Beatles*. "Thank You Girl" was the U.K. flip of "From Me to You," "She Loves You" and "I'll Get You" already appeared together as a single in the States

on the Swan label. The Beatles' own version of "I Call Your Name" made its debut here although it had already been released in Britain as the B-side of a Billy J. Kramer single (it would later be a hit for the Mamas and the Papas). That song, together with the remake here of Little Richard's "Long Tall Sally" were recorded in late February for an EP to be issued in Britain the coming June.

The next official Beatles release in America was not a record but a book of hot-wired prose by John Lennon entitled *John Lennon In His Own Write*. The best description of Lennon's weird way with words as captured here and later in *A Spaniard in the Works* came from McCartney in his daffy introduction to *In His Own Write*. "None of it has to make sense and if it seems funny then that's enough."

In addition to a surplus of crackling Lennon wit, *In His Own Write* included the phrase "a hard day's night" in a piece called "Sad Michael." Those four words would eventually become the title of the Beatles' first feature film, a hit song, and hit soundtrack album in that order. Directed by Richard Lester and written by a Liverpool writer, the late Alun Owen, *A Hard Day's Night* was—to borrow a phrase—a day in the life of the Beatles. From a commercial point of view, it was ostensibly a full-length feature excuse for the boys to play a few new songs and romp across the big screen in their own uninhibited inimitable style. The one-two punch of Lester's quick-paced *cinema verite* style and the Beatles' own natural personal charm scored a knockout at the box office, a victory made even sweeter since the film cost only $600,000 to produce.

The title song was the first tune Lennon and McCartney ever wrote for a specific title and the band won a Grammy that year for Best Vocal Performance by a Group for their troubles (they also scored in the Best New Artist category). Not bad for a song written, arranged, rehearsed, and recorded in just over 24 hours.

Needless to say, "A Hard Day's Night" kicked off the United Artists soundtrack album. "Can't Buy Me Love" finally showed up on the LP here as well. Aside from the schmaltzy instrumental arrangements of "Ringo's Theme (This Boy)," "I Should Have Known Better" (the group's take backed the "A Hard Day's Night" Capitol 45), "And I Love Her," and "A Hard Day's Night," the record featured six other Lennon-McCartney originals making their bows. George Harrison played lead microphone on "I'm Happy Just to Dance With You" and was responsible for the jazzy acoustic guitar break on "And I Love Her." He also played bongos and claves on the tune with Ringo, but the real star of that song was Paul, who was beginning to make a name for himself as a writer of classy romantic pop ballads (in all fairness, John wrote the middle eight bars of that one).

"I'll Cry Instead" never made it into the film— Richard Lester didn't like it. Lennon would later say the line "a chip on my shoulder that's bigger than my feet" was an accurate summation of his personality.

The soundtrack to *A Hard Day's Night* spent August, September, and October at the top of the *Billboard* album chart. Ironically, the number two LP was the Beatles' third Capitol longplayer *Something New*, which was false advertising. "She Loves You" turned up in a German language version; five of the songs were culled from the film soundtrack. The covers of "Slow Down" (a Larry Williams raver) and Carl Perkins' "Matchbox" (Ringo at the mike) had been cut last February at the same sessions as "Long Tall Sally" and "I Call Your Name." Only "Things We Said Today," "Any Time at All," and "When I Get Home" were relatively new, recorded the previous June 1, 2, and 3.

For Capitol single number seven, the band cranked up the guitars and McCartney wailed "Long Tall Sally"-style on his bust-out rocker "She's a Woman." From the guitar feedback drone (accidental, by the way) opening the song to the faint sound of barking dogs at the fade, "I Feel Fine" was only a hint of the guitar experimentation to be taken up over the next few years by the Who's Pete Townshend, Jeff Beck and Jimmy Page of the Yardbirds, and a psychedelicized black man named Jimi Hendrix. Lennon claimed in the 1980 *Playboy* interview it was the first electric guitar feedback ever recorded.

Both songs hit twelve-inch vinyl as part of *Beatles '65*, actually released in the waning days of '64. With the exception of "I'll Be Back" (cut at the same June sessions as the three "new" tunes on *Something New*), the eleven tracks here were recorded in late September and October. Ringo took the lead vocal on "Honey Don't," one of two Carl Perkins numbers on the album (John handled the other, "Everybody's Trying to Be My Baby"). John, Paul, and George Martin all bashed away at the same piano for Chuck Berry's "Rock & Roll Music," while the rather wimped-out melodramatic "Mr. Moonlight" found McCartney at the Hammond organ, George keeping the beat on an African drum, and Ringo adding percussive flourishes on bongos. An interesting approach maybe, but they still sounded like lounge lizards on this one.

"Baby's in Black" was an interesting try at a bluesy waltz, marked by the trademark Lennon-McCartney harmonies, but the dark horse of this collection was Lennon's "I'm a Loser," this one an uptempo rock & roll shade of folk-blues with a blast of Dylanesque harmonica revealing the growing influence of the young American folkie-protest bard on the group. Commenting on the song in that same Playboy interview, Lennon said "Part of me thinks that I'm a loser and the other part of me thinks I'm God almighty."

By the other end of 1964, most American teenagers figured that if the Beatles were not God incarnate, they certainly knew a lot about working miracles.

1965

If 1964 was a very good year for the Beatles, then 1965 would turn out to be even better. They certainly got off to a good start with eight albums on the charts. "Eight Days a Week" b/w "I Don't Want to Spoil the Party" (the latter a personal fave of John's) came out February 15, only four days after Ringo said "I do" to the former Maureen Cox. While the group was busy shooting their second feature film *Help!* and recording new numbers for the soundtrack, Capitol continued to obey the laws of supply and demand by releasing *The Early Beatles*, a compilation of tracks from the U.K. *Please Please Me* LP, songs already released to death the previous year by Vee-Jay.

The first taste of the *Help!* tunes was served April 19 with the single "Ticket to Ride," a flamboyant prototype of the heavy metal sound-to-come (Vanilla Fudge took the song to its logical conclusion in 1967 with their sonic sludge version). Also noteworthy is that the Capitol single bore the legend "from the United Artists release *Eight Arms to Hold You*"—the original title of *Help!*. The flip, "Yes It Is," would later turn up on *Beatles VI*.

June 12 was a big day in the Beatles' lives because that was the day Queen Elizabeth announced each of the boys could be awarded an MBE, better known as Member of the British Empire award. Old war heroes were outraged (did they feel any better when John returned his in 1969 as a protest?). The band took it in stride. John actually took his under the influence of marijuana—years later, he would admit he got high in the bathroom before the official (October 26th) presentation.

Capitol celebrated the event two days later with the release of *Beatles VI*. Of the new numbers, George Harrison's "You Like Me Too Much" featured John on electric piano and Paul and George Martin at the same Steinway. "Bad Boy" and "Dizzy Miss Lizzie" were copped from R&B songwriter Larry Williams' catalogue and "Tell Me What You See" (Lennon-McCartney) found Paul at the electric 88's. All four were cut May 10 and 11.

With the exception of "Yes It Is," the other recordings were pulled from *Beatles For Sale*. For "Every Little Thing," an effervescent number sounding not a little like what the high harmonic Byrds were doing in Southern California, Ringo worked out on tympani, settling for a packing case to keep the beat on in Buddy Holly's "Words of Love."

Pop royalty mixed with the real thing at the July 29 premiere in London of *Help!*, again directed by Richard Lester. More great tunes and more great fun, *Help!* was really contrived slapstick compared to the gritty tongue-in-cheek documentary approach of *A Hard Day's Night*. Paul would later say it was "fun basically as an idea for a film" but was "a bit wrong for us. We were sort of guest stars." For John, "it was like having clams in a movie about frogs."

The single "Help" and "I'm Down" preceded the U.S. release of the *Help!* album by one month. The latter finally appeared on an album with the 1976 *Rock 'N'*

Roll Music compilation. In its review of that album, *Rolling Stone* magazine described "I'm Down" as "all Paul, his best Little Richard vocal plus George's electric metal guitar and astonishingly rough drumming from Ringo."

"Help," though as bright and commercial (if not more so) as all the preceding Beatles singles, was made of more serious stuff as Lennon explained in the 1980 *Playboy* interview. "I was actually crying out for help... It was my fat Elvis period. You see the movie: He—I—is very fat, very insecure, and he's completely lost himself. And I am singing about when I was so much younger and all the rest, looking back at how easy it was... I *was* crying out for help."

Bob Dylan made no guest appearances on that record, yet he was certainly there in spirit. In Anthony Scaduto's biography, Dylan acknowledged the Beatles' sound and success inspired him to go electric—"They were doing things nobody was doing. Their chords were outrageous, just outrageous, and their harmonies made it all valid."

Dylan's songs and their electric treatment by the Byrds (once dubbed "the American Beatles" by Harrison) in turn forced the Beatles to take a closer look at their words as well as music. Although Dylan's influence came through loud and clear on "Help," it was even more blatant on the folksy "You've Got to Hide Your Love Away" from the *Help!* soundtrack, written by Lennon in what he called "my Dylan days." Note, however, that the Beatles used flutes where Lennon's Dylan-like harmonica should have been. The English folkies Silkie had a hit with the song later that year.

Released August 13, the *Help!* album contained a few more gems amid the orchestral dross. George chimed in with "I Need You," written on location in the Bahamas. John took a turn at the electric piano for "The Night Before" while McCartney made a rare appearance on lead guitar for "Another Girl." Last but not least was "You're Gonna Lose That Girl."

Two days after the release of the *Help!* album, the Beatles started a new American tour with a show before their biggest audience to date—55,600 fans at New York's Shea Stadium. Promoter Sid Bernstein claimed that his $304,000 gross was the biggest in show biz history and at the time he was probably right. The group were well paid, however. Brian Epstein negotiated a deal netting the group $160,000, which turned out to be one hundred dollars for every *second* they were on stage.

For all the "biggest" this, "best" that, and number ones, "Yesterday"—issued by Capitol in September with Ringo singing "Act Naturally" hoedown-style on the flip—was a genuine "first." It was the first solo record by a Beatle, written and recorded by McCartney with a string quartet although the group was credited on the label. It was the first time a Beatles record featured musicians who were not Beatles (not including George Martin's occasional appearances on piano). It was the first time Martin used orchestration on a Beatles record. And it was the first record the Beatles could not duplicate in concert (they did try a band version on the 1966 tour.)

"Yesterday" started life with the somewhat inappropriate title of "Scrambled Egg." He had the music for sometime—Paul rolled out of bed one morning and wrote it at a piano—and added the words later.

"I really reckon 'Yesterday' is probably my best," McCartney has been quoted as saying. "I like it not only because it was a big success, but because it was one of the most instinctive songs I've ever written. I was so proud of it. I felt it was an original tune ... the most complete thing I've ever written. It's very catchy without being sickly, too."

"Yesterday" holds the record for cover versions of a Beatles song. As of 1976, there were 75 recorded in America alone. Needless to say, the original recording went number one.

So did "We Can Work It Out" and "Day Tripper," released together as a single in early December and recorded barely a month before. But while it too was a charttopper, come New Year's Day 1966, *Rubber Soul* (issued by Capitol December 6) made everyone do a double take. The influence of the American folk-rock movement and Dylan in particular came through loud and clear. Acoustic guitars meshed with electrics into an organic fabric of sound highlighted by the crystalline Lennon-McCartney-Harrison harmonies and dotted with flashes of piano, organ, harmonium, a bullish "fuzz" bass, and—in its first appearance on a Beatles record—George Harrison's sitar.

Insensitive to the natural musical flow of the British fourteen-song *Rubber Soul*, Capitol saved the songs "Nowhere Man" and "What Goes On" (a Ringo special co-written with John and Paul) for an early '66 single. They also removed "Drive My Car" and George's "If I Needed Someone," replacing them with "I've Just Seen a Face" and "It's Only Love" from the U.K. *Help!*.

Even so, *Rubber Soul* was an embarrassment of riches and an experiment in more than just music. The title was Paul's idea, probably a pun on the idea of English soul. The cover photograph of the boys—all hair and suede and no smiles save for John's Mona Lisa-like smirk—ushered in a new era of hip in album packaging. Their popularity was certainly taken for granted since the name "Beatles" does not even appear on the cover (it does on the back).

Song-by-song: "I've Just Seen a Face" started out as a song entitled "Auntie Gin's Theme." For some reason, Paul once described "Norwegian Wood" as a "comedy song" although John originally wrote it as a song about a secret love affair, lyrically disguised so his wife Cynthia would be none the wiser. George overdubbed his sitar later because he still didn't have the hang of the instrument.

Paul played piano and roadie-confidante Mal Evans the Hammond organ on "You Won't See Me," followed by George's "Think For Yourself" with Paul's grumbling fuzz-tone bass. Of John's song "The Word,"

Paul once commented "to write a *good* song with just one note in it—like 'Long Tall Sally'—is really very hard. It's the kind of thing we've wanted to do for some time. We get near it in 'The Word.'"

The concepts of pain and pleasure — that one leads to another—is an underlying theme in "Girl." "Listen to John's breath on 'Girl,'" notes McCartney. "We asked the engineer to put it on treble, so you get this huge intake of breath and it sounds just like a percussion instrument."

Lennon contributed the middle eight bars to another "girl" song, but the credit for "Michelle" was all McCartney's. A fragile evocative ballad, "Michelle" won a Grammy in '66 for Best Song of the Year. "Wait," "Run For Your Life" (vaguely inspired by the old '50s rave-up "Baby Let's Play House"), and "I'm Looking Through You" (a rare performance on the organ by Ringo) led up to one of the Beatles' and John Lennon's true songwriting triumphs.

As poignant an autobiography as has ever been written, "In My Life" started out as a bus journey through his past. Lennon later rewrote it to include friends and lovers, with Paul helping out on the middle section. A classic with a capital C.

According to *Newsweek*, the Beatles blew away the pop competition with *Rubber Soul*. "The Beatles blend gospel, country music, baroque counterpoint, and even French popular ballads into a style that is wholly their own." The English weekly Melody Maker had their reservations, claiming the album was "not their best" and was even "monotonous." Even with the Beatles, there was no accounting for taste.

—David Fricke

Volume Two (1966-1970)

I think Rubber Soul, *really, was the first of the Beatles' albums which presented a new Beatles to the world. Up till then we had been making albums rather like a collection of singles. Now we were really beginning to think about albums as a bit of art on their own, as entities of their own. And* Rubber Soul *was the first to emerge that way.*

—George Martin

The next Beatles album to "emerge that way" would be *Revolver*, which hit American record stores August 8, 1966, the same day as the "Yellow Submarine"/"Eleanor Rigby" single. In between, however, came George Harrison's January 21 marriage to Patti Boyd, an album cover controversy, an anti-Beatle backlash concerning Lennon and a crack he made about Jesus Christ, and the start of the Beatles' last world tour. There were also a few more records.

The first would be "Nowhere Man" and "What Goes On," refugees from the British *Rubber Soul* coupled as a single and issued February 7. Penned by John, "Nowhere Man" signified the first serious departure from the boy-meets-girl storylines of Beatles songs. But the song has less to do with the social commentary of the post-*Revolver* era than it did with the simple fact that Lennon had just been trying to write a song and as he later said "nothing would come. I was cheesed off and went for a lie down, having given up. Then I thought of myself as a Nowhere Man—sitting in his nowhere land." The song's folkie shuffle no doubt had its roots in Dylan. But his arrogant whine would have played a poor second to the voices raised in fourteen-carat harmony by John, Paul, and George. Ringo got his licks in on the flip, co-writing "What Goes On" with John and Paul as well as singing it.

"Paperback Writer" and "Rain"—two more songs of experience, Paul's and John's respectively—appeared as a double A-side May 30, recorded the month before. The former probably came out of McCartney's frustrating experiences as the in-house flak for the group in the early days, creating mail campaigns and writing hype sheets. "Rain"'s hypnotic quality can be attributed to Lennon's tinkering with backward tape loops on his vocal track, although George's neo-Eastern riffing and Ringo's clever rhythmic punctuation should not be shortchanged.

Besides, John discovered the miracle of playing tapes backwards not in a moment of artistic genius but in a late-night stupor. At home one night, he put a rough mix of "Rain" on a tape recorder and listened to it over and over again—*something* did not sound right—until it hit him. He'd put the tape on backwards by accident. Nevertheless, he liked what he heard as did the band, who would employ reverse tape loops on future recordings. Not surprisingly, though, "Rain" only peaked at number 23 while the comparatively straightforward rocker "Paperback Writer" became the Beatles' twelfth number one single in the States.

In the "stranger than fiction" department, Capitol Records actually lost money on their next Beatles album *Yesterday... and Today*, another jigsaw compilation of singles, U.K. album leftovers, and newly recorded tracks yet to be released in Britain. The cover photograph of the group in bloodied butcher smocks cradling dismembered dolls and hunks of meat caused such a row among outraged disc jockeys and retailers who received advance copies of the album that Capitol was forced (despite John's protest that the shot was "as relevant as Vietnam") to junk 750,000 covers as well as piles of streamers and other promotional accessories at a cost of close to a quarter of a million dollars. (A few "butcher covers" did escape when lazy Capitol employees simply pasted the new cover—an innocuous shot of the band posed around a steamer trunk—over the offending photo, creating an instant collector's item.)

Of the *Yesterday ... and Today* tracks, "Nowhere Man," "What Goes On," George Harrison's "If I Needed Someone," and the campy raver "Drive My Car" came from the British *Rubber Soul*. McCartney singled out "Drive My Car" in a *Newsweek* interview as a "perfect example" of his songwriting collaborations with Lennon. Apparently, Paul first wrote the song with the key line *You can give me golden rings*. At the recording session, John dismissed the line as "crap" and together they came up with *You can drive my car*. Agreeing it was a significant improvement, Paul said "the idea of the girl being a bitch was the same but it made the key line better."

For John's song "I'm Only Sleeping," George fed his guitar breaks backwards into the final mix (the version of this song which later appeared on the U.K. *Revolver* had extra guitar sounds and the verses were rearranged). "Dr. Robert" was a sarcastic Lennon raver about a less-than-scrupulous physician and on "And Your Bird Can Sing," the band stripped down to two electric guitars, bass, and drums. Both songs later showed up on the English *Revolver* as well.

Recent singles padded out the rest of the album—"Yesterday," Ringo's cowboy workout "Act Naturally" (the last non-original to appear on a Beatles LP until "Maggie Mae"), "Day Tripper" with John slapping the tambourine, and "We Can Work It Out." Paul wrote the latter, but John (who played the harmonium) contributed the sadly prophetic line *Life is very short/and there's no time/For fussing and fighting, my friend.*

The dog days of August started with an unprecedented flap over remarks Lennon had made some months earlier in an interview with the London *Evening Standard*: "Christianity will go. It will go. It will vanish and shrink. I needn't argue about that. I'm right and I will be proved right. We are more popular than Jesus now. I don't know which will go first—rock & roll or Christianity. Jesus was all right, but his disciples were thick and ordinary."

When the American fan mag *Datebook* reprinted the remarks (out of context, by the way) shortly before the start of the Beatles' third and last American tour August 12, Lennon and the group became the targets of a backlash just as intense as the euphoria they sparked in 1964. A radio station in Birmingham, Alabama sponsored what was the first of many bonfires of Beatles records and memorabilia across the Bible Belt. Other radio stations in New York, Utah, Texas, and South Carolina joined the fray by banning Beatles records from the air. The outcry against John's "bigger than Jesus" crack was so great he swallowed his words in a public apology at a Chicago press conference the night before the first show.

The tour itself was a bit of a bumpy ride. At that same press conference, when asked if he had called the United States a racist country, McCartney replied in the affirmative. In Toronto, John proclaimed he was in favor of American draft resisters fleeing to Canada. The August 19 show in Memphis was picketed by the Ku Klux Klan, and in Los Angeles, the crowd rioted, forcing the band to escape in an armored car. The highlight of the tour was their second show at Shea Stadium August 23, naturally a sellout.

In the midst of all this arrived *Revolver*, accompanied by the single "Yellow Submarine" b/w "Eleanor Rigby." "Yellow Submarine" was as far out as the Beatles had yet dared to get. Paul wrote it as a kind of kiddie singalong, but the final result sounded like they recorded it in some musical playground of the mind. Among the sound effects used were clinking glasses, rags pushed around in a bucket of water, and bubbles blown through a straw. A military brass band blew a

few licks and an impromptu choir starring Patti Harrison, George Martin, Mal Evans and assorted members of the studio staff chimed in for the chorus, all topped off by Ringo's deadpan vocal.

"Eleanor Rigby" was and still is something else altogether. None of the Beatles actually played on the song, scored by Martin for four violins, two violas, and two cellos. McCartney later won a Grammy for his vocal performance on this tragic tale of urban desolation set in a dark forbidding city that could easily be a double for Liverpool.

The rest of *Revolver* was no less innovative. For "Got to Get You Into My Life," the band hired five of the best hornmen in British jazz—Ian Hamer, Les Condon, and Eddie Thornton on trumpets and Alan Branscombe and Peter Coe on tenor sax. Alan Civil's horn also drifted in and out of Paul's dreamy ballad "For No One." John claimed "For No One" to be one of his favorite Beatle songs while Paul has said "Here, There and Everywhere" (reportedly inspired by the Beach Boys' "God Only Knows") is one of his.

George trotted out all the Indian trappings, including guest tabla player Anil Bhagwat, for his obligatory sitar showcase "Love You To," one of three new Harrison numbers on the album. In "Taxman," he railed against the British tax laws eating up all but five percent of the group's income while Paul stepped out on lead guitar. McCartney also handled piano duties on George's "I Want to Tell You." George Martin took over the ivories for Paul's cheery "Good Day Sunshine."

The "she" in "She Said She Said" who said *I know what it's like to be dead* turned out to be actor Peter Fonda. But things got real strange come album's end with Lennon's spooky surrealist outing "Tomorrow Never Knows," originally dubbed "The Void." Unable to hire the one thousand chanting Tibetan monks he heard in his head, John settled for creating the illusion of same by playing tapes of voices, guitars, and miscellaneous sounds backward, forward, and at a variety of speeds. *Turn off your mind, lay down all thought, surrender to the void* he droned, drawing his inspiration from the Tibetan Book of the Dead. *Love is all and love is everyone.*

But it just goes to show you..."I was in Germany on tour just before *Revolver* came out. I started listening to the album and I got really down because *I thought the whole thing was out of tune.* Everyone had to reassure me it was okay."—Paul McCartney, *Musician Player and Listener*, 1980.

The Beatles closed an important chapter in their story when they played their last concert together August 29 at San Francisco's Candlestick Park. Taking well-deserved vacations, the Beatles temporarily went their own ways—John to Spain to star in Richard Lester's film *How I Won the War*, Paul to do his first film score for *The Family Way*, and George to further his studies in Indian religion, culture, and music. It was the end of an era, yet there was another one just around the corner.

1967

Welcome to "The Studio Years." Retired once and for all from live performances as a group (with the sole exception of the prankish *Let It Be* rooftop gig), the Beatles took up extended residence at Abbey Road to learn how to play a new instrument—the studio. They'd had plenty of practice on *Rubber Soul* and particularly *Revolver*, but the double A-side single "Penny Lane"/"Strawberry Fields Forever" was the first of what would be many virtuoso performances.

Recorded the previous December and released in America February 13, "Penny Lane" and "Strawberry Fields Forever" were among the first three tracks recorded for the album eventually to be called *Sgt. Pepper's Lonely Hearts Club Band*. The third was "When I'm Sixty-Four."

"When the new year came," recalled George Martin in a 1978 interview, "Brian [Epstein] said 'We do need another single' and I said 'We're working on this album at the moment and we've got three titles.' Brian said, 'We'll take two of them.' "

Taking one from column John and one from column Paul, they settled on "Strawberry Fields Forever" and "Penny Lane." The former, Martin continued, "wasn't any more experimental than 'Tomorrow Never Knows' on *Revolver*. 'Strawberry Fields' was very much John's way of expressing himself at the time. 'Penny Lane' was very much Paul's. We only had three to choose from and Paul much preferred 'Penny Lane' over 'Sixty-Four.' Wouldn't you?

"Ironically," he added, "the coupling of 'Strawberry Fields' and 'Penny Lane,' which I think is one of the best singles ever made, was the first Beatles record in England that didn't make number one. We had nine number one's up to that point from our start and the tenth record didn't make number one. It made number two. That's justice for you."

In addition to being one of the best—if not *the* best—pop singles of all time, "Penny Lane" and "Strawberry Fields Forever" was the official starting gun for rock musicians to seriously experiment with and beyond their medium. A fan of the high rippling trumpets in Bach's *Brandenburg Concerto*, Paul came up with the idea of the trumpet obligatos in "Penny Lane," humming the notes to George Martin who in turn transcribed them on paper for soloist Philip Jones. Paul and George Martin played piano, John beat a conga drum, and string bassist Frank Clark and David Mason on B flat piccolo trumpet completed the studio troupe here.

Just as "Penny Lane" took its name from a busy Liverpool street where Lennon grew up, "Strawberry Fields Forever" was named after a Liverpool house called Strawberry Fields where the young John attended garden parties with his neighborhood pals (the house, ironically, was located near a boy's reformatory). Musically, the song was a miracle of then-current studio technology. Lennon conceived the song as a slow, dreamy flashback, but the first take apparently turned out to be too rock & roll for his taste. After he wrote a new score in a different key and tempo, George Martin took the first half of the initial recording and spliced it together (on a variable control tape machine) to the second half of the new version, speeding up the latter by five percent to match the original key and tempo. Martin and the group also employed a startling array of instruments for the songs, including flutes, cellos, harpsichord, brass, an electric drum track, and mellotrons. But for all its innovations, "Strawberry Fields Forever" stands as a classic because, as Lennon said, it was one of his best and most honest songs ever.

The completed *Sgt. Pepper* showed up the following June (June 1 in England, the next day in the States). With the passing of time, *Sgt. Pepper* sounds more and more like a period piece, a soundtrack for turning on, tuning in, and dropping out. There is no question, nevertheless, that *Sgt. Pepper's Lonely Hearts Club Band* forced the world to look at and listen to pop music as a social force, not just adolescent confection. The cosmic counterculture based on peace, love, and rock & roll already had a head start on the West Coast, headquartered at the corner of Haight and Ashbury in San Francisco, but it was *Sgt. Pepper* that disseminated the psychedelic message to the masses.

It also set the standard for rock & roll-to-come. Consider the new tricks the Beatles pulled out of their

collective musical bag: folk, baroque, classical, and music hall flourishes; rhythms, keys, and tempos turned inside out and upside down; lyrics as poetry, even further removed from the hand-holding anthems of '64; an inspired assortment of makeshift studio effects; and a collection of instruments brand new to big beat music. Paul alone played bass, organ, piano, harpsichord, lead guitar, and comb-on-paper. George exerted even more of his Indian influence, and whole orchestras were called in for even bit parts. When you realize that today it takes the Eagles and Bruce Springsteen two to three years to cut albums and Fleetwood Mac blew a cool million on *Tusk* alone, it stands as a tribute to the striking immediacy as well as artistic worth of *Sgt. Pepper* that it only took four months and $100,000 to complete.

From the Burroughsian cut-and-paste way that George Martin spliced together the steam organ parts in "Being for the Benefit of Mr. Kite" to the extravagant packaging (lyrics printed on the back, Sgt. Pepper cutouts, the "band" cover photo), *Sgt. Pepper* was an album that demanded to be taken seriously and a new "serious" school of rock criticism epitomized by new over- and underground publications like *Crawdaddy* and *Rolling Stone* arose as a direct result.

Actually, the rather stodgy *Newsweek* hit *Pepper's* nail right on the head in its review: "*Sgt. Pepper* is such an organic work…a rollicking, probing language-and-sound vaudeville, which grafts skin from all three brows—high, middle, and low—into a pulsating collage about mid-century manners and madness."

Declared the first true rock concept album, *Sgt. Pepper* did not start out that way and the song "Sgt. Pepper's Lonely Hearts Club Band" only appeared halfway through the sessions. "It was spread over a long time," George Martin has said of the album. "The boys were very much into their psychedelic business and they weren't too aware of what was going on."

"I guess the thing really happened once we got started. It almost seemed to grow by itself, automatic writing. When I started editing it together, it just started to flow that way. I don't think it was any one person's planning or thought. We never sat down and said 'Let's make a conceptual record.'"

After the rousing "calling all ears" opener, the band introduces Billy Shears a.k.a. Ringo crooning "With a Little Help From My Friends," a song tailormade for him by Paul with a little help from his friend Lennon who added the line *What do you see when you turn out the light/I can't tell you but I know it's mine.*

There must also be some connection between the fact that the song was first titled "Badfinger Boogie" and barely two years later Paul would rechristen Apple Records signing the Iveys as Badfinger.

To this day, people still cannot believe—as Lennon claimed—"Lucy in the Sky with Diamonds" was inspired by his four-year-old son Julian's painting of a little girl in a black sky dotted with stars and not by Hippiedom's number one hallucinogen. Described by George Martin as an "aural Salvador Dali," Lennon came on more like a pop art cross between Peter Max and Lewis Carroll here with his *tangerine trees, marmalade skies, plasticene porters with looking glass ties.* Note the shift from 3/4 time on the verses to 4/4 at the chorus, a high contrast between the dream-like imagery in the lyrics and Lennon's basic rock & roll instincts. That heavy metal-like celeste sound was actually Paul overdubbing his bass with organ.

John Lennon had substitute drummer Jimmy Nicol—who stepped in for an ailing Ringo on a few European and Far East concert dates in '64—to thank for the key line in "Getting Better." During that tour, whenever asked how things were going, he usually replied "It's getting better." The Beatles' jack-of-all-jobs Mal Evans had a hand in writing "Fixing a Hole" with Paul but settled for payment instead of a songwriting credit.

Based on a London newspaper account of a girl who really did leave home, "She's Leaving Home" features but one Beatle—Paul in a remarkably melodramatic vocal performance. The string section was in fact arranged by Mike Leander. George Martin could not make the session because of a previous recording commitment to British pop thrush Cilla Black.

Martin nearly drove his engineers batty with his unorthodox approach to the circus calliope effects on John's "Being for the Benefit of Mr. Kite." In addition to a basic track featuring Lennon and Martin on organs and Mal Evans on bass harmonica, Martin instructed his studio staff to cut a tape of Victorian steam organ recordings into foot-long sections, fling them into the air, and reconstruct them at random, in addition to which the snippets were speeded up, slowed down, distorted, played backwards, and even dipped in a bottle of Coke. If the final result really sounds like a circus, the session surely must have looked like one.

Pepper's Side Two opened with George starring on sitar and vocal backed by musicians from the Indian Music Association on "Within You Without You." Harrison wrote the tune on a harmonium belonging to long-time Beatle friend Klaus Voorman (he also did *Revolver*'s black-and-white cover drawing). In scoring the tune, however, George Martin told the background string section to bend and slur their notes to blend with those of the Indians. The laughter at the end was meant to deflate the overwhelming spiritual seriousness of the song, but that did not stop rocker Stephen Stills from later carving the lyrics *With our love, with our love, we can save the world* on a stone in his garden.

"When I'm Sixty-Four"—the odd song out in the "Strawberry Fields Forever"/"Penny Lane" single saga—was penned by Paul on the occasion of his father's sixty-fourth birthday. Martin got that "tooty kind of sound" Paul wanted to accent the vaudevillian cut of the tune with two clarinets and a bass clarinet.

While the idea for "Lovely Rita" came to McCartney after someone informed him that parking meter women are called meter maids in America, Lennon titled "Good Morning Good Morning" after a television cornflakes commercial. For the latter, George Martin created his own *Animal House* band, overdubbing a score of sounds from the animal kingdom, from baying hounds to your basic farmyard oink. He was particularly pleased once he discovered he could segue a chicken clucking straight into the wailing guitar signalling the reprise of the *Sgt. Pepper* theme.

Over a decade after *Pepper*'s release, John Lennon's "A Day in the Life" remains *the* highpoint on an album of nothing but highpoints. *Newsweek* hailed it as "the Beatles' 'Waste Land,' a superb acheivement of their brilliant and startlingly effective popular art." And still the BBC banned it because of the line *I'd love to turn you on.*

George Martin described the session:

"John had a song called 'A Day in the Life' [inspired by separate newspaper accounts of a Guiness heir dying in a car crash and of 4000 potholes in the streets of Blackburn] and he couldn't think of how to get out of it. Paul said 'I've got a song'—which was quite different—and they said 'Okay, let's try that in the middle and see what happens.' 'But they don't really connect up. What do we do in between?' 'Well, let's just play twenty-four bars and we'll worry about that later.'

"And that was how we did it. We got twenty-four bars of Mal counting out the beat and we got an alarm clock [which can be heard on the record] on the side just in case we fell asleep. But what are we going to do eventually? He says, 'Well, we'll fill it up with a big orchestral sound. Let's have a symphony orchestra.' But I

said, 'What should I make them play?' 'They can just come in and busk it.' 'But you can't have eighteen musicians just come in and busk it!' "

But that is exactly what Martin had them do—to be more precise, forty-one musicians from the London Philharmonic sawing away, every man for himself. As for that last lingering piano chord which goes on for forty-two seconds, Martin said that was he, John, and Paul slamming down on three separate pianos at the same time—Paul hitting the top end of the chord, Martin the middle, and John the bottom—with each piano superamplified as to catch every last harmonic drop.

Sgt. Pepper's Lonely Hearts Club Band was enough to keep pop fans and critics occupied for months, even years. Yet a mere two months after its release, the Beatles hit the market with a new single coupling the anthemic singalong "All You Need is Love" and Lennon's "Baby You're a Rich Man," a cryptic self-interview in song on which he played an electronic keyboard called the clavioline and Rolling Stone Brian Jones blew away on oboe.

"All You Need is Love" had already been premiered on the British television show *Our World* to a global audience estimated at 700,000,000 through the miracle of satellites. Opening with the blare of trumpets playing the French national anthem and fading out to the strains of "Greensleeves" with a flash of "She Loves You" for good measure, "All You Need is Love" was the right song at just the right time, the perfect theme for the Summer of Love currently in progress. Rock & roll was the medium, love was the message, and the Beatles delivered it first class, with help from an all-star chorus featuring Stones Mick Jagger and Keith Richards, the Who's Keith Moon, Graham Nash, Jagger's girl Marianne Faithfull, Jane Asher, and Patti Harrison.

The sudden death August 27 of manager Brian Epstein at age 32 brought the Beatles crashing back to the material world. The group was in India learning the secrets of life according to the Maharishi Mahesh Yogi when they got the news. Returning immediately to London, the group found themselves forced to take a crash course in the secrets of life according to the music business. They refused to even consider a replacement, insisting as Paul succinctly put it "no one could possibly replace Brian."

Left to their own device, the Beatles set off on their first post-Epstein adventure, a one-hour film musical entitled *Magical Mystery Tour*. Mostly McCart-

John listens avidly to the Maharishi in 1967 as Ringo, with his wife Maureen and George look on.

ney's idea, *Magical Mystery Tour* was—on paper—a zany anarchic bus trip through a wigged-out English countryside starring a host of eccentric characters, the Beatles among them, in a kind of psychedelic Rolling Thunder Revue.

On record (a lavish double EP set in England, a full-length LP in America filled out with recent singles including the bouncy "Hello Goodbye"), *Magical Mystery Tour*'s six songs came off like half a *Pepper*, trying to cover the same expansive musical territory in only half the time. The title song, like the "Sgt. Pepper" theme, was like a commercial for the fun to follow and McCartney apparently sent Mal Evans out to hunt down some real mystery tour posters to give him some idea for the lyrics (Evans returned unsuccessful).

Both "The Fool on the Hill" and "Your Mother Should Know" were classic McCartney, the first a simple but poignant three-minute ballad with a sharp philosophical point and the second a reprise of the music hall clowning of "When I'm Sixty-Four" minus the latter's sugary but sincere expression of love. On "Flying," an eerie instrumental filler credited to all four Beatles, Lennon played the melody on a mellotron—an electronic keyboard with near-orchestral possibilities—as well as doing the backward tape loops in the coda with Ringo. George Harrison got a similar effect on "Blue Jay Way," an evocative adaption of his Indian ideas to a more Western arrangement with a cello and Hammond organ instead of sitar and tablas. The song, by the way, was written by George for former Beatles press agent Derek Taylor who was visiting Harrison at his house on Blue Jay Way in Los Angeles.

What "A Day in the Life" was to *Sgt. Pepper*, John's "I Am the Walrus" was to *Magical Mystery Tour*, a psychedelic centerpiece full of oblique Dylanesque wordplay and exotic sonic sensations. Not so much a song as an experience, "I Am the Walrus" was compiled from bits and pieces of incomplete Lennon songs hinged on the image of the Walrus in Lewis Carroll's poem "The Walrus and the Carpenter" in *Alice in Wonderland*. Lennon noted in the 1980 *Playboy* interview that he later discovered that in Carroll's poem the walrus was the bad guy, not the carpenter. "I should have said 'I am the carpenter.' But that wouldn't have been the same, would it?"

The sound of a police car, siren going full blast, racing by John's country home gave him the idea for the "Walrus" musical score. The siren-like sound of two alternating notes repeated throughout the track were the foundation upon which George Martin built a manic orchestral arrangement of cellos, violins, horns, and choir. Those voices floating in and out of the mix at the end came courtesy of the BBC, in fact a radio dramatization of Act V, Scene 6 of *King Lear*.

When the completed *Magical Mystery Tour* finally hit British television screens December 26, the film and its stars took a considerable beating at the hands of the press. Among the words used to describe the film were "witless rubbish," "lamentable," "a great big bore," "colossal conceit," and "tasteless nonsense." In retrospect, *Magical Mystery Tour*—as record or film—does not seem nearly as lame as the critics suggested. Naive maybe, amateurish probably, but certainly not the total artistic bomb they claimed. Still, it was not a great end to an otherwise generally triumphant year.

1968

The hippie dream of peace and love that looked like such a sure thing in 1967 burst like a bubble in 1968. Both Martin Luther King and Robert Kennedy lost their lives to separate assassins' bullets. Chicago erupted in blood and violence at the Democratic National Convention there. America stood waist deep in the rice paddies of Vietnam, fighting a war that did not so much separate the men from the boys as it did the hawks from the doves.

And that was just for starters. If the hippie was dead—the San Francisco freak community actually staged a mock burial—it was because it didn't look like he had much to live for.

The Beatles had their problems as well. Cynthia Lennon sued husband John for divorce as a result of the Beatle's blossoming romance with Japanese avant-gardist Yoko Ono. The Apple boutique the group had opened in London the previous December shuttered a few months later with a going-out-of-business sale that quickly turned into a free-for-all when the inventory was given away. The Beatles nevertheless founded Apple Corp., Ltd. as a corporate umbrella for all manner of multi-media activity (including records), although it soon became apparent that a lot of Beatles money was being wasted by people other than the Beatles. Finally, in a surprising reversal of their soapboxing on behalf of the Maharishi and transcendental meditation the year before, John, Paul, and Ringo all disavowed any further interest in enlightened Indian paths, leaving George to continue walking them alone.

But none of this stopped them from making records, and great ones at that. The first one of the year came out in England on the Ides of March (March 15) and that pairing of Paul's "Lady Madonna" and George's "The Inner Light" must stand as one of the most schizophrenic Beatles 45s ever. Based on an old record called "Bad Penny Blues" and recorded shortly before the Beatles set out on their last pilgrimage as a group to India, "Lady Madonna" was Paul doing his best Fats Domino imitation backed by a quartet of saxophonists led by renowned British jazzman Ronnie Scott. George recorded the flip in Bombay with Indian musicians (no other Beatles were present) and nicked the lyrics from a Japanese poem. (For reasons unknown, "The Inner Light" was not issued on a U.S. album until the 1980 *Rarities* LP.)

On July 17, John, Yoko, Paul and Mr. and Mrs. Starr attended the world premiere in London of the animated film *Yellow Submarine*, a *Fantasia*-like outing based on the song of the same name, starring Sgt. Pepper and animated versions of the individual Beatles, and written by Erich *Love Story* Segal. Four new songs recorded in 1967 and early '68 appeared in the movie, but the soundtrack would not be released until next January.

August 26 marked Apple Records' debut in America and with it that of the Beatles' first single on the label, "Hey Jude" b/w "Revolution." At seven minutes and eleven seconds, "Hey Jude" was the longest pop single to date. At sales in excess of five million copies, "Hey Jude" was also the band's most successful single to date. The use of almost fifty instruments, nearly as many voices, and a forty-piece orchestra also called on to sing and clap their hands smacked of Phil Spector's Jericho wall-of-sound. But it was rather extravagant stuff for a song first written by Paul as "Hey Jules," a message of consolation to Lennon's son Julian after the collapse of his parents' marriage.

The Beatles' first political tract in song, "Revolution" (released at the same time as the Rolling Stones' incendiary "Street Fighting Man") was Lennon's challenge to the Bastille-style politics of the Yippies with his demand to *see the plan* and his Gandhi-like insistence on non-violence (or *you can count me out*). They recorded two versions, one a fast proto-punk rocker with fuzzed-up guitars—and effect achieved by overloading one of the pre-amps—and the other a slower bluesy take Lennon wanted issued as the single. George and Paul voted for the faster, more commercial take and won, although John would continue to play "the singing reporter" (as he called himself) with a poetic vengeance on his own records.

The other "Revolution" did appear on *The Beatles*. Released in November, it was the group's first double album not counting Capitol's '64 cash-in documentary *The Beatles Story* and was soon subtitled "The White Album" for its ultra-simple white cover, itself a reflection of the basic rock & roll roots showing through in the thirty songs here. The first Beatle solo albums, Harrison's *Wonderwall* soundtrack and John and Yoko's controversial *Two Virgins* with its notorious nude cover shot, were already out and on *The Beatles* the individual members concentrated on their own conceptual and musical trips, more together in name than spirit. By matching song with songwriter, *The Beatles* emerges as a sprawling road map of their soul(s) and starts, appropriately, with a blast of hot rock & roll …

Ever the pop formalist, Paul got the album off to a rousing start by grafting the Beach Boys' "California Girls" to Chuck Berry's "Back in the U.S.A." and calling the end result "Back in the U.S.S.R.," although he first wrote it with more patriotic fervor as "I'm Backing the U.K." Later he would dabble in Jamaican ska with "Ob-La-Di, Ob-La-Da," play the cowboy troubadour on "Rocky Raccoon" (with John on harmonium, George Martin on piano), and even rewrite his own '64 song "I'll Follow the Sun" as "I Will."

He also recreated the music hall ambience of "When I'm Sixty-Four" and "Your Mother Should Know" with "Martha My Dear" (in truth, a song for his English sheepdog) and "Honey Pie," which came complete with authentic old 78 RPM scratches. Still, the score relied more on its feeling than its form as a disguised acoustic tribute to the Black Power movement in America, "Blackbird," and the touching "Mother Nature's Son," written and recorded by McCartney all by his lonesome self (the brass came later).

When John indulged in parody or pastiche, he took dead aim. "Yer Blues" was a wicked raunchy parody of the British blues scene, as though the title weren't clue enough. He, too, had a go at the Beatles songbook in "Glass Onion," referring to five different songs—"Lady Madonna," "Fixing a Hole," "Strawberry Fields Forever," "The Fool on the Hill," "I Am the Walrus"—and even fingering Paul as the Walrus. Later, that would turn out to be a big clue in the "Paul is Dead" hoax although Lennon insisted he meant it as a joke.

Another good practical joke was his juxtaposition of the nerve-wracking "Revolution 9" tape collage and the absolutely syrupy "Good Night" at the end of the

album. He wrote the latter for Ringo to sing, accompanied by a thirty-piece orchestra and children's choir. He also deflated the ego of a mighty jungle hunter, modeled on one he met in India, in "The Continuing Story of Bungalow Bill" which also marked Yoko's first vocal appearance (here with Ringo's wife Maureen) on a Beatles record. John originally got the idea for "Happiness is a Warm Gun" from a gun magazine. Yet the combination of the sinister doo-wop chorus and the string of non-sequitur references to Yoko was merely a product of John's mischievous wit.

As often as he was cutting, he was also tender. Compare Lennon's vicious crack at the Maharishi in "Sexy Sadie" (written first as "Maharishi" when John thought the guru was taking more than a spiritual interest in student Mia Farrow) to his poignant revamp of "I'm Only Sleeping" in "I'm So Tired." And his touching tribute to his late mother Julia and Yoko in the acoustic "Julia," with lyrics derived from the Persian poet Kahlil Gibran's *Sand and Foam*, remains one of his most beautiful songs.

George's four songs ranged from the Far Eastern fragility of "Long Long Long" to the bitter protest of "Piggies," written like a kind of *Animal Farm* in reverse. He wrote an instant classic with "While My Guitar Gently Weeps" even though it was Eric Clapton's guitar that did the weeping on the record and then paid tribute to Clapton's sweet tooth with "Savoy Truffle," whose meaty sax sound would later become a trademark of George's solo LPs. Even Ringo chimed in with his first recorded original, a hoedown called "Don't Pass Me By" on which he also played piano. Add to that Harrison's "Not Guilty" and Lennon's "What's the New Maryjane," both pulled from the album at the last minute.

The elemental, almost anti-*Pepper* simplicity of *The Beatles* sounded psychedelia's deathknell. Most of the songs were written during the group's Indian sojourns, then recorded at breakneck speed during the summer and fall of '68. Sure, they continued trying their amateur hands at new noisemakers (Paul's got the fluegelhorn on "Dear Prudence," but they consciously stuck very much to basics. John handled most of the instruments on "Cry Baby Cry;" Paul played all of them on "Wild Honey Pie" and the jokey "Why Don't We Do It in the Road?" And where they might have used a string section on "Dear Prudence," they got that electric string ensemble sound by overdubbing half a dozen guitars.

The Beatles, said Jann Wenner in his *Rolling Stone* review, "is the history and synthesis of Western music." Even for the Beatles, that was no small accomplishment.

1969

The *Yellow Submarine* soundtrack showed up a good seven months after the film. Released in the States January 13, the album contained only four "new" Beatles songs sandwiched between the title tune and "All You Need is Love" and backed with a side of George Martin's orchestral film themes. And of those four, only George Harrison's six-minute screeching feedback fest "It's All Too Much" took more than a few hours to write and record. George himself dashed off "Only a Northern Song" in one hour when the Beatles were informed they still shy one song in the film. "All Together Now" could not have taken much longer, being a Paul-style campfire singalong the group sang in *Yellow Submarine*'s live-action finale.

John's "Hey Bulldog" was wrapped up in a day. In February, 1968, the group arrived at the studio to do a promotional film for the "Lady Madonna" single. To prevent wasting precious studio time, Paul suggested whipping up a song while they were there. They quickly came up with an arrangement for some words John had with him, recording the tune with the film crew working around them. The reference in one line to a bullfrog made Paul start barking as a joke. The barking stayed on the track and Lennon changed it to "Hey Bulldog." McCartney also made some alterations in John's words as they sang them, but that was only because he could not read John's handwriting.

Talk began to emanate from the Beatles camp late in '68 that the group would soon play some concerts featuring material from a new album and to be filmed for television. Indeed, Lennon played two concerts of a sort in December, appearing at the Royal Albert Hall with Yoko in their "bagism" debut (they simply squirmed in a big white sack) and singing "Yer Blues" on the Rolling Stones' unreleased *Rock'n'Roll Circus* TV special.

But when the group finally went into Twickenham Film Studios in January, it was to make a combination live-in-the-studio album and film documentary, neither of which would be released until a year and a half later. The contradiction between the genius-in-action concept of the project and the Beatles' own perfection phobia brought already simmering tensions to a boil and the tentatively titled *Get Back* album and movie went on standby.

The first songs released from those sessions were "Get Back" and "Don't Let Me Down" (April 11 in the U.K., May 5 Stateside). Paul wrote the first one as a reactionary White Power raver with lines *Don't dig no Pakistanis taking all the people's jobs* but later toned it down. In addition to ripping off the Chuck Berry-fied

lead guitar on the A-side, John penned and sang "Don't Let Me Down" as a gripping bluesy ballad to Yoko.

John then chronicled the most recent adventures of pop's most daring duo on the next single "The Ballad of John and Yoko" (the flip went to George and his "Old Brown Shoe"). McCartney married New York rock photographer Linda Eastman in London with relatively little fanfare on March 12. In high contrast, John and Yoko were wed in Gibraltar a week later and immediately hit the headlines by turning their honeymoon into a week-long Bed-In for peace in Amsterdam. The line *Christ, you know it ain't easy* kept the record from going past number eight on the U.S. charts, but the fact that Ringo was off making a film and George was nowhere around did not keep John and Paul from recording it themselves with the former on guitars and the latter overdubbing the drums.

Throughout the year, the individual Beatles busied themselves with Apple solo recordings and productions featuring an astonishingly eclectic roster of artists, from Welsh warbler Mary Hopkin and American troubadour James Taylor to London's singing Radha Krishna Temple and the black R&B pianist Billy Preston earlier heard tinkling the ivories on "Get Back." Apple also launched and then scuttled in quick succession its "paperback records" label Zapple, but not before George issued an album of transistorized noodling called *Electronic Sound* and the Lennons put out their *Two Virgins* followup entitled *Unfinished Music No. 2: Life With the Lions.*

But the big Apple winner of '69 turned out to be a new Beatles album, dubbed *Abbey Road* after the EMI studio where it was recorded with lightning-fast speed during July and August. *Abbey Road* was the group's last recording together, as George Martin described it in a 1968 interview, "an attempt to refind ourselves because we'd been through a very unhappy experience with *Let It Be* [the retitled *Get Back*]."

They certainly came close, working at the peak of their creative powers and weaving those four gradually unraveling threads of talent into one last brilliant fabric of sound. All four Beatles played on nearly all of *Abbey Road*'s seventeen songs and their three-part harmonies still stand as among the richest they ever put on record.

Over to George Martin again ...

"That whole album was a compromise. One side was a whole series of titles which John preferred and the other side was a program Paul and I preferred. I had been trying to get them to think in symphonic terms and think of the entire shape of the album and getting some form to it—symphonic things like bringing songs back in counterpoint to other songs, actually shaped things.

"And I think if we had gone on making records, that was the way I would have done it. But we were already breaking up. *Abbey Road* was the death knell."

It hardly sounded like one. From John's greasy jock-rock salvo "Come Together" to the whimsical twenty-three-second coda "Her Majesty," *Abbey Road* showed the Beatles' kaleidoscopic talents in full colorful bloom. Even when they borrowed, they borrowed from the best. He based the enchanting "Because" on a backwards version of Beethoven's *Moonlight Sonata* first played for him by Yoko on the piano. For his brilliant ballad "Something"—proclaimed by Frank Sinatra as "the greatest love song of the past fifty years"—George Harrison copped his opening line from a tune on James Taylor's Apple LP.

The majority of kudos naturally should go to the McCartney-Martin symphonic pop collage on Side Two that opened with Paul's lament on Apple's financial mess called "You Never Give Me Your Money" and concluded with the three-way guitar battle and Ringo's first recorded drum solo on "The End." In between, of course, were John's three entries—"Sun King," "Mean Mr. Mustard," "Polythene Pam"—followed by Paul's perverse pairing of the down-and-dirty "She Came in Through the Bathroom Window" (a leftover from the *Get Back* sessions) and the orchestral glory of "Golden Slumbers."

But also destined to take their place among Beatle classics were George's bright'n'cheery "Here Comes the Sun," written in the spring as a reaction to the Apple hassles; Ringo's campy update of the *Yellow Submarine* saga in "Octopus's Garden;" Paul's punchy R&B workout "Oh! Darling" for which he practiced by screaming the lyrics at the top of his voice for several days. "Maxwell's Silver Hammer" may have been too "fruity" for George's taste (he plays synthesizer, Ringo the anvil, on Paul's Kink-ee little ditty about a murderer). But John more than made up for it with his seven-minute-plus gonzo guitar exercise "I Want You (She's So Heavy)," a raw neo-heavy metal ballad written for Yoko that soon turned into a wall of white noise.

By late 1970, *Abbey Road* had already sold over five million copies, eclipsing both *Meet the Beatles* and

Sgt. Pepper. The furor that arose over the "Paul is Dead" hoax that fall no doubt accounted for at least a few of those sales. Ghoulish Beatlemaniacs came up with a host of convincing "clues" that Paul had indeed joined that great rock band in the sky and been replaced by a look-and-soundalike who had been gainfully employed by the three surviving Beatles since 1966. Even when Paul issued a statement to the contrary, some people laughed it off as a red herring meant to throw them off the trail.

None of the Beatles, of course, was dead. Still, the group did not have long to live.

1970

After recording *Abbey Road*, the Beatles never worked together as a group in the studio ever again. Apple would release a collection of singles under the title *Hey Jude* (also titled *The Beatles Again*) in February and all four of the Beatles would release their first bonafide solo albums during 1970—the homemade one-man show *McCartney*; *Sentimental Journey*, a program of mom-and-pop sounds by Ringo; George's extravagant triple-album opus *All Things Must Pass*; the brutally confessional *John Lennon/Plastic Ono Band*. But it was left to legendary American producer Phil Spector to get the *Let It Be* album in shape for release.

Over ten years later, the jury is still out on whether Spector really did the Beatles any favors in "reproducing for disc" the original George Martin-produced *Get Back* tracks. What the originals (already extensively bootlegged) lacked in studio gloss, they more than compensated in honesty and warmth. And hidden amid Spector's lavish overproduction of some songs and the gruff rock & roll treatment of others are some real gems.

One of them is the title track, released as a single in March in its original Martin-ized take. Convinced he had another "Yesterday" in the wings, Paul locked himself up with his piano for a week to write this one. For the album version, Spector tacked on strings, horns, and a female chorus in his own typically DeMille-like style. He did the same for Paul's "The Long and Winding Road," which turned out to be the Beatles' last single, released in May almost concurrently with *Let It Be*. (Incidentally, the flip of the "Let It Be" single was a bizarre 1967 recording called "You Know My Name [Look Up The Number]," a fragmented studio lark very similar to the group's annual nonsensical Christmas fan club records.)

"Two of Us" recalled the folky charm of *Rubber Soul*. Lennon dug out one of the first songs he'd ever written, "One After 909," for the album and finally got one of his personal favorites "Across the Universe" on the LP. First slated as an early '68 single until "Lady Madonna" got the nod, "Across the Universe" initially turned up in more acoustic form on a benefit album issued in 1969 entitled *No One's Gonna Change Our World* after a line in the song. This, too, got the big treatment from Spector on *Let It Be*.

George Harrison was all present and accounted for with "For You Blue" and "I Me Mine," the second one actually recorded January 3, 1970. It also served as the title of his limited edition autobiography published in 1980. Of only passing interest were John's rough-hewn blues waltz "I Dig a Pony," the R-rated traditional tune "Maggie Mae," and the snatch of a jam called "Dig It," the last two accounting for only a minute and a half of the whole album.

Let It Be nevertheless went out not with a whimper but a bang with the live version of "Get Back," recorded at an impromptu lunchtime performance on the Apple office roof in the dead of winter. Not only was it the Beatles' first live performance in over three years, "Get Back" was also the first officially released live Beatles recording (the 1964 and '65 Hollywood Bowl shows would be issued several years later). But even the thought of history in the making did not stop the chief officer of a nearby bank from calling the cops.

Let It Be is not the Beatle's best album, nor is it their worst (to a Beatles' fan, does such a thing exist?). It *is* an anticlimactic album. On April 10, a month before its release, Apple press agent Derek Taylor announced Paul McCartney was leaving the Beatles. John, George, and Ringo threatened to quit not long before, but Paul saved them the trouble. As John would put it later, the dream was over.

To this day, there is a silver lining to that cloud in the form of the music they made and would continue to make as solo artists. In "The End," they explained how *the love you take is equal to the love you make*." How could we ever have repaid them?

—David Fricke

55

Paul McCartney Interview:

The following interview with Paul McCartney was conducted at McCartney's Soho Square offices in London in May of 1980. I'd been given the usual *caveats* about Paul's reluctance to talk about the Beatle years but early in our conversation, I decided to take the plunge anyway. Paul responded eagerly and in considerable depth to my first question about the inter-relation between stress and creativity on the Beatles *White Album*, confessing that he finally felt ready to break what he called "the voodoo against talking about the Beatles."

For the next two hours, he spoke candidly about everything from Hamburg to *Abbey Road*. The resulting interview is less soul-searching and personally revealing than John Lennon's last conversations, but because it covers such topics as their early days in Hamburg, *Sgt. Pepper*, and the Beatles' arrival in the States that Lennon only briefly touched on, and because this is the first time McCartney had talked openly about the Beatles to the press in almost a decade, it provides a crucial perspective of the Beatles years.

Musician: Some of the early Beatle material was obviously coming out of Chuck Berry and Buddy Holly, but most of it seemed strikingly original. How did that Merseybeat sound come about?

Paul McCartney: When we started the Beatles, John and I sat down and wrote about fifty songs, out of which I think "Love Me Do" is the only one that got published. Those songs weren't very good because we were trying to find the next beat—the next new sound. *New Musical Express*—which was a much gentler paper at the time—was talking about calypso, and how latin rock was going to be the next big thing. The minute we stopped trying to find that new beat the newspapers started saying it was us; and we found we'd discovered the new sound without even trying. That's what made me suspicious of categories like heavy metal or pop. My musical tastes range from Fred Astaire to the Sex Pistols and everything in between: Pink Floyd, Stevie Wonder, the Stones . . .

Musician: The first major cultural experience of my generation was in February 1964 when we saw you on the *Ed Sullivan Show*. It was like something just swept over the whole country, a new, open energy . . .

Paul McCartney: We had cooked up this whole new British thing; we had a long time to work it out and make all our mistakes in Hamburg with almost no one watching. We were very different, having taken all the American influences and stewed them up in a British way. A lot of things had been happening with our own chemistry. 'Cos John and I were strong writers, George was like a third writer, Ringo who had a good head on his shoulders and was by no means thick . . . We'd put in a lot of work. In Hamburg we'd work eight hours a day, while most bands never worked that hard. So we had developed our act and by the time we came to America we had worked all that out. All the success we'd had in Britain—the British newspapers were saying, well, what's left to do, you've conquered everything, and we'd say AMERICA. We got the Number One, did Ed Sullivan . . . by then we'd distilled our stuff down to an essence, so we weren't just coming on as any old band. We had our own totally new identities.

Musician: But when did you realize "My God, it worked!" This is more than just a musical event; this is a whole generation . . .

Paul McCartney: Very early on. When we started off in Hamburg we had no audience, so we had to work our asses off to get people in. People would appear at the door of the club while we were on stage, and there would be nobody at the tables. We used to try to get them in to sell beer. The minute we saw someone we'd kick into "Dancing In The Streets"—which was one of our big numbers at the time—and just rock out, pretending we hadn't seen them. And We'd find we'd got three of them in. We were like fairground barkers: see four people—have to get them in. We eventually sold the club out, which is when we realized it was going to get really big. Then we went back to England and played the Cavern; same thing happened there. First nobody came; then they started coming in; finally they came in droves. There was this incredible excitement. So we knew something we were doing must have been right. By the time we started playing tours it really didn't surprise us anymore, though we were still thrilled by it all. When we were on the Chris Montez tour he was on the top of the bill; halfway through they switched it and put us on top. It was embarrassing as hell for him—I mean, what could you say to him? Sorry, Chris? He took it well and stuff, but we expected it by then. Everywhere we'd gone it seemed to work.

Musician: At that point no European group had ever really conquered America—no pop group. How did you determine when you were ready to take the plunge and come to the U.S.?

Paul McCartney: The thing we did—which I always think new groups should take as a bit of advice—was that we were cheeky enough to say we wouldn't go to the States until we had a No. 1 record there. We were offered tours, but we knew we'd be second to someone and we didn't want that. There was a lot of careful thought behind it. There were a lot of artists from here who'd go over and vanish. Cliff Richard's still trying to make it in the States. We always looked at it logically and thought, well that's the mistake. You've got to go in a No. 1. So there was a lot of careful thought there, we were cooking up this act, the Beatles. It was very European, very British as opposed to the standard American way of doing things, Ed, couple of jugglers, Sinatra, Sinatra Jr., even Elvis from the waist up. The American Dream.

Musician: What about your composing and writing? Do you have a set way of going about putting together a song, or is it all pretty free-flowing?

Paul McCartney: I'm suspicious of formulas: the minute I've got a formula I try and change it. People used to ask us what comes first, the music or the words? Or Lennon and McCartney, who does what? We all did a bit of everything. Sometimes I wrote the words and

sometimes John did; sometimes I'd write a tune and sometimes he would ... We all did a bit of everything. Sometimes I wrote the words and sometimes John did; sometimes I'd write a tune and sometimes he would ... We used to nick songs, titles, John and I. I've even been inspired by things in the press. "Helter Skelter" came about because I read in *Melody Maker* that the Who had made some track or other that was the loudest, most raucous rock'n'roll, the dirtiest thing they've ever done. I didn't know what track they were talking about but it made me think, "Right. Got to do it." And I totally got off on that one

Musician: little sentence in the paper, and I said, "We've got to do the loudest, most raucous ..." And that ended up as "Helter Skelter." But that's great. We were the greatest criminals going.

Musician: How did *Sgt. Pepper* come about?

Paul McCartney: I think the big influence was *Pet Sounds* by the Beach Boys. That album just flipped me. Still is one of my favorite albums—the musical invention on that is just amazing. I play it for our kids now and they love it. When I heard it I thought, "Oh dear, this is the album of all time. What the hell are we going to do?" My ideas took off from that standard.

Musician: Wasn't the initial concept some kind of fantasy thing?

Paul McCartney: Yeah, I had this idea that it was going to be an album of another band that wasn't us—we'd just imagine all the time that it wasn't us playing. It was just a nice little device to give us some distance on the album.

Musician: I remember listening to it and thinking it was the perfect fantasy album; you could put yourself into a whole other world. That's really the way you went about creating it, then.

Paul McCartney: Right. That was the whole idea. The cover was going to be us dressed as this other band in crazy gear; but it was all stuff that we'd always wanted to wear. And we were going to have photos on the wall of all our heroes: Marlon Brando in his leather jacket, Einstein—it could be anybody who we'd ever thought was good. Cult heroes. And we kind of put this other identity on them to do it. It changed a lot in the process; but that was the basic idea behind it.

Musician: Thinking back on that period, which album would you say caught the feeling of expansion and creativity that was going on at its height?

Paul McCartney: *Pepper* probably ...

Musician: What about *Rubber Soul?* That was a real departure ...

Paul McCartney: All I can remember is that it was a kind of straightforward album ...

Musician: It was so acoustic though, compared to the previous stuff.

Paul McCartney: Those were the sounds we were into at the time. "You've Got To Hide Your Love Away" is just basically John doing Dylan. Dylan had just come out and we were big fans of his.

Rubber Soul was just a catchy title; that's the bit I remember most about it. A lot of people liked that as an album.

Musician: Among connoisseurs it's considered one of the early high points, *Revolver* too ...

Paul McCartney: Just to show you how wrong one can be: I was in Germany on tour just before *Revolver* came out. I started listening to the album and I got really down because I thought the whole thing was out of tune. Everyone had to reassure me that it was OK.

Musician: I've heard that with the Beatles you sometimes gave Ringo directions regarding what he should play.

Paul McCartney: We always gave Ringo direction— on every single number. It was usually very controlled. Whoever had written the song, John for instance, would say "I want this." Obviously a lot of the stuff came out of what Ringo was playing; but we would always control it.

Musician: Did musical disagreements or conflicts have anything to do with the breakup?

Paul McCartney: They were some of the minor reasons, yeah. I remember on "Hey Jude," telling George not to play guitar. He wanted to echo riffs after the vocal phrases, which I didn't think was appropriate. He didn't see it like that, and it was a bit of a number for me to have to dare to tell George Harrison—who's one of the greats, I think—not to play. It was like an insult. But that was how we did a lot of our stuff.

Musician: About creative tension—even if it's a pain in the ass it can be useful. Are there any particular Beatle albums that ...

Paul McCartney: *The White Album.* That was the tension album. We were all in the midst of the psychedelic thing, or just coming out of it. In any case, it was weird. Never before had we recorded with beds in the studio and people visiting for hours on end; business meetings and all that. There was a lot of friction during that album.

Musician: That was the one that sounded the most fragmented to me, whereas Abbey Road sounded the smoothest. Yet I imagine there was a lot of tension at that point, too.

Paul McCartney: No, not really, there was ... no, come to think of it there was actually, yes.

There were one or two tense moments. But it didn't feel like a tense album to me; I was busy getting into a lot of new musical ideas, like the medley thing on the second side. I think the *White Album* was the weirdest experience because we were about to break up. And that was just tense in itself.

Musician: I want to ask you about your bass playing. To me you've always played bass like a frustrated guitar player. Those melodic lines that started to show up on *Sgt. Pepper*—there was no precedent for that in rock music. How did that style of playing come about?

Paul McCartney: I'd always liked those little lines that worked as support, and yet had their own identity instead of just staying in the background. Also, bass was beginning to come to the fore in mixes at that point. If you listen to early Beatle mixes the bass and bass drum aren't there. We were starting to take over mixing ourselves, and to bring those things out, so I had to do something with it. I was listening to a lot of Motown and Stax at the time, Marvin Gaye and people like that ... The Hofner violin bass is like balsa wood. It's so comfortable after a Fender or a Rickenbacker. I now play a Rickenbacker or a Yamaha, which are quite heavy.

Musician: Why did you switch?

Paul McCartney: It was given to me. Back in the mid-sixties Mr. Rickenbacker gave me a special left-handed bass. It was the first left-handed bass I'd ever had, 'cause the Hofner was a converted right hand. It was a freebie and I loved it; I started getting into it on *Sgt. Pepper*. And now I'm playing a Yamaha.

Musician: How come?

Paul McCartney: Because they gave me one—I'm anybody's for a free guitar! Sometimes I think I should research what instrument I like to play best. But generally I seem to play stuff that's been given me. Naturally I only play the stuff that I like—I've been given stuff that I don't care for—but I like it like that. I don't like things to be too thought out and logical. If someone asked me what strings I used I honestly couldn't tell you—they come out of a little bag. To me these things are just vehicles. They're beautiful and I love

them, but I don't want to find out too much about them. It's just the way my mind is; I'd prefer to be non-technical.

Musician: A great deal of the criticism you've come in for seems to be because you use pop as a medium. What is it about pop you're attracted to?

Paul McCartney: I just like it. I'm like a lot of people—when I get in my car and turn on the radio I want to hear some good sounds. So whatever I write, I write for that. What are the alternatives? To write a "serious" piece of music? Or modern classical music? No thanks, I'd bore myself stiff after a couple of bars.

Musician: Looking back over your career do you feel satisfied? Do you feel content when you consider your musical legacy?

Paul McCartney: I'd say I've done some songs that I think are really good; some that I think didn't quite come off; some I hate. But I've done enough to satisfy myself that I'm O.K. That's basically all I'm looking for. Like most people.

—Vic Garbarini

Something About George Harrison:

It was no cosmic accident that, four years after the breakup of the Beatles, George Harrison named his own record company and later his third solo album *Dark Horse*. But in the wake of everything the Beatles accomplished in popular music and culture during their ten extraordinary, tumultuous years together, it is true—if somewhat hard to believe in retrospect—that Harrison was always the group's dark horse, laboring as a musician, songwriter, and producer in the overwhelming shadow cast by his more celebrated bandmates John Lennon and Paul McCartney. Unlike Ringo Starr, who made up in personal charm and dry wit what he may have lacked in musical or compositional chops, George—the "quietest" Beatle as well as the youngest—had to prove to a world mesmerized by the Beatles' spell that he was more than just the cute guitar player in a band specializing in hits by Lennon and McCartney.

There is no arguing that, as founders of the group, Lennon and McCartney were also its driving forces as well as chief songwriters. Of the 186 original songs recorded by the group appearing in this book, only 22 were written by Harrison, starting with "Don't Bother Me" which first appeared on the Beatles' second U.K. album *With the Beatles* and later turned up on their American Capitol debut *Meet the Beatles*. But one of those Harrisongs, the classic ballad "Something" recorded in 1969 and included on *Abbey Road*, was proclaimed by no less a crooner than Frank Sinatra as "the greatest love song of the past fifty years."

Although they were either never released as singles or relegated only to B-sides, Harrison-penned Beatles songs like "Think for Yourself" on *Rubber Soul*, *Revolver*'s "Taxman," the dramatic "While My Guitar Gently Weeps" from the so-called *White Album*, and the simple but charming "Here Comes the Sun" which kicked off Side Two of *Abbey Road* have all come to be regarded as hits in and of themselves. True, Lennon and McCartney were considerably more prolific as songwriters, but it is worth noting that George's first solo album *All Things Must Pass* had to be a triple album just to accommodate the mountainous backlog of songs Harrison had accumulated during his Beatle years. Even as late as 1979 he was releasing the odd Beatles-era relic like "Not Guilty," a 1968 *White Album* outtake which appeared on his Dark Horse LP *George Harrison*.

As a guitarist and student of both Indian music and culture, George's influence as a Beatle is immeasureable. His prowess on six strings was certainly never in doubt. Though never considered a "guitar hero" *a la* Eric Clapton (with whom he later recorded), Jeff Beck, or Jimmy Page, Harrison's guitar style—an invigorating, innovative fusion of Chuck Berry grit, Duane Eddy cool, rockabilly moxy, and jazzy harmonics—became the standard by which others were judged, the precedent for the '60s guitar revolution that came to a head with Jimi Hendrix. His solos on "I Saw Her Standing There," "Can't Buy Me Love," and the poignant acoustic break on "And I Love Her," to take just a few examples, were more class than flash, pithy distillations of melody and muscle. He could say more in twelve bars than later "axe" murderers could explain in epic fifteen-minute solos.

The sitar may have died a fad's death among pop musicians by the time the '60s turned into the '70s. But George's introduction of the exotic Indian stringed instrument on *Rubber Soul*'s "Norwegian Wood (This Bird Has Flown)" in 1965 not only made his musical guru Ravi Shankar a household name but was the first endorsement of Indian modality as a tool in rock composition. He also got some of India's best traditional players on the pop charts when he brought Anil Bhagwat to play tabla on the *Revolver* track "Love You To" and recorded *Sgt. Pepper*'s "Within You, Without You" and the single B-side "The Inner Light" with Indian musicians (the latter was actually recorded in Bombay).

George's fascination with the secrets of the East prompted the Beatles' brief but sensational splash in Indian mysticism and transcendental meditation in 1967 and '68. He was the first Beatle to visit India—he took sitar lessons from Ravi Shakar there in October, 1966—and long after the other three lost interest in the Maharishi and his karmic rap, Harrison continued to pursue his spiritual interests, later producing records for Shankar and London's Radha Krishna Temple as well as proselytizing on Top 40 radio with songs like "My Sweet Lord."

For someone so obsessed with things of a higher plane, George was born February 25, 1943 to rather lowly circumstances, the youngest of four children to Harold and Louise Harrison who lived in one of the most impoverished sections of Liverpool. Young George attended Dovedale Primary School near Penny

Lane, three classes behind Lennon (their paths had yet to cross), and later enrolled at Liverpool Institute, whose future alumni would also include James Paul McCartney and his brother Michael (he'd later change his surname to McGear). By the age of thirteen, bored by his bout with the three R's, George had a go at two more R's, rock & roll, after scoring his first guitar from a school buddy who let him have it for less than four pounds. That same year he got his first electric guitar and not long after that his first "pro" music gig, playing with his brother Peter and a couple of barely competent pals as the Rebels at Speke British Legion Club. They split ten shillings for the evening.

Fate pointed its fickle finger in his direction in 1958 when George met Paul McCartney, who had already been playing around Liverpool with Lennon as the Nurk Twins and in the latter's skiffle group the Quarrymen. Through McCartney, Harrison met Lennon, who auditioned him for the band on the condition that "if you can play as good as Eddie Clayton [a

local guitar hotshot], you're in." One mean version of "Raunchy" later, he was "in."

The next ten years are a matter of public record, an incredible story already become legend and fast approaching myth. Anecdotes about George alone could fill a book—how in the Silver Beatles days he played for a time under the semi-pro name of Carl Harrison after his idol Carl Perkins; his deportation from Germany during the band's first visit there in 1960 for being underage and not having appropriate papers; his classic wisecrack to producer George Martin at the "Love Me Do" session (Martin: "Let me know if there's anything you don't like." Harrison: "Well, for a start, I don't like your tie.").

George eventually did write a book, his lavish limited edition 1980 autobiography *I Me Mine*. And in it, in one brief, almost parenthetical passage, he managed to sum up the epidemic insanity that was Beatlemania...

It was all so silly anyway, all the way through. Ringo's story was funny, you know. We were talking about school once and he said that he had been in hospital so much, that when he went back to school he had to get a note, an official note, to say he had left and come back from hospital and the school said to him: "You never went to this school" and he said "Yes, I did. I've just been in hospital a lot." Then, he said, a couple of years later, they were saying, proudly, "This was Ringo's desk. The great man sat here." Madness. There was always plenty of that. We were always meeting the wrong people, Lord Mayors and Police Chiefs, and so on. It would depend on what mood you were in how you behaved. That's why the fab four were good, because if one of us was in a bad mood, the others would cover. We protected each other.

Considering the "madness" that surrounded the Beatles—the screaming teenage girls, the press that crowned them media messiahs, the flower children and hustlers that wormed into Apple Corps., the internal squabbles that eventually broke up the band—it's a miracle they were able to make any music at all. George was lying sick in a Bournemouth, England hotel bed during a '63 tour when he wrote "Don't Bother Me," as he says in *I Me Mine*, "as an exercise to see if I *could* write a song." "Here Comes the Sun" was written by George in Eric Clapton's garden on a beautiful spring day when he was playing hookey from Apple, the accountants, the lawyers, etc. Even later Harrison songs reflected the traumas as well as the triumphs of the period. "Wah Wah," recorded for *All Things Must Pass*, was written during the *Let It Be* mess—turns out that here "wah wah" means headache.

Ironically, George was one of the busiest Beatles outside the group. Not counting Paul's '67 soundtrack *The Family Way*, Harrison's *Wonderwall Music* (recorded in London and Bombay in late '67/early '68) was the first Beatles solo album, beating the release of John and Yoko's *Two Virgins* by less than a month. His *Electronic Sound* was one of the only two releases on the short-lived Zapple label (the other was the Lennons' *Life With the Lions*). He co-wrote "Badge" with Eric Clapton for Cream's *Goodbye* album, turned up on sessions often under pseudonym, and even briefly went out on tour with Delaney and Bonnie. And his production

credits both during and after the Beatles include British soul man Jackie Lomax, Billy Preston's classic *That's the Way God Planned It* LP and single, and the singing-songwriting duo Splinter.

After the Beatles went their separate ways in April, 1970, George went from strength to strength. *All Things Must Pass* was a Number One album and ultimately outsold many of the Beatles albums. "My Sweet Lord," which became the subject of litigation when George was accused of copping the melody from the Chiffons' "He's So Fine," nevertheless went on to become the best-seller of the ex-Beatles solo singles.

But his greatest triumph may well be the two Concerts for Bangla Desh staged at New York's Madison Square Garden August 1, 1971. Eventually released both as a film and triple live album, the Bangla Desh shows not only highlighted the plight of the victims of the Pakistani civil war and brought together an unprecedented collection of superstar talent (Ringo, Bob Dylan, Eric Clapton, Leon Russell, etc.), but it showed George Harrison to be a man who practiced what he preached. As *Rolling Stone* put it, "the Bangla Desh

benefit, in the magnificence of its music and the selflessness of its motives, was proof that the art and the spirit are still alive."

He still makes albums occasionally (the last was *George Harrison* in 1979), but it seems that these days George Harrison is more interested in his second wife Olivia (the first, of course, was Patti Boyd), son Dhani, Formula I auto racing (see "Faster" on *Thirty-Three and 1/3*), and films (he was the executive producer and played a bit part in Monty Python's *Life of Brian*). And yet if he never makes another record again, George Harrison has left a pop music legacy behind him that proves he wasn't such a quiet Beatle after all.

Funny thing, too: at a press conference during the Beatles' '64 U.S. tour, a woman reporter turned to Harrison and asked him, "Mr. Starr is known for his rings, Mr. McCartney obviously for his looks, and Mr. Lennon for his wife. What about you, Mr. Harrison?" He quite calmly answered, "As long as I get an equal share of the money, I'm willing to stay anonymous."

He was only kidding.

—David Fricke   63

John Lennon:

A Last Interview

Playboy: Generally speaking, what did each of you contribute to the Lennon-McCartney songwriting team?

John Lennon: Well, you could say that he provided a lightness, an optimism, while I would always go for the sadness, the discords, a certain bluesy edge. There was a period when I thought I didn't write melodies, that Paul wrote those and I just wrote straight, shouting rock'n'roll. But, of course, when I think of some of my own songs—"In My Life"—or some of the early stuff —"This Boy"—I was writing melody with the best of them. Paul had a lot of training, could play a lot of instruments. He'd say, "Well, why don't you change that there? You've done that note 50 times in the song." You know, I'll grab a note and ram it home. Then again, I'd be the one to figure out where to go with a song—a story that Paul would start. In a lot of the songs, my stuff is the "middle eight," the bridge.

Playboy: For example?

John Lennon: Take "Michelle." Paul and I were staying somewhere, and he walked in and hummed the first few bars, with the words, you know [sings verse of "Michelle"], and he says, "Where do I go from here?" I'd been listening to blues singer Nina Simone, who did something like "I love you!" in one of her songs and that made me think of the middle eight for "Michelle" [sings]: "I love you, I love you, I l-o-ove you...."

Playboy: What was the difference in terms of lyrics?

John Lennon: I always had an easier time with lyrics, though Paul is quite a capable lyricist who doesn't think he is. So he doesn't go for it. Rather than face the problem, he would avoid it. "Hey Jude" is a damn good set of lyrics. I made no contribution to the lyrics there. And a couple of lines he has come up with show indications of a good lyricist. But he just hasn't taken it anywhere. Still, in the early days, we didn't care about lyrics as long as the song had some vague theme— she loves you, he loves him, they all love each other. It was the hook, line and sound we were going for. That's still my attitude, but I can't leave lyrics alone. I have to make them make sense apart from the songs.

Playboy: What's an example of a lyric you and Paul worked on together?

John Lennon: In "We Can Work It Out," Paul did the first half, I did the middle eight. But you've got Paul writing, *We can work it out/We can work it out*—real optimistic, y' know, and me, impatient, *Life is very short and there's no time/ For fussing and fighting, my friend....*

Playboy: Paul tells the story and John philosophizes.

John Lennon: Sure. Well, I was always like that, you know. I was like that before the Beatles and after the Beatles. I always asked why people did things and why society was like it was. I didn't just accept it for what it was apparently doing. I always looked below the surface.

Playboy: When you talk about working together on a single lyric like "We Can Work It Out," it suggests that you and Paul worked a lot more closely than you've admitted in the past. Haven't you said that you wrote most of your songs separately, despite putting both of your names on them?

John Lennon: Yeah, I was lying. [Laughs] I was when I felt resentful, so I felt that we did everything apart. But, actually, a lot of the songs we did eyeball to eyeball.

Playboy: But many of them were done apart, weren't they?

John Lennon: Yeah. "Sgt. Pepper" was Paul's idea, and I remember he worked on it a lot and suddenly called me to go into the studio, said it was time to write some songs. On *Pepper*, under the pressure of only ten days, I managed to come up with "Lucy in the Sky" and "Day in the Life." We weren't communicating enough, you see. And later on, that's why I got resentful about all that stuff. But now I understand that it was just the same competitive game going on.

Playboy: But the competitive game was good for you, wasn't it?

John Lennon: In the early days. We'd make a record in 12 hours or something; they would want a single every three months and we'd have to write it in a hotel room or in a van. So the cooperation was functional as well as musical.

Playboy: All right, but get back to the music itself: You don't agree that the Beatles created the best rock'n'roll that's been produced?

John Lennon: I don't. The Beatles, you see—I'm too involved in them artistically. I cannot see them objectively. I cannot listen to them objectively. I'm dissatisfied with every record the Beatles ever made. There ain't one of them I wouldn't remake—including all the Beatles records and all my individual ones. So I cannot possibly give you my assessment of what the Beatles are.

When I was a Beatle, I thought we were the best group in the goddamned world. And believing that is what made us what we were—whether we call it the best rock'n'roll group or the best pop group or whatever.

But you play me those tracks today and I want to remake every damn one of them. There's not a single one. . . . I heard "Lucy in the Sky with Diamonds" on the radio last night. It's abysmal, you know. The track is just terrible. I mean, it's great, but it wasn't made right, know what I mean? But that's the artistic trip, isn't it? That's why you keep going. But to get back to your original question about the Beatles and their music, the answer is that we did some good stuff and we did some bad stuff.

Playboy: Many people feel that none of the songs Paul has done alone match the songs he did as a Beatle. Do you honestly feel that any of your songs—on the Plastic Ono Band records—will have the lasting imprint of "Eleanor Rigby" or "Strawberry Fields?"

John Lennon: "Imagine," "Love" and those Plastic Ono Band songs stand up to any song that was written when I was a Beatle. Now, it may take you 20 or 30 years to appreciate that, but the fact is, if you check those songs out, you will see that it is as good as any fucking stuff that was ever done.

Playboy: Do you listen to the radio?

John Lennon: Muzak or classical. I don't purchase records. I do enjoy listening to things like Japanese folk music or Indian music. My tastes are very broad. When I was a housewife, I just had Muzak on—background music—'cause it relaxes you.

Playboy: The inevitable question, John. Do you listen to your records?

John Lennon: Least of all my own.

Playboy: Even your classics?

John Lennon: Are you kidding? For pleasure, I would never listen to them. When I hear them, I just think of the session—it's like an actor watching himself in an old movie. When I hear a song, I remember the Abbey Road studio, the session, who fought with whom, where I was sitting, banging the tambourine in the corner.

Playboy: Your songs are performed more than most other songwriters'. How does that feel?

John Lennon: I'm always proud and pleased when people do my songs. It gives me pleasure that they even attempt them, because a lot of my songs aren't that doable. I go to restaurants and the groups always play "Yesterday." I even signed a guy's violin in Spain after he played us "Yesterday." He couldn't understand that I didn't write the song. But I guess he couldn't have gone from table to table playing "I Am the Walrus."

Playboy: How does it feel to have influenced so many people?

John Lennon: It wasn't really me or us. It was the times. It happened to me when I heard rock'n'roll in the Fifties. I had no idea about doing music as a way of life until rock'n'roll hit me.

Playboy: Do you recall what specifically hit you?

John Lennon: It was "Rock Around the Clock," I think. I enjoyed Bill Haley, but I wasn't overwhelmed by him. It wasn't until "Heartbreak Hotel" that I really got into it. I don't mean to belittle the Beatles when I say they weren't thus, overblow their importance as separate from society. And I don't think they were more important than Glenn Miller or Woody Herman or Bessie Smith. It was our generation, that's all. It was Sixties music.

Playboy: What do you say to those who insist that all rock since the Beatles has been the Beatles redone?

John Lennon: All music is rehash. There are only a few notes. Just variations on a theme. Try to tell the kids in the Seventies who were screaming to the Bee Gees that their music was just the Beatles redone. There is nothing wrong with the Bee Gees. They do a damn good job. There was nothing else going on then.

Playboy: Wasn't a lot of the Beatles music at least more intelligent?

John Lennon: The Beatles were more intellectual, so they appealed on that level, too. But the basic appeal of the Beatles was not their intelligence. It was their music. It was only after some guy in the London *Times* said there were Aeolian cadences in "It Won't Be Long" that the middle classes started listening to it—because somebody put a tag on it.

Playboy: Did you put Aeolian cadences in "It Won't Be Long?"

John Lennon: To this day, I don't have any idea what they are. They sound like exotic birds.

Playboy: It's interesting to hear you talk about your old songs such as "Lucy in the Sky" and "Glass Onion." Will you give some brief thoughts on some of our favorites?

John Lennon: Right.

Playboy: Let's start with "In My Life."

John Lennon: It was the first song I wrote that was consciously about my life. [Sings] *There are places I'll remember/all my life though some have changed....* Before, we were just writing songs *a la* Everly Brothers, Buddy Holly—pop songs with no more thought to them than that. The words were almost irrelevant. "In My Life" started out as a bus journey from my house at 250 Menlove Avenue to town, mentioning all the places I could recall. I wrote it all down and it was boring. So I forgot about it and laid back and these lyrics started coming to me about friends and lovers of the past. Paul helped with the middle eight.

Playboy: "I Am The Walrus."

John Lennon: The first line was written on one acid trip one weekend. The second line was written on the next acid trip the next weekend, and it was filled in after I met Yoko. Part of it was putting down Hare Krishna. All those people were going on about Hare Krishna, Allen Ginsberg in particular. The reference to *Element'ry penguin* is the elementary naive attitude of going around chanting, "Hare Krishna," or putting all your faith in any one idol. I was writing obscurely, *a la* Dylan, in those days.

Playboy: The song is very complicated musically.

John Lennon: It actually was fantastic in stereo, but you never hear it all. There was too much to get on. It was too messy a mix. One track was live BBC Radio— Shakespeare or something—I just fed it whatever lines came in.

Playboy: What about the walrus itself?

John Lennon: It's from "The Walrus and the Carpenter," *Alice in Wonderland.* To me it was a beautiful poem. It never dawned on me that Lewis Carroll was commenting on the capitalist and social system. I never went into that bit about what he really meant, like people are doing with the Beatles' work. Later, I went back and looked at it and realized that the walrus was the bad guy in the story and the carpenter was the good guy. I thought, Oh, shit, I picked the wrong guy. I should have said, "I am the carpenter." But that wouldn't have been the same, would it? [Singing] "I am the carpenter."

Playboy: "I Feel Fine."

John Lennon: That's me, including the guitar lick with the first feedback ever recorded. I defy anybody to find an earlier record —unless it is some old blues record from the twenties—with feedback on it.

Playboy: "A Day in the Life."

John Lennon: Just as it sounds: I was reading the paper one day and I noticed two stories. One was the Guinness heir who killed himself in a car. That was the main headline story. He died in London in a car crash. On the next page was a story about 4000 holes in Blackburn, Lancashire. In the streets, that is. They were going to fill them all. Paul's contribution was the beautiful little lick in the song "I'd love to turn you on." I had the bulk of the song and the words, but he contributed this little lick floating around in his head that he couldn't use for anything. I thought it was a damn good piece of work.

Playboy: May we continue with some of the ones that seem more personal and see what reminiscences they inspire?

John Lennon: Reminisce away.

Playboy: For no reason whatsoever, let's start with "I Wanna Be Your Man."

John Lennon: Paul and I finished that one off for the Stones. We were taken down by Brian to meet them at the club where they were playing in Richmond. They wanted a song and we went to see what kind of stuff they did. Paul had this bit of a song and we played it roughly for them and they said, "Yeah, OK, that's our style." But it was only really a lick, so Paul and I went off in the corner of the room and finished the song off while they were all sitting there, talking. We came back and Mick and Keith said, "Jesus, look at that. They just went over there and wrote it." You know, right in front of their eyes. We gave it to them. It was a throwaway. Ringo sang it for us and the Stones did their version. It shows how much importance we put on them. We weren't going to give them anything great, right? That was the Stones' first record. Anyway, Mick and Keith said, "If they can write a song so easily, we should try it." They say it inspired them to start writing together.

Playboy: How about "Strawberry Fields Forever?"

John Lennon: "Strawberry Fields" is a real place. After I stopped living at Penny Lane, I moved in with my auntie who lived in the suburbs in a nice semidetached place with a small garden and doctors and lawyers and the ilk living around —not the poor slummy kind of image that was projected in all the Beatles stories. In the class system, it was about half a class higher than Paul, George and Ringo, who lived in government-subsidized housing. We owned our house and had a garden. They didn't have anything like that. Near that home was Strawberry Fields, a house near a boys' reformatory where I used to go to garden parties as a kid with my friends Nigel and Pete. We would go there and hang out and sell lemonade bottles for a penny. We always had fun at Strawberry Fields. So that's where I got the name. But I used it as an image. Strawberry Fields forever.

Playboy: What memories are jogged by the song "Help!"?

John Lennon: When "Help!" came out in '65, I was actually crying out for help. Most people think it's just a fast rock'n'roll song. I didn't realize it at the time; I just wrote the song because I was commissioned to write it for the movie. But later, I knew I really was crying out for help. It was my fat Elvis period. You see the movie: He—I—is very fat, very insecure, and he's completely lost himself. And I am singing about when I was so much younger and all the rest, looking back at how easy it was. Now I may be very positive— yes, yes—but I also go through deep depressions where I would like to jump out the window, you know. It becomes easier to deal with as I get older; I don't know whether you learn control or, when you grow up, you calm down a little. Anyway, I was fat and depressed and I was crying out for help.

In those days, when the Beatles were depressed, we had this little chant. I would yell out, "Where are we going fellows?" They would say, "To the top Johnny," in pseudo-American voices. And I would say, "Where is that, fellows?" And they would say, "To the toppermost of the poppermost." It was some dumb expression from a cheap movie—*a la Blackboard Jungle*—about Liverpool. Johnny was the leader of the gang.

Playboy: Was "I'm A Loser" a similarly personal statement?

John Lennon: Part of me suspects that I'm a loser and the other part of me thinks I'm God Almighty.

Interview by David Sheff

Don't Pass This Boy By:

Ringo and the Beatles

Queen of England: Are you the one
who started it?
Ringo: No, I was the last to join. I'm
the little fellow.

*Perhaps it was providential that the
Beatles, having found ordinary Ringo,
discovered the extraordinariness that made
them legendary.*
—Wilfred Mellers, *Twilight of the Gods*

Ringo couldn't make up his mind when Brian Epstein and the Beatles asked him to replace Pete Best in August of 1962. The Beatles were on their way to London, to record their very first record with George Martin at Parlophone. The reasons for Best's sacking were highly mysterious. After years of hard work, the Beatles were on the very precipice of success. Epstein had claimed that George Martin was behind the move and the other Beatles had supposedly claimed that "Pete just doesn't fit in." Ringo was puzzled. Pete Best had been the Beatles' drummer for two years and had developed a strong following in Liverpool, particularly among the girls at the Cavern. "The birds loved Pete. Me, I was just a skinny, bearded scruff. Brian didn't want me either. He thought I didn't have the personality. And why get a bad-looking cat when you got a good-looking one?"

In the end, Ringo later admitted, it was the extra five pounds a week in wages offered by the Beatles that finally prevented him from returning to Rory Storme and the Hurricanes for another season at Butlin's (a fortuitous decision for Ringo; a depressing one for Mr. Best!). And so Richard Starkey, ex-skiffle player, ex-Teddy boy, self-styled "beat" and drummer decided to wash the grease from his hair and throw in his lot with John, Paul, and George. McCartney later recalled waiting for Ringo to join the group before their departure and wondering if Ringo had shaved his beard or would grow his hair Beatle-style, figuring that "he'd need some talking to on that account." "The beard was gone," Paul remembered. "And his hair—it wasn't quite long enough yet—but there it was, drooping over his forehead, limply. We all shook hands and joked a bit. And then Ringo looked at us all and he said, '*Well, mates, where do we go from here?*'"

Richard Starkey was born on July 7, 1940, in a house on Madryn Street as German bombs fell on Liverpool. He grew up down by the docks, in the Dingle, the roughest neighborhood in the city.

Although he bore his childhood with equanimity and typical good cheer, it was a difficult one. His parents divorced when he was three and his mother worked as a barmaid, leaving him at his grandmother's house. At six, peritonitis from a burst appendix put him in St. Silas' for ten months; at thirteen, he was hospitalized with pleurisy for another two years and fell further behind at school. "I'm beginning to see now that I am what I am because of the sort of upbringing I had," he told Hunter Davies in 1967. "With no father and my mother always out of work. It did make me quiet and introverted, though I was happy at the time." He worked as a messenger and a joiner's apprentice for a short time after school until his grandfather put down the deposit for a new 'kit' of drums—the drums, of course, won out. "I banged me thumb the very first day" he later said. "I became a drummer because it was the only thing I could do!"

And drum he did, learning his craft like all of the self-taught drummers of the time—by listening to Elvis and Chuck Berry and Buddy Holly and by playing rave-ups with the Hurricanes at Butlin's in Liverpool, at U.S. air force bases in France, and in the loud, smoky, crowded cellar clubs of Hamburg, where English bands like the Hurricanes and the Beatles punched out American R&B until the morning light.

Ringo was nervous on September 11, 1962, terrified of the EMI studio in London—and George Martin wasn't impressed at first. "I didn't rate Ringo very highly" he said of the session. "He couldn't do a roll..." Ringo played drums through seventeen takes of "Love Me Do" until Martin was satisfied, but not before he'd substituted a studio drummer named Andy White on "Please Please Me" and had given Ringo the tambourine to play, much to his consternation ("I was shattered. What a drag. How phoney the record business was, I thought."). It didn't take long, however, before George Martin began to recognize Ringo's unique talents as a drummer. "I did quickly realize that Ringo was an excellent drummer for what was required," he explained in his memoir, *All You Need Is Ears*. "He's not a 'technical' drummer. Men like Gene Krupa and Buddy Rich would run rings around him. But he's a good solid rock drummer with super steady beat, and he knows how to get the right sound out of his drums. Above all, he does have an individual sound. You can tell Ringo's drums from everyone else's, and that char-

acter was a definite asset to the Beatles early recordings."

Indeed, Ringo Starr was more than merely "excellent." Within the specific context and scope of the Beatles' oeuvre as it developed and blossomed through its multi-faceted stages to encompass not only rock 'n' roll but all forms of pop, Ringo became the perfect drummer for the Beatles. Moreover, as he became integrated into the tightly-knit fraternity, and as the magic and bedlam of Beatlemania engulfed the globe, he emerged as a unique personality in his own right who, in addition to serving as a vehicle for his own style of music, served to counterbalance the personalities of the other Beatles, keeping the group in a state of creative equipoise.

As a drummer, he was a natural—purely intuitive, remarkably tasteful, spirited but always basic, a proponent of the "less is more" school of minimal drumming. With a sense of endearing modesty, Ringo has often disparaged his drumming over the years ("Whenever I hear another drummer I know I'm no good...I'm no good on the technical things but I'm good with all the motions, swinging my head, like. That's because I like to dance but I can't dance on drums..."); but the fact of the matter was that his willingness to lay back and take directions and feed the others—a quality which seemed intrinsically rooted in his very background and character—was what allowed the Beatles' sound to take such powerful flight. He was, in essence, the perfect team player, a character musi-

cian whose ingenuity grew directly out of a sublime ability to make his deficiencies and flaws as a musician work to accentuate and liberate rather than hold back their music. He had an uncanny understanding of John's rhythm guitar and Paul's bass line. Time and again, the Beatles rode his backbeat to glory, and precisely because he never overstated a beat or over-accented a phrase (unless it was appropriate), he managed to get more mileage out of his licks than most drummers could ever dream of. The results were extraordinary: the rare clash of the ride cymbal or tom-tom roll imparted cataclysmic style and a powerful identity to passages—the machine-gun snare of "Ticket to Ride"; the explosive roll and cymbals of "Day Tripper" —the examples are endless (everyone has their favorites).

As the Beatles rose to successive creative challenges over the years, so did Ringo, in his own way; he improved from album to album and his growth as a musician paralleled the musical-cultural directions of the group. In a curious way though, his utter simplicity remained a large part of his appeal as a drummer. He grew but he remained the same; he improved technically, but only enough to accommodate his mates. In the end, he remained an original. If I could think of a single passage in which Ringo's quintessential "style" as a drummer is most identifiable, it could well be something as late as, say, the drumming behind George's guitar solo in Paul's "Let it Be," after the organ trails off. There, in simple 4/4 time, Ringo comes in with the

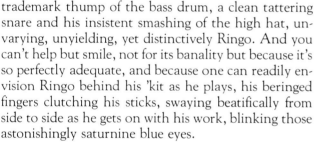

trademark thump of the bass drum, a clean tattering snare and his insistent smashing of the high hat, unvarying, unyielding, yet distinctively Ringo. And you can't help but smile, not for its banality but because it's so perfectly adequate, and because one can readily envision Ringo behind his 'kit as he plays, his beringed fingers clutching his sticks, swaying beatifically from side to side as he gets on with his work, blinking those astonishingly saturnine blue eyes.

As a vocalist, he was no less unique. Unlike his compadres, he wasn't a composer: "I used to wish I could write songs like the others," he once remarked wistfully, "and I've tried but I just can't." No matter. The fact that Ringo could even carry a tune was a pleasant discovery when he recorded Dixon-Farrel's classic "Boys" in 1963 and followed it up with John and Paul's "I Wanna Be Your Man," both ferocious renditions of raucous R&B numbers on which he displays a viable set of pipes—slightly off-key, perhaps, nasal but not muddy, a bluesy, droning wail filled with his personality and a sense of fun. These two songs actually began a tradition on the Beatles albums of a special track for a "Ringo sort of song." At first, he displayed his considerable affinities for country-western-rockabilly by recording two Carl Perkins tunes, "Matchbox" and "Honey Don't." Eventually, John and Paul began to use the motif of Ringo's character and image to create material for him. As the individual Beatles emerged over the years as separate identities with interests and directions, Ringo's presence was a stark contrast to the others. As Greil Marcus once aptly wrote: "John was cultivating his rebellion and anger; Paul was making his decision for Pop; George was making his decision for Krishna; and Ringo was having his house painted." Yes, Ringo was the homebody, always less publicly visible than the others. To the world, he was shy, soft, puerile, down-to-earth, funny, friendly, cute, lovable, vulnerable. Appropriately, the music his friends created for him, in addition to being perfectly tailored for his range and style, embodied the above characteristics as well as reflected his tastes—the immortal "Yellow Submarine," "Octopus' Garden," and, perhaps his finest vocal moment with the Beatles, "With A Little Help From My Friends." "Don't Pass Me By" was the only tune that Ringo both composed by himself and sang with the Beatles.

Of all the Beatles, it was fitting that Ringo would be the one to remain on amicable terms with the others in the aftermath of the group's break-up, when the polar friction between John and Paul was strongest. He was, after all, always the innocent, the quiet one, the bloke who was always just "doing his job" and was least inclined toward politics within the group. And precisely because the world somehow expected much less of him than the others when the group split, the critical failures of several of his solo ventures into crooning were less disappointing, even palatable, and the success (the LP *Ringo*) was all the more delightful.

—**Martin Torgoff**

George Martin Remembers:

George Martin was born in England in 1926. Trained as a classical musician, he studied the oboe with Margaret Asher, the mother of Jane and Peter. In 1950, he joined EMI Studios as an Artists and Repertoire Man for Parlophone Records. In June 6, 1962, he auditioned the Beatles at EMI Studio 3 on London's Abbey Road and on September 11, produced their first Parlophone recording, "Love Me Do." He produced every Beatles recording until they disbanded and was also musical director for the soundtracks of such films as A Hard Day's Night, Yellow Submarine, Live and Let Die *and* Sgt. Pepper's Lonely Heart's Club Band. *His many awards include four Grammys and the Queen's Silver Jubilee Award for Best Producer 1952-1977.*

Date: Friday, December 5, 1980.
Place: George Martin's office at Chrysalis Records in a quiet cul de sac behind London's busiest thoroughfare, Oxford Street.

It is three days before the grotesque event at the Dakota apartments three thousand miles away in New York City and the meeting with George Martin is recalled in the wistful retrospect of its innocence of the tragedy to come.

George Martin is in the midst of producing a new LP with Paul and Linda and Wings, the first time in eight years that he is working with McCartney. "Not that he really needs *me*—" he smiles diffidently. "He's such a clever bloke—a melder of sounds, not a straight ahead rock and roller. All that he needs from me is a person who can see the whole picture. And hear it. He trusts me not to give the psychiatric view."

One of nature's truly elegant men, he looks like the hero of a stiff upper lip movie set during World War II and, in fact, did serve as a flyer in the Royal Navy. Low key and courteous of manner, he conveys a sense of fierce integrity and gentle strength. Sitting opposite him over a morning cup of tea, the recipient of his full attention, it's easy to understand the emotional trust and professional confidence the Beatles felt for this extraordinary man.

Among his fondest Beatles memories this sunny Friday morning are the making of "Strawberry Fields Forever" and "Penny Lane." "Two masterpieces" is how American music critic Jack Kroll assessed them from the retrospect of 1981, asserting that they demon-strate McCartney and Lennon's greatest gifts as artists, "their genius blending images of Utopia and loss, a beautiful but tough idealism about reality and its way of dissolving into a dream."

Contrasting Paul's "Penny Lane"'s surreal characters, the barber, the banker and the fireman beneath blue suburban skies, with John's "Strawberry Fields' school where he was taken to the annual garden party by his Aunt Mimi, Kroll concluded, "These are great songs. If they are pop, then clearly pop is capable of greatness in expressing the gathering pathos of mass society."

George Martin remembers the day in November, 1966, when John first played "Strawberry Fields" for him and Paul. "I was sitting on my usual high stool and Paul was beside me. John stood before us with his acoustic guitar and sang it. It was absolutely lovely."

But something happened during the recording session. "It had somehow lost the gentle quality. It was good heavy rock which was something else."

Up to that time, the Beatles had never re-recorded anything. Spontaneous energy was central to the creative process. "We always thought that if it didn't work out the first time around, we shouldn't try it again."

As it turned out, John shared Martin's uneasiness and suggested the producer score something for trumpets and cellos to add a new dimension to the effort. It wasn't long before the Beatles were back in the studio to record a new, improved "Strawberry Fields Forever."

Now came the dilemma. John liked the beginning of the first cut and the end of the second. How would it be if George Martin simply joined the two parts together?

"There were two small problems," the producer remembers with obvious delight. "The two cuts were in different keys and different tempos."

Challenged by what seemed an insurmountable task, he listened to the two versions again and again, waiting for inspiration. Suddenly, he realized that the way the keys were arranged, the slower version was a semi-tone flat compared to the faster one.

"If I could speed up one and slow down the other, I could get the pitches the same and, with any luck, the tempos would be sufficiently close so one wouldn't notice the difference—I hoped!"

Using a variable control tape machine, he joined the two versions together. The combination worked and that's how it was released.

"Penny Lane" presented a challenge of a different kind. At a concert performance of Bach's Brandenburg Concerto, Paul had heard a piccolo trumpet and suggested the Beatles include the high piping instrument in the recording of "Penny Lane". The piccolo trumpet plays an octave above a traditional trumpet and is therefore half its length, almost like a toy, about ten inches long.

The ever-accommodating Martin hired David Mason of the London Symphony Orchestra to bring his piccolo trumpet and join the recording session.

"It was something that had never been done in rock before. Paul would decide which notes he wanted and I would write them down for David. The result was unique and it gave "Penny Lane" a distinct character."

When it was decided to release both songs together as a single, there could be no B-side. Both were A-side and were acclaimed and reviewed as such. In George Martin's estimation, "It was the best record we ever made." His only disappointment was that it failed to reach Number One on the charts during the first week of issue.

"Unlucky Thirteen" he still calls it exactly thirteen years after the event. The twelve previous Beatles releases had soared instantly to top chart position: "Please Please Me," "From Me To You," "She Loves You," "I Want To Hold Your Hand," "Can't Buy Me Love," "A Hard Day's Night," "I Feel Fine," "Ticket To Ride," "Help!," "Day Tripper," "Paperback Writer" and "Yellow Submarine."

Not that the Double-A was exactly a failure. It zoomed to the Number Two spot that first week. Ironically, the song that topped them was Englebert Humperdinck's "Release Me," produced by Peter Sullivan who was to become George Martin's partner in later years.

A pioneer in the development of recording processes, George Martin's favorite description is to compare making a record to painting a picture with sound. "Orchestration is different from composition. Orchestration is what gives color to what's written. Composition is musical line and harmony. Whether it's performed on a synthesizer or a hundred piece orchestra, it's still the basic composition. Orchestration is painting a picture with a subtle coloring and a three dimensional form. I get a mental picture of how the sound picture will turn out."

With "Yesterday," for example, he points out that they used orchestration for the first time and from then on progressed to whole new areas. This had two results. On the one hand, the increasing sophistication of the records meant that George Martin, producer, was having a greater influence, technical and otherwise, on the music and the final result.

But on the other hand, the personal relationship between him and the Beatles changed, too.

"At the start, I was like the master with his pupils and they did what I said. They knew nothing about recording but heaven knows they learned quickly so

that soon I was to become the servant and they the masters."

As to comparisons of the Beatles with such classical composers as Beethoven, Bach and Schubert, George Martin shrugs amiably. It's a subject he's frequently asked to comment upon. "Not the same category, of course, although Beethoven wrote for bands and Schubert could be said to have written 'pop' music in that his songs were sung for the pleasure of ordinary people. If Bach were alive today, I'm sure he'd be working at music in the same way that we do in the business today. Above all, he was a worker and a craftsman and he didn't enjoy much reverence in his time."

Where he would place the Beatles historically is in comparison with such American composers as George Gershwin, Cole Porter and Jerome Kern. "The Beatles output is concentrated. They wrote nearly three hundred songs in ten years. Just remember that in Bach and Beethoven's time, the working class never heard of them. There was no such thing as music for the masses. Even in the 1930s you had to be able to afford Gershwin and Kern records and sheet music. In the 1960s, it was the first time in history that young people had the money and influence to start a musical revolution. The Beatles music and lyrics are of its generation."

George Martin's assistant, Shirley Burns, has been holding calls but now there is one that cannot be postponed. Paul McCartney wants to schedule the afternoon recording session at the studio in Sussex for the LP-in-progress that will be interrupted by the trauma of John Lennon's death and only completed many

desolate weeks later at George Martin's studios on the Caribbean island of Montserrat.

Since Martin's wife, Judy, and the children are at their country house, he has been staying on his own at their London flat. As he gets ready to leave for Sussex, a concerned and protective Shirley wants to know, "What time did you get back from the studio last night?"

"After midnight."

"Did you have your supper, then?"

Martin's manner becomes that of a guilty schoolboy. A man who could easily order in a gourmet feast, he confesses to having cooked himself a "nursery tea" consisting of three rashers of bacon, baked beans on toast and a steaming mug of Horlicks, a malted milk concoction cherished by generations of British children.

The veteran producer's departure for the recording studio suddenly personalizes the statistical fact that this kind self-effacing man was a crucial participant in the recording of over two hundred Beatles songs. The enormity of this prompts a final record collector's question.

"Do you have a complete set of all the Beatles records?"

A pause. A smile. "I have them all in my head."

—Jeannie Sakol

Musical Innovations:

How the Beatles Broke the Rules and Made New Ones

When I think back on those days when they first exploded across the country, I realize I still don't understand exactly how or why. To the extent that I anticipated a new Beatles record, through the entire course of their career, I was constantly wondering just exactly how much more experimental, even atonal-edged, they were going to allow themselves (or, possibly more accurately, George Martin was going to allow them) to get. There's never been any denying that in almost more ways than anyone could ever count the Beatles really did reinvent rock 'n' roll from the ground up.

Everybody knows the Beatles were innovators, but seldom is it precisely explained *how* they did it. Either you get some mustydusty old music prof croaking on about how "Love Me Do" was the introduction of Lydian Chromatic Theorems to rock (Musicologist Wilfrid Mellers informed us that in "She Loves You," "the opening phrase is pentatonic, or perhaps in an Aeolian C which veers towards E flat," while the more downtown Ned Rorem reassured everybody that "The best of these memorable tunes—and the best is a large percentage ('Here, There and Everywhere,' 'Good Day Sunshine,' 'Michelle,' 'Norwegian Wood')—compare with those by composers from great eras of song: Monteverdi, Schumann, Poulenc."), or you get the geegoshwow weren't they *neat* school of pure fan gush. Neither of which is necessarily bad for what it is and who it's directed at, but still both fail to answer for the layman unschooled in harmony, theory etc. the question: "Just what did them dudes do to make 'em *sound* like that?"

To show you what exactly their innovations were, I'll go through their LP output as originally recorded and released, and list an example or two from each album which represents what I feel to be some of the Beatles' prime innovations/contributions/most influential moves:

Introducing The Beatles (Vee Jay), later reissued as **The Early Beatles** (Capitol): Okay, in this instance a mustydusty was right, and in terms anybody could understand: namely Leonard Bernstein, when he pointed out on CBS-TV how "Love Me Do" incorporated a drone effect which of course foretold the later inclusion of Indian ragas and suchlike as source materials. Did the Beatles know this when they recorded it? Nah. They were just having a little fun with Everly Brothers type harmonies and harmonica. (Which maybe means it wasn't so innovative after all. Leonard and I will have to sit down with a copy of "Bird Dog" or maybe "Cathy's Clown" one of these days and hash this out.)

Meet the Beatles (Capitol—as all future releases be till **The Beatles** a.k.a. "White Album"): The first time I heard "I Wanna Hold Your Hand," all I could think was "The Beatles in the sky." I'd heard of these guys, but nothing quite prepared me for that sunblindingly brilliant high note they hit on "I get *hiiiiiigh*" (or I can't hide," as you will). Nobody previously in rock 'n' roll had hit a high note quite so blazingly resonant (Elvis being basically a baritone, Little Richard a screamer, etc.). Result: countless million teenage girls round the world shrieking along, trying to beat the band (literally) to hit it and all failing (maybe if Wilfrid Mellers'd tried). That got called "charisma."

The Beatles' Second Album: The Stones were the official Bad Boys always, and to this day a lot of people including your reporter have tended to prefer them for precisely that ultimately juvenile reason, but it's also fact that they could generally be found trotting along a few months later in the Beatles' very wake stylewise (as Lennon pointed out in *Lennon Remembers*, and that aside from a couple of goodies like "Brown Sugar" and "Jumping Jack Flash" most of the certified Hall of Fame bronzetone RIFFS purloined and run into the ground by every would be-badass heavy metal band as well as most other rockbands for over a decade now came straight from the Beatles. Crucial early example on this album: "You Can't Do That," built on one of the bitterest and most iron-indestructible riffs ever conceived. It's like, if somebody steals a Stones riff everybody goes "Oh yeah, that's 'Satisfaction'" or whatever, but when "You Can't Do That" or "Day Tripper" or any one of a hundred other Beatles frames is lifted, nobody says anything because *everybody's* already stole 'em so many times they've sort of entered the *lingua franca*, public domain, etc.

Something New: With "Matchbox," the Beatles proved they had the smarts to go back farther than Chicago blues (i.e., farther than vaunted blues kings Rolling Stones) for source material, all the way back to Blind Lemon Jefferson (the Stones wouldn't get that far back till they recorded Robert Johnson's "Love in Vain" in '69). Even if they did have to stop off by Carl Perkins' place to borrow it.

Beatles '65: For years a controversy has been raging between fans and occasionaly in the press over just exactly who "invented" feedback: Jeff Beck, Jimmy Page, Eric Clapton, Pete Townshend or Dave Davies? Overlooking the fact that feedback could never be "invented" at all, still one must grant that its first appearance introduced deliberately into a rock 'n' roll side (as pointed out by Lennon in his and Yoko's January 1981 *Playboy* interview) was in "I Feel Fine," presaging the contributions of Mssrs. Beck-Page-Clapton-Townshend-Davies *et. al.* by a good 6–12 months at least.

Beatles VI: Before the Beatles (well, all right, and Bob Dylan, but he was—don't try to deny it—always basically a folkie), almost all rock songs fell into one of a handful of basic categories: "I love you but you don't love me," "You love me yuch buzz off," "You don't love me just yet but how 'bout it huh okay pretty please?" etc. This left no room for ambiguity, which the Beatles almost singlehandedly introduced and which has dominated much of the rock made since because half the time in lyrics by say Blondie or Elvis Costello you haven't a clue what these creeps are on about. The Beatles sometimes achieved higher drama by underplaying, *e.g.* George's "You Like Me Too Much," probably the first song in rock history whose lyrics admitted that neither party loved the other but neither had the guts to call it quits. Real adult stuff, ambiguity here deriving from the listener's implicit knowledge that inasmuch as he was even bothering to say all this stuff in the first place, they might very well break up after all, either that or end up spending their whole lives living a lie. Either way, the tension is palpable: "Could this be *me?*" we all thought, and looked across the carseat at our girlfriends/boyfriends.

Help: Introduction of sitars of course, even if only in soundtrack instrumentals as yet. But the real move is in the title song, which was the first admission in rock history that superstardom just might not be all it was cracked up to be. Since then, of course, we have drowned in nauseatingly bathetic depositions re same. The only previous thing that came close was probably Paul Anka's "Lonely Boy," and hell, he was just a spoiled rich kid, which of course is far different: "I've got everything you could think of/But all I want is someone to love." The condition of superstardom is never explicitly mentioned in "Help." but you can't help being aware of it, it's implicit, these are the BEATLES talkin' (where Elvis mouthed other folks' words and Chuck Berry told stories), as dank clouds of self-consciousness for both them and us formed on the horizon.

Rubber Soul: "Norwegian Wood" was of course the first use of sitar in a rock 'n' roll song, but what probably made it more important in the long run was that it was also the first time in rock that a male protagonist turned down a lusty woman for non-macho reasons (and not because "we should wait to get married" either)—i.e., here comes *sensitivity*, which will ultimately decay into the horrid likes of "You've Got a Friend."

Yesterday and Today: "Dr. Robert" was first-ever use of backwards guitar tapes, later employed extensively by everybody from the Byrds to Quine/Harris. Also, "We Can Work It Out" was the first application of Beatles-spirit to self-consciously "social"/"topical"/"political" implications beyond love songs or the group itself, i.e. first implication anybody actually thought that the Beatles could save the world.

Revolver: "Eleanor Rigby"—first use of string quartet *sans* guitars or rhythm section in fact as *sole* backing for a rock vocal. "Love You To"—first injection of ersatz Eastern Wisdom into rock. "Good Day Sunshine" was wonderful at the time but responsible for

"Feelin' Groovy" and a whole generation of ersatz good vibey airhead salutations (well, okay, the Lovin' Spoonful hadda share some blame). "Tomorrow Never Knows" was the second injection of ersatz Eastern Wisdom into rock, plus the first example of why you should never put books (in this case *The Tibetan Book of the Dead*, no less) into the hands of most rockers, eager-beaver for cultural status and social relevance as they are (*cf.* whoever gave the Clash a copy of Orwell's *Homage to Catalonia* resulting in "Spanish Bombs").

Sgt. Pepper: First rock opera—Richard Goldstein was right, in his much-vilified review in the New York *Times* when it first came out, predicting that this record had the power to almost singlehandedly destroy rock 'n' roll. Also the first album in which we realized with what absolute solemnity the Beatles were beginning to take their Mission (again, shades of the Clash, except it took the Beatles so much longer); take "With a Little Help From My Friends"—where the Stones always sneered or at least smirked at their "personas," Ringo's is presented as positively *noble* somehow. "Getting Better" was certainly one of the first instances of Beatles As Paternal Comforters, while with "A Day in the Life" wretched excess set in for real (remember that picture in *Time* magazine of McCartney in a butcher's smock and shades up there *conducting* that orchestra?) —all suggesting that they were beginning to believe their worst-informed writeups.

Magical Mystery Tour: "Flying" was the Beatles' first instrumental and McCartney's first venture into FM muzak. "Your Mother Should Know" was the first anti-generation gap song in rock written from *that* side of the gap. Lewis Carroll enters with his "Walrus," shudders, leaves the room. "Strawberry Fields Forever" meanwhile boasts not only the first false ending in rock history, but the first time a hardcore rock 'n' roll singer imitates Barbra Streisand (the way Lennon phrases

"fore*vah!*" coulda come right out of "Second Hand Rose").

The Beatles a.k.a "The White Album" (Apple): The first album by the Beatles or in the history of rock by four solo artists in one band; later, of course, this practice would become commonplace (C.F. *Tusk*, the works of Crosby, Stills, Nash & Young, etc.). Also first rock album to albeit indirectly inspire mass murders.

Abbey Road: (Apple): "You Never Give Me Your Money" was the first example of insider's biz-bitching pettiness in a Beatles song (later examples abound: Graham Parker's "Mercury Poisoning," Lynyrd Skynyrd's "Working for MCA," Lou Reed's "Dirt" addressed to his former manager/lawyer), although George's "Taxman" off *Revolver* must stand as the first rock 'n' roll song wherein a millionaire star complained on record about his financial situation. *Abbey Road* was also the first album to spark rumors that one of the Beatles was dead, which means the fans sensed *something* was wrong almost a year before the Beatles formally broke up.

Let It Be (Apple): First Beatles LP tied in with a movie that was totally boring and depressing. First time any of the Beatles had to bring in an outside producer (Phil Spector) to do a cleanup job (and some say even that was botched).

Hey Jude (Apple): In "Rain," first use of backwards voices in rock, later carried on by Roger McGuinn in the Byrds' "Mr. Spaceman" among others.

—Lester Bangs

LET IT BE

Transformations:

From the Beatles' nova-like emergence in late 1963 until Paul McCartney's official announcement of the group's disintegration on April 10, 1970, the fabulous four never once truly faltered. They did some crazed, even foolish, things, but none of it ever diminished their collective mystique; and in the most important area—the music—they almost never put out even a mediocre song, let alone a bad one. One might describe the Beatles as having been for seven straight years the world's most successful recording artists—in both commercial and artistic terms—but that would only be the half of it. One might say they were the preeminent symbols of a cultural revolution among the youth of Europe, Britain, America, and the rest of the English-speaking world, but that doesn't quite do them justice either. As their press officer Derek Taylor once said, they became an abstraction, like Christmas. In a word, the Beatles were magic.

Having transformed everything from the look of album covers and male hairstyles to the sound and sense of the modern popular song, John, Paul, George, and Ringo went their separate ways. But they were still viewed as Beatles, even if the group was no more, and the world's expectations remained enormous. Everyone eagerly waited for Paul McCartney to fulfill the dazzling promise of *Abbey Road*'s "Pop Symphony," for John Lennon to point the way toward new pinnacles of revelation and enlightenment, for the Magical Mystery Tour to go on indefinitely. Only slowly would it dawn on Beatlemaniacs that—as Lennon himself sang on his first solo LP—the dream was over. As surely as the Sixties and the Beatles had passed into history, so had the magic sparked by the interaction of those times and those personalities and talents.

Because the split was so bitter, the solo fortunes of Lennon, McCartney, Harrison, and Starr took on the aspect of a competition in the minds of both the ex-Beatles and their audience. Fans and critics lined up behind one or another, taking sides as their estranged heroes battled each other in the press, in the courts, and even on the covers and within the grooves of their solo records.

Since Lennon and McCartney had always constituted the major creative force behind the Beatles' music, expectations for these two were particularly high. In the case of Paul McCartney, the disappointment came almost immediately.

The fact that Paul had timed his break-up bombshell to tie in with the release of his first solo album left the *McCartney* LP in a rather bad odor to begin with. Paul's celebrated gift for P.R. must have deserted him when he assumed all the "credit" for the split that he, of all the Beatles, had most struggled to avoid. The problem was only compounded upon his initiation of court proceedings, on the last day of 1970, to dissolve the partnership. (No matter that Paul's real aim was to extricate himself from the clutches of Allen Klein, the three other Beatles' manager.)

Furthermore McCartney, in breaking with his past, also appeared to turn his back on much that the Beatles had come to represent, at least within the so-called counterculture. In both packaging and content, *McCartney* blatantly celebrated the bourgeois pleasures of (as Paul put it) "home, family, love." *McCartney* and its sequels offered little in the way of poetry or musical innovation; they were in no sense even remotely hip. Upon launching his post-Beatles career, Paul seems to have decided that his only mission was to entertain.

Perhaps this was an astute assessment of the direction rock was soon to take, but even as Paul won his case in court, the countercultural rags like *Rolling Stone* and *Crawdaddy* found him guilty of betraying the Beatles and all they had stood for, and McCartney was effectively banished to the Siberia of teenybopperdom. His critics overlooked the very real off-the-cuff charm of his first solo album, which was something of a tour-de-force in that Paul overdubbed all the instruments himself, mostly at home on his Scottish farm. Doors slam, birds chirp, Linda titters, you can almost taste the fresh country air.

Stung by the barbs, however, McCartney abandoned this do-it-yourself approach for "the top people in the top studio." The result was the hollow chocolate *Ram* (1971), which was sweet at first taste but fell to pieces if you tried to sink your teeth in—an album cluttered with self-conscious production gimmicks and superb snatches of melody that go nowhere. Paul's critics called it the worst disaster ever, which it wasn't, and said he was obviously out of touch on his own and needed to interact with a band. McCartney took the hint and formed Wings, with his unmusical wife Linda spotlighted on keyboards and back-up vocals—not the first time an ambitious Beatle wife staked a claim on her husband's professional turf.

Yet another album, *Wild Life* (1971) was hastily assembled, some of it made up on the spot in an attempt to emulate the immediacy Bob Dylan was said to bring

to his recording sessions. One side was fast for dancing and the other slow for smooching (as Linda helpfully explained), but both were equally lame. And so we leave McCartney in late 1971, limping well at the back of the pack.

John and George, meanwhile, continued to view themselves as Artists with a message and a mission, working in a medium that both still believed could change the world. The messages of these two ex-Beatles, however, couldn't have been more different from one another.

After secluding himself in California with Yoko for two months of Dr. Arthur Janov's harrowing Primal Scream therapy, John reemerged to exorcise his demons with his so-called Primal Album (*John Lennon/Plastic Ono Band*) (1970), and the remarkable book-length "Lennon Remembers" interview with *Rolling Stone*'s Jann Wenner. Both on record and in print, John savagely dismantled every "myth" (from the Bible to the Beatles) that he and his listeners had ever believed in. His new music and lyrics were pared to the bone and straight to the point, truly stripping this extraordinary artist naked to the world. *Plastic Ono Band* is a fascinating and disturbing self-portrait, a monumental feat of both self-indulgence and sheer guts. As art, however, much of this myth-breaking derived its power largely from the context of Lennon's previous myth-making; and the sound of his "pain" certainly didn't qualify as entertainment. The critics raved, but the album didn't exactly fly out of the stores.

Imagine (1971) offered a few more concessions to popular taste; the guts and sensitivity were still evident, but so too were compelling melodies, irresistible hooks, and rich, full arrangements. With his second solo album at Number One, Lennon's stature seemed virtually undiminished. But there were danger signals: a single, "Power to the People," on which John indiscriminately parroted the cliches of his new radical politico friends; and *Imagine*'s "How Do You Sleep?," a self-righteous character assassination of McCartney, whom Lennon charged with becoming a has-been, a Muzak monger, and (perhaps most unforgivably) a "straight" family man. (In all fairness, it should be pointed out that Paul's *Ram* had allegedly baited Lennon with its coy digs at people "going underground" and "preaching practices," not to mention its symbolic photograph of one beetle buggering another.)

Yet it was the Dark Horse (as George Harrison later styled himself) who took the early lead in the ex-Beatles sweepstakes. Having blossomed as a songwriter

towards the end of the group's history, with "While My Guitar Gently Weeps" and "Here Comes the Sun" and "Something," George launched his solo career with an enormous backlog of quality material for which the Beatles' original songsmiths had deemed there "no room" on the band's albums. Ably assisted by legendary "wall-of-sound" producer Phil Spector and a veritable pop orchestra comprising many of the top names in the business, George created rock's first elegantly boxed three-record set, the overwhelming *All Things Must Pass* (1970). To towering, painstakingly crafted productions, characterized by *Rolling Stone*'s reviewer as "music of mountain tops and vast horizons," Harrison set his Hindu-influenced parables and sermons: there were also a few folk- and country-flavored confections that owed more to George's hero and friend Bob Dylan. The album clung to the Number One slot for much of the winter, as did the single "My Sweet Lord."

The following summer George organized and starred in New York's historic benefit concerts for Bangla Desh, and even coaxed Dylan out of retirement for the occasion. What with Lennon and McCartney's tacky bickering and all, Harrison appeared to many in late 1971 to be the only real hero to have survived the wreckage of the Beatles.

Another performer at the concerts for Bangla Desh was Ringo Starr, from whom few had expected much in the way of solo accomplishments: after all, he had composed but two Beatles tunes, or about 1% of the group's songbook, and was hardly a great singer or versatile musician. In 1970, Ringo issued two rather unsuccessful "specialty" albums, one of pre-rock ballads (*Sentimental Journey*) and one of country music (*Beaucoups of Blues*). (A third, electronic LP was never released.) But then the little drummer boy took everyone by surprise with a catchy, self-penned, Harrison-produced hit single, "It Don't Come Easy." The B-side, "Early 70," offered afficionados a fascinating insight into Ringo's view of his ex-colleagues. Paul was portrayed as too busy with family and farm to bother with his former sidekick, John as willing to play when he could find the time; but George was "always in town playing for you with me."

Paul, however, soon showed signs of coming out of his shell to get his act together. After puttering round Britain in a van playing surprise gigs at universities on a few hours' notice, Wings toured Europe and in 1973 managed a full-scale swing though the U.K. that was marred only by Paul's refusal to sing any of his Beatles

In the Bahamas, 1965, for "A Hard Day's Night."

songs. Dreadful flop singles (e.g., "Mary Had a Little Lamb") gave way to respectable hits ("Hi Hi Hi") and, finally, an almost unbroken string of million sellers (starting with "My Love" and the theme from the James Bond flick *Live and Let Die.*)

Red Rose Speedway, an endearing and well-produced collection of silly love songs, gave Wings their first American Number One album in mid-1973, after which McCartney took a working vacation in Nigeria —where, galvanized by a string of disasters, including the untimely departure of their drummer and lead guitarist, the remnants of Wings—Paul, Linda, and the ever-faithful Denny Laine—produced their first and only masterpiece. Chock-full of inventive and uplifting melodies whose lyrics all followed the theme of flight, escape, and freedom, *Band on the Run* (1973) caused the aging hipsters to welcome Paul back to the fold, yielded three hit singles, and literally stayed on the charts for years.

Lennon, meanwhile, had stumbled badly with a commercially disastrous collection of heavy-handed political "statements," *Some Time in New York City* (1972), and became embroiled in a debilitating legal battle with a Nixon regime bent on expelling this young subversive from the land of the free. With *Mind Games* (1973) John rediscovered the sense of humor so conspicuously missing from his earlier solo work, but for the first time he was largely recycling his old ideas.

A painful separation from Yoko followed, with Lennon departing for Los Angeles to record a rock 'n' roll "oldies" LP with Phil Spector. When the enigmatic producer disappeared with the unfinished tapes, John made the headlines with his new persona of an obnoxious drunkard; and eventually returned to New York to chronicle the emotional traumas of his "Sinbad's Voyage" to California with *Walls and Bridges* (1974) an American Number One album that brilliantly combined the soul-bearing of *Plastic Ono Band*, the tunefulness of *Imagine*, and the humor of *Mind Games*.

Lennon subsequently reconciled with Yoko, completed the *Rock 'n' Roll* album (1975) without Spector, and was awarded his Green Card entitling him to permanent residence in the United States. On his thirty-fifth birthday Yoko gave birth to their first child, Sean, and Lennon retired from the music business for a full five years to devote himself to his family and the acquisition of American real estate.

Harrison, for his part, followed *All Things Must Pass* 18 months later with an album that successfully duplicated the former's painstaking production, melodic richness, and elegiac tone. *Living in the Material World* (1973), in fact, remains the only LP by an ex-

Beatle to have hit Number One on *Billboard* within two weeks of its release. But many critics gagged on an excess of Krishna Consciousness pervading both the packaging and the lyrics. The slipshod *Dark Horse* (1974) and the poorly planned and executed North American tour (the first by an ex-Beatle) that followed, gave them all the ammunition they required to shoot Harrison off his pedestal with a vengeance. Matters hardly improved with the dismal *Extra Texture* (1975), and holy George was further bedeviled by court proceedings that found him guilty of plagiarizing his biggest hit, "My Sweet Lord," from the Chiffons' "He's So Fine."

Ringo Starr, that darkest horse of them all, briefly outpaced the other three after he cajoled each into lending a helping hand on his first "real" solo LP, *Ringo* (1973). Thanks no doubt to their lingering rivalry, each strove to outshine the others by providing material of a somewhat higher caliber than the usual Beatle solo outing; and on John's "I'm the Greatest" all save McCartney could be heard playing together on what remains the closest approximation of a recorded Beatles reunion. Bolstered by Richard Perry's slick yet inventive production and a supporting cast of dozens of other celebrity "friends" the album proved an almost endless source of hit singles, among them Harrison and Starr's "Photograph" and the "oldie" "You're Sixteen." But when Ringo attempted to repeat the winning formula on *Goodnight Vienna* (1974) and *Rotogravure* (1976), spontaneous excitement and charm only gave way to excruciating dullness.

By that time, though, it really didn't matter anymore. Fans had come to realize that, on their own, John, Paul, George, and Ringo neither could nor should be equated with the Beatles. By 1976, the Beatles had become an untouchable myth, and the subject of an unprecedented revival. Their legend was commemorated in books and films, TV specials and Broadway musicals, and fanzines and fan conventions— whose giant flea markets offered circa-1964 Beatle toys and trinkets and rare editions of Beatle records for tens of times their original retail value. Meanwhile, reissues and repackages of their recordings took over the charts and the airwaves all over again, sounding fresh as ever. There was more to it than nostalgia; the Beatles at their best had proved timeless.

The pressure for the group to reunite was enormous, but the ex-Beatles wisely ignored all the astronomical offers. As John would tell *Newsweek*: "Whatever made the Beatles the Beatles also made the Sixties the Sixties, and anyone who thinks that if John and Paul got together with George and Ringo, 'The Beatles' would exist, is out of their skulls." Said George: "The Beatles are for the history books, like the year 1492."

Of all the former Fabs, only Paul continued to produce at anything like the old pace. Unlike the others, he re-signed with Capitol in 1975 for an unprecedented sum, only to break his own record four years later when he switched to Columbia. In 1976, his heavy international touring schedule culminated in Wings Over America, where McCartney's professionalism and showmanship—and a generous sampling of Beatles classics—earned him widespread and well-deserved acclaim. But for all Paul's efforts to establish Wings as a *group*, the constant turnover of musicians emphasized the fact that they were little more than a back-up band for an ex-Beatle. And though McCartney's commercial sense seldom failed him during the mid-to-late Seventies, many critics soon soured once again on the triviality and sentimentality of Wings' output.

Recording for his own Dark horse label, a less strident George Harrison appeared to recapture his muse on a series of finely crafted yet somewhat low-key albums. Commercially, however, he was out of the big leagues, content to concentrate on gardening, racecars, and pursuing a quiet family life with his new Mexican bride Olivia.

Ringo hit an all-time low when former Bee Gees producer Arif Mardin was brought in to perpetrate some formula disco in the ex-Beatle's name. But Atlantic's *Ringo the Fourth* (1977) didn't sell, and Starr resumed his customary role of "the world's most charming bit-part player," doing cameos in films and designing classy, off-beat furniture on the side. On the set of *Caveman* (1980), he met *his* second wife, sometime *Playboy* pin-up Barbara Bach.

Throughout the late Seventies, any lingering hopes that an ex-Beatle might yet set the music scene on its ear devolved upon John Lennon—the one who, prior to his retirement, had issued the most interesting solo albums, and the only ones to suggest any continuing artistic growth—until the clamor for John's "return" almost resembled that for the Beatles themselves. For those harboring such inflated expectations, *Double Fantasy* (1980) proved a disappointment. With Yoko claiming half the vocals and songwriting credits, it was only half a Lennon album to begin with, and even that half seemed to lack much of the old fire and wit, poetry and vision.

Perhaps what was missing was simply Lennon's old demons; he had finally found real happiness and fulfillment as a "househusband," being for young Sean both the father and the mother John himself had

lacked. By stressing that getting one's own house in order must take precedence over any attempt to make the world at large a better place, John felt he was making as important a statement as ever—which he underlined by giving his wife "equal space" on the album. Still, in their own more sophisticated celebrations of "home, family, love," John and Yoko inevitably recalled their antitheses of a decade earlier, the Paul and Linda of *McCartney* or *Red Rose Speedway*.

Then again, nobody had any right to demand otherwise, at a time when most teenagers (the age group that had comprised the original audiences for both the Beatles and rock music) hadn't even been born when the Magical Mystery Tour first got underway. Thoughtful Beatlemaniacs could only be glad that their heroes all appeared to be approaching middle-age so happily, that everything in their own lives had turned out so well.

As solo artists, all the ex-Beatles had their moments, even if none (except, perhaps, John) truly amounted to much without the others. Certainly, they failed on their own to set a single trend in or out of music, or even, when you come down to it, to write one Great Song on the order of a "Yesterday" or a "Hey Jude," let alone a "Strawberry Fields" or a "Day in the Life." But that was no reason to make one think any less of John, Paul, George, or Ringo; they had already accomplished far more than their share.

Even as I was finishing this piece, John Lennon's life was cut short by a psychotic assassin who—like Charles Manson—was himself a Beatlemaniac. I don't wish to dwell here on the unspeakable horror of December 8, 1980—or on its aftermath, that recalled to so many original Beatles fans their childhood memories of the wake of President Kennedy's assassination (for which the Fab Four originally provided something of an antidote). Only John Lennon probably touched his millions of followers in a far more profound and personal way than any president ever could.

The hail of an assassin's bullets seemed to end, once and for all, that era that had been ushered in in much the same manner on November 22, 1963. But despite our deep regret over the senseless and tragic passing of John Lennon, the great man and artist (made more poignant by our knowledge the personal happiness he had finally achieved), it must be said—in the context of this piece—that the erratic solo careers of Paul, George, Ringo, and even John had already made plain that the amazing Beatles story was no longer an ongoing saga, but, rather, a closed book.

—Nicholas Schaffner

Sgt. Pepper:

Sgt. Pepper
· Recording produced by George Martin
· Cover by MC Productions and the Apple
· Staged by Peter Blake and Jann Haworth
· Photographed by Michael Cooper
· Wax Figures by Madame Tussauds
· A splendid time is guaranteed for all

Who's Who
in Sgt. Pepper's Band

The first "rock concept" album. *The* bridge between art and pop. *The* most famous pop album in history.

Sgt. Pepper's Lonely Heart's Club Band is known not only for its brilliant musical imagery and biting lyrics, but for the cover of assembled luminaries ranging from childhood heroes (Lawrence of Arabia, Livingstone) to nostalgic movie stars (Mae West, Fred Astaire, Tom Mix) to public figures (Karl Marx and C.J. Jung) to original Beatle Stu Sutcliffe. To say nothing of the Fab Four themselves! When asked about the origin of the cover, the Beatles replied, "We wanted to put on people we like!"

1, Guru (Indian holy man); 2, Aleister Crowley (The Beast 666—black magician); 3, Mae West; 4, Lenny Bruce (American comedian); 5, Stockhausen (Modern German composer); 6, W.C. Fields; 7, C.J. Jung (psychologist); 8, Edgar Allan Poe; 9, Fred Astaire; 10, Merkin (American artist); 11, Drawing of a girl; 12, Huntz Hall (Bowery Boy); 13, Simon Rodia (folk artist—creator of Watts Towers); 14, Bob Dylan; 15, Aubrey Beardsley (Victorian artist); 16, Sir Robert Peel (Police pioneer); 17, Aldous Huxley (philosopher); 18, Dylan Thomas (Welsh poet); 19, Terry Southern (author).

20, Dion (American pop singer); 21, Tony Curtis; 22, Wallace Berman (Los Angeles artist); 23, Tommy Handley (wartime comedian); 24, Marilyn Monroe; 25, William Burroughs (author of "The Naked Lunch"); 26, Guru; 27, Stan Laurel; 28, Richard Lindner (New York

artist); 29, Oliver Hardy; 30, Karl Marx; 31, H.G. Wells; 32, Guru; 33, Stuart Sutcliffe (former Beatle who died before group became famous); 34, Drawing of a girl; 35, Max Miller; 36, Drawing of a girl; 37, Marlon Brando; 38, Tom Mix (cowboy film star); 39, Oscar Wilde; 40, Tyrone Power; 41, Larry Bell (modern painter).

42, Dr. Livingstone (in wax); 43, Johnny Weissmuller (former Tarzan); 44, Stephen Crane (nineteenth century American writer); 45, Issy Bonn (comedian); 46, George Bernard Shaw (in wax); 47, Albert Stubbins (Liverpool footballer); 48, Guru; 49, Einstein; 50, Lewis Carroll; 51, Sonny Liston; 52, 53, 54, 55, The Beatles (in wax); 56, Guru; 57, Marlene Dietrich; 58, Diana Dors; 59, Shirley Temple (child star); 60, Bobby Breen (singing prodigy); 61, T.E. Lawrence (Lawrence of Arabia); 62, American Legionnaire.

Who's who in Sgt. Pepper's Band

Because:

John Lennon

FOR SEAN LENNON

their voices
have changed
as much as
their ears

we who were older
just danced
and made love

but their voices
have changed

the children
will never be
what we were

lem sat
on my bed
at seven-fifteen
in the morning
while i told him
john had died
sat silent
with his voice
this one time stopped

until he wrote
his poem for john

and nat
late that night
writing his

as we all have learned
to try to handle grief

but i wouldn't
have written a poem
at nine or fourteen

john helped them
do that

taught more
than a school
or a father
of the power of words
and how they move us
and how they serve
to carry grief

and how they
preserve life
in the midst
of murder

—joel oppenheimer

THE SONGWRITER

songwriter sits, overworked, overtired,
        writes songs day and night nonstop.
he writes songs for him, yoko, and us,
        we like him, he likes us.
someone stalks him, shoots, the killer
        doesn't care, he just wants to get into
        papers.
he shot a songwriter, he shot a legend.

—lem oppenheimer

FOR JOHN LENNON

hey bulldog sitting in the rain
why?

sixteen days before his
fortieth christmas
        he was shot

all together now,
he said,
to unite people,
to bring peace.

he will now say
hello to lucy with her
diamonds
up in those
marshmallow skies

he says hello and
we say
goodbye

—nat oppenheimer

Most Beatles singles, EPs and albums were released in the United States and England at different times, on different labels and often with different album titles. This discography lists the following information for the songs included in the two volumes of THE COMPLEAT BEATLES:

Abbreviations for arrangements: CH (Chorals); OR (Orchestra); CB (Concert Band); JB (Jazz Band); MB (Marching Band)

for Singles: songwriter; label and release number (US/UK); release date (US/UK); gold certification (US/UK); other awards; weeks on chart; producer; additional musicians who performed on the songs; arrangements available; and versions covered by other artists.

for EPs and Albums: EP title (US/UK); EP label and release number (US/UK); EP release date (US/UK); Album title (US/UK); Album label and release number (US/UK); Album release date (US/UK); gold certification (US/UK).

An addendum following the listings includes: a list of other Beatles albums, such as early releases by Tony Sheridan, and special compilation albums released before and after 1970; information on American and British chart listings; and Grammy awards for albums.

ACT NATURALLY

Written by:	Johnny Russell - Vonie Morrison
Single #:	USA: Capitol 5498
Released:	USA: Sept. 1965
Weeks on chart:	USA: 7
Produced by:	George Martin
EP:	UK: Yesterday, Parlophone GEP 8948 March 1966
Album:	USA: "Yesterday..." And Today, Capitol ST 2553 UK: Help! Parlophone PCS 3071
Released:	USA: June 1966 UK: August 1965
Gold:	USA: July 8, 1966
Additional Musicians:	Paul, Back-up vocals

ALL I'VE GOT TO DO

Written by:	Lennon/McCartney
Produced by:	George Martin
Album:	USA: Meet the Beatles!, Capitol ST 2047 UK: With the Beatles, Parlophone PCS 3045
Released:	USA: January 1964 UK: Nov 1963
Gold:	USA: Feb 3, 1964
Additional musicians:	Paul, Back-up vocals
Cover versions:	

The Beatles, Louise Goffin, Gene Johnson, Lester Lanin, George Martin, Moon Martin, The Merseyboys

ALL MY LOVING

Written by:	Lennon/McCartney
Awards:	Outstanding British song, 1963 (Ivor Novello Award)
Weeks on chart:	USA: 6
Produced by:	George Martin
EP:	USA: Four By The Beatles, Capitol EAP 2121, May 1964 UK: All My Loving, Parlophone GEP 8891, Feb 1964
Album:	USA: Meet the Beatles, Capitol ST 2047 UK: With the Beatles, Parlophone PCS 3045
Released:	USA: January 1964 UK: Nov 1963
Gold:	USA: Feb 3, 1964
Additional Musicians:	John & George, Back-up vocals
Arrangements:	JB, CB, CH
Cover Versions:	

All Star Pop Orchestra, Herb Alpert & The Tijuana Brass, Richard Anthony, Band of the Irish Guards, Count Basie, Terry Baxter Orchestra, The Beatles, The Beavers, The Bennetts, Harry Betts Chorale, The Big Ben Banjo Band, The Brothers Four, Cafe Creme, The Carefrees, The Chipmunks, Current Event, Sonny Curtis, Ray Davis, The Destitutes, Val Doonican, The Dowlands, Duke Ellington, The Frivolous Five, Annette Funicello, Johnny Gibbs & Orchestra, Francois Glorieux, Jim Gregory, Jimmy Griffin, Jimmie Haskell, The Hollyridge Strings, Iguana Brass, Paula Kelly & The Modernaires, Lester Lanin, Donald Lautrec, Bob Leaper, Don Leaper, The Leasebreakers, Les Gams, Les Lionceaux, Liverpool Sound, David Lloyd and Orchestra, Los Norte Americanos, Johnny Maddox, Henry Mancini & His Orchestra, Johnny Mann Singers, George Martin & His Orchestra, The Merseyboys, Mexicali Singers, Dale Miller, Matt Monro, Lamar Morris, Werner Muller, The Mustangs, Jack Nietzsche, The Pair, The Panics, George Paris, Polakin Orchestra, Johnny Puleo & The Harmonicats, Billy Lee Riley, The Rollers, Tony Romandini, The Sandpipers, Santo & Johnny, David Seville, Keely Smith, Sounds of Tijuana, Squirrel, The Surrey Strings, Sydney Thompson Orchestra, George Van Eps, The Velvet Strings, Roger Webb & His Trio, Mary Wells, The Windjammers, Windsor Strings, Leon Young, Leon Young String Quartet, Young World

AND I LOVE HER

Written by:	Lennon/McCartney
Single #:	USA: Capitol 5235
Released:	USA: July 1964
Awards:	Million performance song: June 1974
Weeks on chart:	USA: 9
Produced by:	George Martin
EP:	UK: A Hard Day's Night I, Parlophone GEP 8920, Nov 1964
Album:	USA: A Hard Day's Night, United Artists Uas 6366 USA: Something New, Capitol ST 2108 UK: A Hard Day's Night, Parlophone PCS 3058
Released:	USA: June 1964 USA: July 1964 UK: July 1964
Additional Musicians:	George & Ringo, Claves & Bongos; George, acoustic guitar solo
Arrangements:	MB, JB, CH
Cover versions:	

Wiomara Alfaro, All-Star Pop Orchestra, T.W. Ardy, Chet Atkins, Nick Ayoub, Count Basie, Terry Baxter, The Beatles, Big Ben Banjo Band, Boss Guitars, Brazilian Echoes, Brian Brown Trio, Brothers Four, Gilles Brown, Ray Bryant, Button Down Brass, Lee Castle, Gary Chester, The Chords, Renee Claude, Ray Coniff Singers, Lawrence Cook, Dick Crest Orchestra, Stuart Crosby, King Curtis, Xavier Cugat, Ray Davies, Lolita De Carlo, Detroit Emeralds, Bobby Engemann, Enoch Light, Jose Feliciano, Ferrante & Teicher, Arthur Fiedler & Boston Pops Orchestra, Buddy Fo, Connie Francis, Friends of Distinction, Rafael Gonzales, The Gophers, Eddie Graff, Julio Gutierrez, George Hamilton, Bob Hammer, Al Hirt, The Hollyridge Strings, Bob Holmes, Shirley Horn, Lena Horne, Jerry Inman, Jackie & Roy, Willis Jackson, Jack Jones, Sammy Kaye, Alan Keaton, Manny Keller, Roshaan Roland Kirk, Lester Lanin, Billy Larkin, The Lettermen, Ramsey Lewis Trio, David Lindup, Julie London, Roger Lorendo, Freddie McCoy, Gary McFarland, Carman McRae, George Maharis, Henry Mancini & his Orchestra, Johnny Mann Singers, W. Marambio, Mariachi Mexico, Ralph Marterie, George Martin & His Orchestra, Sergio Mendes & Brazil '66, Reggie Milner, Vincente Moroccoy, Tony Mottola, Peter Nero, David Newman, The Now Generation, Tony Osborne, Other Company, Overton Berry Trio, The Pair, George Paris, Rene Paulo, Jan Peerce, Peter & Gordon, Esther Phillips, John Pike, Pucho, Walter Raim, Randy Rayment, Smokey Robinson, The Rollers, The Romantic Strings, David Rose, Sacha, The Sandpipers, Santo & Johnny, Pete Schofield, Serendipity Singers, Bud Shank, Keely Smith, The Irv Spice Trio, Stargazers, Grady Tate, Teamates, The Ten Tuff Guitars, Sydney Thompson, Toc Band, Michele Torr, Leslie Uggams, The Uniques, George Van Eps, The Vibrations, Mary Wells, Ian Whitcomb, Roger Williams, Nancy Wilson, Hugo Winterhalter, Wisconsin Youth Symphony, Bobby Womack, Xylos, Inc., Si Zentner

AND YOUR BIRD CAN SING

Written by:	Lennon/McCartney
Produced by:	George Martin
Album:	USA: "Yesterday"...and Today, Capitol ST 2553 UK: Revolver, Parlophone PCS 7009
Released:	USA: June 1966 UK: August 1966
Gold:	USA: July 8, 1966
Additional Musicians:	Paul & George, Back-up vocals
Cover versions:	

The Beatles, The Charles River Valley Boys, E.F. McKay, George Martin & His Orchestra, Snail, Spanky & Our Gang

ANNA (GO TO HIM)

Written by:	Arthur Alexander
Produced by:	George Martin
EP:	USA: The Beatles, Vee Jay VJEP-1-903, March 1964 UK: The Beatles #1, Parlophone GEP 8883, Nov 1963
Album:	USA: Introducing the Beatles Vee Jay VJLP 1062 USA: The Early Beatles, Capitol ST 2309 UK: Please Please Me, Parlophone PCS 3042
Released:	USA: July 1963 March 1965 UK: March 1963

ANOTHER GIRL

Written by:	Lennon/McCartney
Produced by:	George Martin
Album:	USA: Help!, Capitol SMAS 2386 UK: Help!, Parlophone PCS 3071
Released:	USA: Aug 1965 UK: Aug 1965
Gold:	USA: August 23, 1965
Additional Musicians:	Paul, Lead Guitar; John & George, Back-up vocals
Cover versions:	

Beatles, David Budin, Lester Lanin, George Martin

ANYTIME AT ALL

Written by:	Lennon/McCartney
Produced by:	George Martin
EP:	UK: A Hard Day's Night II, Parlophone GEP 8924, Nov 1964
Album:	USA: Something New, Capitol ST 2108 UK: A Hard Day's Night, Parlophone PCS 3058
Released:	USA: July 1964 UK: July 1964
Gold:	USA: August 24, 1964
Additional Musicians:	Paul & George, Back-up vocals
Cover versions:	

The Beatles, The Big Ben Banjo Band, Blue Ash, Bob Hammer Band

ASK ME WHY

Written by:	Lennon/McCartney
Single #:	USA: VeeJay VJ 498
	UK: Parlophone R4983
Released:	USA: Feb 1963 UK: Jan 1963
Produced by:	George Martin
EP:	USA: The Beatles, VeeJay VJEP 1-903, March 1964
	UK: All My Loving, Parlophone GEP 8891, Feb. 1964
Album:	USA: The Early Beatles, Capitol ST 2309
	UK: Please Please Me, Parlophone PCS 3042
Released:	March 1965 UK: March 1963

BABY IT'S YOU

Written by:	Hal David - Burt Bacharach - Barney Williams
Produced by:	George Martin
Album:	USA: Introducing the Beatles, VeeJay VJLP 1062
	The Early Beatles, Capitol ST 2309
	UK: Please Please Me, Parlophone PCS 3042
Released:	USA: July 1963
	March 1965
	UK: March 1963
Additional Musicians:	George Martin, piano; George & Paul, Back-up vocals

BABY'S IN BLACK

Written by:	Lennon/McCartney
Produced by:	George Martin
EP:	UK: Beatles for Sale II, Parlophone GEP 8938, June 1965
Album:	USA: Beatles '65, Capitol ST 2228
	UK: Beatles for Sale, Parlophone PCS 3062
Released:	USA: Dec 1964 UK: Dec 1964
Gold:	USA: December 31, 1964

Cover versions:
The Applejacks, The Beatles, Bill Black, Charles River Valley Band, Jerry Inman, The Other Company, The Rollers, Sound Alike

BAD BOY

Written by:	Larry Williams
Produced by:	George Martin
Album:	USA: Beatles VI, Capitol ST 2358
	UK: A Collection of Beatles Oldies, Parlophone PCS 7016
Released:	USA: June 1965 UK: Dec 1966
Gold:	USA: July 1, 1965

Cover versions:
The Beatles, Shaun Cassidy

BOYS

Written by:	Luther Dixon - Wes Farrell
Single #:	USA: Capitol Starline 6066
Released:	USA: Oct. 1965
Produced by:	George Martin
Album:	USA: Introducing the Beatles, VeeJay VJLP 1062
	The Early Beatles, Capitol ST 2309
	UK: Please Please Me, Parlophone PCS 3042
Released:	USA: July 1963
	March 1965
	UK: March 1963

CAN'T BUY ME LOVE

Written by:	Lennon/McCartney
Single #:	USA: Capitol 5150
	UK: Parlophone R5114
Released:	USA: March 1964
	UK: March 1964
Gold:	USA: March 31, 1964
	UK: March 1964
Awards:	Most performed pop song: 1964, USA and England

Other:	1964, Highest Certified British Sales (Ivor Novello Awards)
Weeks on chart:	USA: 10 UK: 15
Produced by:	George Martin
EP:	UK: The Beatles' Million Sellers, Parlophone GEP 8946, Dec 1965
Album:	USA: A Hard Day's Night, United Artists UAS 6366
	Hey Jude, Apple SW 385/ SO 385
	UK: A Hard Day's Night, Parlophone PCS 3058
Released:	USA: June 1964
	February 1970
	UK: July 1964
Gold:	USA: March 6, 1970
Arrangements:	CB, CH

Cover versions:
Chet Atkins, Ena Baga, Band of the Irish Guards, Count Basie, Terry Baxter, Beatlemania, The Beatles, Madame Catherine Berberan, Big Ben Banjo Band, George Brooks, Sascha Burland, Cafe Creme, Chipmunks, The Chords, Dave Cortez, Elimination, The Eliminators, Tanya Falan, Arthur Fiedler & Boston Pops, Ella Fitzgerald, Sam Fletcher, Francois Glorieux, The Gophers, Sandy Gurley, Bob Hammer, Jimmie Haskell, The Hollyridge Strings, Jackie & Roy, Karlheinz Kastel, Kings Road, Lester Lanin, James Last, Brenda Lee, Les Lionceaux, Hank Levine, Liverpool 5, Los Hermanos Carrion, Henry Mancini, Grace Markay, Freddy Martin, George Martin & His Orchestra, Peter Matz, Jo Ment, Dale Miller, Werner Moller, Gerry Mulligan, The Musicmakers, The Now Generation, Don Randi, Michele Richard, Billy Lee Riley, Johnny Rivers, The Rollers, Rostal and Schaefer, Bela Sanders, Santo & Johnny, Shirley Scott, The Senate, Hal Serra, Keely Smith, Sound Alikes, The Supremes, David Clayton Thomas, Sydney Thompson, Stanley Turrentine, Unknown, Roger Webb, Mary Wells, Stan Worth, Zacharias

CHAINS

Written by:	Gerry Goffin - Carole King
Produced by:	George Martin
EP:	UK: The Beatles #1, Parlophone GEP 8883, Nov. 1963
Album:	USA: Introducing the Beatles, VeeJay VJLP 1062
	The Early Beatles, Capitol ST 2309
	UK: Please Please Me, Parlophone PCS 3042
Released:	USA: July 1963
	March 1965
	UK: March 1963

DAY TRIPPER

Written by:	Lennon/McCartney
Single #:	USA: Capitol 5555
	UK: Parlophone R5389
Released:	USA: Dec 1965 UK: Dec 1965
Awards:	Most performed pop song: 1966
Weeks on chart:	USA: 10 UK: 12
Produced by:	George Martin
Album:	USA: "Yesterday"...and Today, Capitol ST 2553
	UK: A Collection of Beatles Oldies, Parlophone PCS 7016
Released:	USA: June 1966 UK: Dec 1966
Gold:	USA: July 8, 1966
Additional Musicians:	John, Tambourine; George, Back-up vocals
Arrangements:	MB, JB, CH

Cover versions:
Amanda Ambrose, Astromusical Orchestra, J.J. Barnes, Terry Baxter, Beatlemania, The Beatles, The Baroque Brass, Odell Brown, Cafe Creme, The Chords, The Cornbread, Dave, Stan & Robbie, David Cloverdales White, Electric Light Orchestra, Jose Feliciano, Fever Tree, Steve Gibbons Band, Marty Gold Orchestra, The Gophers, The Heads, Jimi Hendrix, The Hollyridge Strings, Dee Irwin & Mamie Ghlore, Jalopy Five, The Jazz-3, Lafayette, Lester Lanin, Ramsey Lewis, Liverpool 5, London Festival Orchestra, Longines Symphonette, Lulu, The McCoys, Herbie Mann, Mann & Jones, Sergio Mendes & Brazil '66, Lee Moses, Anne Murray, Sandy Nelson, The New World Generation, The Now Generation, The

Orchestra of Sagittarius, The Other Company, Billy Preston, Otis Redding, Rene & Rene, The Rocklanders, The Rollers, The Rondeus, Mongo Santamarie, Sapodilla Punch, Nancy Sinatra, Sound Alike, Tartaglia, James Taylor, Ozzie Torrens, Cheap Trick, Vanilla Fudge, Vontastics, Geno Washington, Mae West, Yellow Magic Orchestra

DEVIL IN HER HEART

Written by:	Richard B. Drapkin
Produced by:	George Martin
Album:	USA: The Beatles' Second Album, Capitol ST 2080
	UK: With the Beatles, Parlophone PCS 3045
Released:	USA: April 1964 UK: Nov 1963
Gold:	USA: April 13, 1964
Additional Musicians:	Ringo, Maracas; John & Paul, Back-up vocals

DIZZY MISS LIZZIE

Written by:	Larry Williams
Produced by:	George Martin
Album:	USA: Beatles VI, Capitol ST 2358
	UK: Help!, Parlophone PCS 3071
Released:	USA: June 1965 UK: Aug 1965
Gold:	USA: July 1, 1965

Cover versions:
The Beatles, David Brown, Plastic Ono Band, Cliff Richard

DO YOU WANT TO KNOW A SECRET

Written by:	Lennon/McCartney
Single #:	USA: VeeJay VJ 587
Released:	USA: March 1964
Weeks on chart:	USA: 11
Produced by:	George Martin
EP:	UK: Twist and Shout, Parlophone GEP 8882, July 1963
Album:	USA: Introducing the Beatles, VeeJay VJLP 1062
	The Early Beatles, Capitol ST 2309
	UK: Please Please Me, Parlophone PCS 3042
Released:	USA: July 1963
	March 1965
	UK: March 1963

DON'T BOTHER ME

Written by:	George Harrison
Produced by:	George Martin
Album:	USA: Meet the Beatles!, Capitol ST 2047
	UK: With the Beatles, Parlophone PCS 3045
Released:	USA: Jan 1964 UK: Nov 1963
Gold:	USA: Feb 3, 1964
Additional Musicians:	Paul, Claves; John, Tambourine; Ringo, Bongos

DR. ROBERT

Written by:	Lennon/McCartney
Produced by:	George Martin
Album:	USA: "Yesterday"...And Today, Capitol ST 2553
	UK: Revolver, Parlophone PCS 7009
Released:	USA: June 1966 UK: Aug 1966
Gold:	USA: July 8, 1966

Cover versions:
The Beatles

DRIVE MY CAR

Written by:	Lennon/McCartney
Produced by:	George Martin
EP:	UK: Nowhere Man, Parlophone GEP 8952, July 1966
Album:	USA: "Yesterday"...And Today, Capitol ST 2553
	UK: Rubber Soul, Parlophone PCS 3075
Released:	USA: June 1966 UK: Dec 1965
Gold:	USA: July 8, 1966
Additional Musicians:	Paul, Piano; George, Back-up vocals

Cover versions:
Ted Alexander, Steve Bateman, The Beatles, Black Heat, Cafe Creme, Charles River Valley Boys, The Gophers, The Hollyridge Strings, Humble Pie, Bob Kuban, The McCoys, Magne-Tronics Combo, The Other Company, The Rollers, Sound Alike, Thundermug, Gary Toms Empire

EIGHT DAYS A WEEK

Written by:	Lennon/McCartney
Single #:	USA: Capitol 5371
Released:	USA: Feb 1965
Gold:	USA: September 16, 1965
Awards:	Most performed pop song: 1965
Weeks on chart:	USA: 10
Produced by:	George Martin
EP:	UK: Beatles for Sale, Parlophone GEP 8931, April 1965
Album:	USA: Beatles VI, Capitol ST 2358
	UK: Beatles for Sale, Parlophone PCS 3062
Released:	USA: June 1965 UK: Dec 1964
Gold:	USA: July 1, 1965
Additional Musicians:	George, Back-up vocals
Arrangements:	CH

Cover versions:
Baroque Ensemble, The Beatles, The Big Ben Banjo Band, Cafe Creme, The Chords, Stuart Crosby, The Decibels, Enoch Light, Francois Glorieux, The Gophers, The Hollyridge Strings, Jalopy Five, Jamie & The J Silvia Singers, Maryside Kammermusik, Sammy Kaye, Lester Lanin, James Last Band, Liverpool 5, Magne-Tronics, The Now Generation, The Other Company, Billy Preston, Procol Harum, Joshua Rifkin, The Rollers, Sound Alike, Bill Strange, Billy Stranson, Mary Wells

EVERY LITTLE THING

Written by:	Lennon/McCartney
Produced by:	George Martin
Album:	USA: Beatles VI, Capitol ST 2358
	UK: Beatles for Sale, Parlophone PCS 3062
Released:	USA: June 1965 UK: Dec 1964
Gold:	USA: July 1, 1965
Additional Musicians:	John, Lead guitar; Ringo, Timpani Drums; George was not present

Cover versions:
The Beatles, Left End, The Yak, Yes

EVERYBODY'S TRYING TO BE MY BABY

Written by:	Carl Perkins
Produced by:	George Martin
EP:	USA: 4 By The Beatles, Capitol R 5365, Feb 1965
Album:	USA: Beatles '65, Capitol ST 2309
	UK: Beatles for Sale, Parlophone PCS 3062
Released:	USA: December 1964 UK: Dec 1964
Gold:	USA: December 31, 1964
Additional Musicians:	Paul, Back-up vocals

FROM ME TO YOU

Written by:	Lennon/McCartney
Single #:	USA: VeeJay VJ 522
	UK: Parlophone R 5015
Released:	USA: March 1963 UK: April 1963
Gold:	UK: May 1963
Weeks on chart:	USA: 6 UK: 21
Produced by:	George Martin
EP:	UK: The Beatles' Hits, Parlophone GEP 8880, Sept. 1963
Album:	UK: A Collection of Beatles' Oldies, Parlophone PCS 7016
Released:	UK: Dec 1966

GIRL

Written by:	Lennon/McCartney
Produced by:	George Martin
Album:	USA: Rubber Soul, Capitol ST 2442
	UK: Rubber Soul, Parlophone PCS 3075
Released:	USA: December 1965 UK: Dec 1965
Gold:	USA: December 24, 1965
Additional Musicians:	Paul & George, Back-up vocals

Cover versions:
The Beatles, Madame Catherine Berberia, The Brothers Four, Gene Bua, Charlie Byrd, Cafe Creme, Hector Delfosse, Electronic Concept Orchestra, Francois Glorieux, Johnny Hallyday, The Hollyridge Strings, Paul Horn Quintet, Lester Lanin, Raymond Lefevre, George Martin & His Orchestra, Paul Mauriat, Bob Moline, 101 Strings, Frank Pourcel, The Rovin Kind, St. Louis Union, Bud Shank, Ivor Raymonde Singers Etcetera, Susan Smith, Truth, The Vanguards, Waikikis

Recorded by THE BEATLES

CAN'T BUY ME LOVE

By PAUL McCARTNEY and JOHN LENNON

A HARD DAY'S NIGHT

Written by:	Lennon/McCartney
Single #:	USA: Capitol 5222
	UK: Parlophone R5160
Released:	USA: July 1964 UK: July 1964
Gold:	USA: August 25, 1964
	UK: June 1964
Awards:	Million performance song: December 1974
	Most performed pop song: 1964, USA and England
	Grammy: 1964 "Best Performance by a Vocal Group"
	Other: 1964 Outstanding Theme From Radio, T.V. or Film (Ivor Novello Awards)
Weeks on chart:	USA: 13 UK: 13
Produced by:	George Martin
EP:	UK: A Hard Day's Night I, Parlophone GEP 8920, Nov 1964

Album:	USA: A Hard Day's Night, United Artists Uas 6366
	UK: A Hard Day's Night, Parlophone PCS 3058
Released:	USA: June 1964 UK: July 1964
Additional Musicians:	George Martin, piano; Paul, Back-up vocals
Arrangements:	MB, JB, SOR, CH

Cover versions
All-Star Pop Orchestra, Ray Anthony, Chet Atkins, Average Disco Band, Ena Baga, Band of Irish Guards, The Bar Keys, Charlie Barnet & His Orchestra, Count Basie, Terry Baxter Orchestra, Bearcuts, Beatles, Beavers, Catherine Berberian, Big Ben Banjo Band, Bill Blacks Combo, Boss Guitars, Lenny Breau, Teresa Brewer, Cafe Creme, Al Caiola, Eddie Cano & Nino Tempo, Carlin's World of Strings, Frank Chaksfield, Gary Chester, Chipmunks, The Chords, Columbia Musical Treasure Orch., Chris Conner, Dick Contino, J. Lawrence Cook, Country Limited, The Curios, Sonny Curtis, The Doodletown Pipers, Don Elliot & Nutty Squirrel, Enoch Light & The Light Brigade, Face Dancer, Arthur Fiedler & The Boston Pops Orch., Ella Fitzgerald, Francois Glorieux, The Going Thing, Marty Gold, Dickie Goodman, The Gophers, Earl Grant, Bob Hammer Band, Jimmy Haskell, Hey Jude, Mieko Hirota, Hollyridge Strings, Ian & The Zodiacs, Jerry Inman, Willis Jackson, Pete Jolly Trio, Quincy Jones & Orchestra, George Joravin, Meryside Kammermusik, Jean King, Kingsmen, Jack LaForge & Orchestra, Lester Lanin, James Last Band, Andre Lauzon, Bob Leaper, Peggy Lee, Les Baronets, Les Lionceaux, The Lettermen, Ramsey Lewis Trio, Lifeguards, Johnny Littrell, Liverpool 5, London Philharmonic Orchestra, London Sound 70 Orchestra, Gary McFarland, Magne Tronics Quartet, George Maharis, Frank '88' Malone, Henry Mancini, George Martin, Peter Matz, John Mayall, Jo Ment, Mrs. Elva Miller, Gerry Mulligan, Mustangs, Ray Nance, Sandy Nelson, The New Generation, 101 Strings, The Pair, George Paris, Johnny Pate, Perez Prado & Orchestra, Perth Amboy High School, Billy Preston, Arthur Prysock, Ginette Rend, Ronnie Reno, Joshua Rifkin, Billy Lee Riley, Johnny Rivers, Riviera Strings, Howard Roberts Quartet, The Rollers, Diana Ross & The Supremes, Kenny Russell, Santo & Johnny, Peter Sellers, Keely Smith, Billy Strange, Irv Spice Strings & Orchestra, Karl Swoboda, Tee & Cara, Teemates, Ten Tuff Guitars, Lloyd Thaxton, Sydney Thompson, Threads of Glory, Top of the Poppers, The Unifics, Claudette Vandel, Johnny Warrington, Dionne Warwick, Windjammers, World of Strings, Stan Worth, Si Zentner & Orchestra

HELP!

Written by:	Lennon/McCartney
Single #:	USA: Capitol 5476
	UK: Parlophone R 5305
Released:	USA: July 1965 UK: July 1965
Gold:	USA: September 2, 1965
Awards:	Most performed pop song: 1965
	Other: 1965, Highest Certified British Sales (Ivor Novello Awards)
Weeks on chart:	USA: 13 UK: 14
Produced by:	George Martin
Album:	USA: Help!, Capitol SMAS 2386
	UK: Help!, Parlophone PCS 3071
Released:	USA: Aug 1965 UK: Aug 1965
Gold:	USA: August 23, 1965
Additional Musicians:	George & Paul, Back-up vocals
Arrangements:	SOR

Cover versions:
Stefan Anderson, Average Disco Band, Band of
Irish Guards, Baroque Ensemble, Count Basie,
Terry Baxter & Orchestra, Roger Bean &
Orchestra, Beatlemania, The Beatles, Catherine
Berberian, Blades of Grass, Brothers Four, Cafe
Creme, Al Caiola, The Carpenters, Charles River
Valley Boys, J. Lawrence Cook, Country Limited,
Stuart Crosby, Deep Purple, Roy Evans, Family
Frog, Jose Feliciano, Francois Glorieux, The
Gophers, Buddy Greco, Henry Gross, Hollyridge
Strings, Hullabaloo Show Singers, Jerry Inman,
Jalopy Five, Andre Kostelanetz and His Orchestra,
Lester Lanin, Leasebreakers, Liverpool Five,
London Sound '70, Los Mustang, Ed Lyman, Mary
McCaslin, Mariachi Mexico 70, George Martin,
Peter Matz, Roy Meriweather Trio, Peter Nero, The
Newbeats, Ninapinata Orchestra, Now
Generation, The Other Company, Dolly Parton,
David Porter, Frank Pourcell & Orchestra, Joshua
Rifkin, Lon Ritchie, The Rollers, Peter Sellers,
Sound Alikes, Michael Stanley, Ray Stevens,
Those Fabulous Strings, Clara Ward, Mary Wells,
Wild Honey Singers

HOLD ME TIGHT

Written by:	Lennon/McCartney
Produced by:	George Martin
Album:	USA: Meet the Beatles! Capitol ST 2047
	UK: With The Beatles, Parlophone PCS 3045
Released:	USA: Jan 1964 UK: Nov 1963
Gold:	USA: February 3, 1964
Additional Musicians	John & George, Back-up vocals

Cover versions:
Baroque Ensemble, Count Basie, Beatles, Merside
Kammermusik, Lester Lanin, Les Baronets,
Merseyboys, Joshua Rifkin

HONEY DON'T

Written by:	Carl Perkins
Produced by:	George Martin
EP:	USA: 4 By the Beatles, Capitol R 5365, February 1965
Album:	USA: Beatles '65 Capitol ST 2228
	UK: Beatles for Sale, Parlophone PCS 3062
Released:	USA: Dec 1964 UK: Dec 1964
Gold:	USA: December 31, 1964

I CALL YOUR NAME

Written by:	Lennon/McCartney
Produced by:	George Martin
EP:	UK: Long Tall Sally, Parlophone GEP 8913, June 1964
Album:	USA: The Beatles' Second Album Capitol ST 2080
Released:	USA: April 1964
Gold:	USA: April 13, 1964

Cover versions:
Terry Baxter, The Beatles, Donnie Brooks, Brothers
& Sisters, The Buckinghams, Hollyridge Strings,
Billy J. Kramer & The Dakotas, The Mamas & The
Papas, The Rollers, The Shags, Sound Alike,
Stapleton-Morley Expression, Your Gang

I DON'T WANT TO SPOIL THE PARTY

Written by:	Lennon/McCartney
Single #:	USA: Capitol 5371
Released:	USA: Feb 1965
Weeks on chart:	USA: 6
Produced by:	George Martin
EP:	UK: Beatles for Sale II, Parlophone EP 8938, June 1965
Album:	USA: Beatles VI Capitol ST 2358
	UK: Beatles for Sale, Parlophone PCS 3062
Released:	USA: June 1965 UK: Dec 1964
Gold:	USA: July 1, 1965

Cover versions:
Beatles, Jerry Inman, Lester Lanin, Andy Martin,
Peter & Gordon

I FEEL FINE

Written by:	Lennon/McCartney
Single #:	USA: Capitol 5327
	UK: Parlophone R5200
Released:	USA: Nov 1964 UK: Nov 1964
Gold:	USA: December 31, 1964
Awards:	Most performed pop song: 1964
	Other: 1964, Highest Certified British Sales (Ivor Novello Awards)
Weeks on chart:	USA: 11 UK: 14
Produced by:	George Martin
EP:	UK: The Beatles' Million Sellers, Parlophone GEP 8946, Dec 1965
Album:	USA: Beatles '65 Capitol ST 2228
Released:	USA: Dec 1964
Gold:	USA: December 31, 1964
Additional Musicians:	John & George, Guitar Duet

Cover versions:
Nancy Amer, Chet Atkins, Gene Barge, Beatles,
The Big Ben Banjo Band, Stanley Black, The Boss
Guitars, Cafe Creme, Frank Chacksfield, Charles
River Valley Boys, The Floyd Cramer Piano,
Penny De Haven, Ray Ellis, Enoch Light, Roy
Glover, Jimmie Haskell, Hollyridge Strings, Lester
Lanin, James Last, Liverpool 5, George Martin, Jo
Ment, The Now Generation, Johnny Pate, Tim
Reynold, The Rollers, Sound Alike, Billy Strange,
Vanilla Fudge, The Ventures

I NEED YOU

Written by:	George Harrison
Produced by:	George Martin
Album:	USA: Help! Capitol SMAS 2386
	UK: Help! Parlophone PCS 3071
Released:	USA: Aug 1965 UK: Aug 1965
Gold:	USA: August 23, 1965
Additional Musicians:	John & Paul, Back-up vocals

Cover versions:
Beatles, Lester Lanin, George Martin Orchestra,
The Sunshine Company, Maynard Williams

I SAW HER STANDING THERE

Written by:	Lennon/McCartney
Single #:	USA: Capitol 5112
Released:	USA: Jan 1964
Weeks on chart:	USA: 11
Produced by:	George Martin
EP:	UK: The Beatles #1, Parlophone GEP 8883, Nov 1963

Album:	USA: Introducing The Beatles, Vee Jay VJLP 1062
	Meet The Beatles! Capitol ST 2047
	UK: Please Please Me, Parlophone PCS 3042
Released:	USA: July 1963
	Jan 1964
	UK: March 1963
Additional Musicians:	John, Back-up vocals

I SHOULD HAVE KNOWN BETTER

Written by:	Lennon/McCartney
Single #:	USA: Capitol 5222
	UK: Parlophone R6013
Released:	USA: July 1964 UK: Feb 1976
Weeks on chart:	USA: 4
Produced by:	George Martin
EP:	UK: A Hard Day's Night I, Parlophone GEP 8920, November 1964
Album:	USA: A Hard Day's Night United Artists Uas 6366
	Hey Jude, Apple SW 385/SO 385
	UK: A Hard Day's Night, Parlophone PCS 3058
Released:	USA: July 1964
	Feb 1970
	UK: July 1964
Gold:	USA: March 6, 1970

Cover versions:
Richard Anthony, The Bantams, The Beach Boys,
Beatles, The Big Ben Banjo Band, Sascha Burland
& D Elliot, Cafe Creme, Gary Chester, Terry
DeSario, Dino I Kings, Jan & Dean, Johnny & The
Hurricanes, James Last, Les Baronets, Los
Mustang, The Machine, George Martin Orchestra,
Jo Ment, The Naturals, George Paris, Billy Lee
Riley, Johnny Rivers, Mary Wells

I WANNA BE YOUR MAN

Written by:	Lennon/McCartney
Produced by:	George Martin
Album:	USA: Meet The Beatles! Capitol ST 2047
	UK: With the Beatles Parlophone PCS 3045
Released:	USA: Jan 1964 UK: Nov 1963
Gold:	USA: February 3, 1964
Additional Musicians:	John, Hammond Organ

I WANT TO HOLD YOUR HAND

Written by:	Lennon/McCartney
Single #:	USA: Capitol 5112
	UK: Parlophone R5055
Released:	USA: Jan 1964 UK: Aug 1963
Gold:	USA: February 3, 1964
	UK: November 1963
Weeks on chart:	US: 15 UK: 22
Produced by:	George Martin
EP:	UK: The Beatles Million Sellers, Parlophone GEP 8946, Dec 1965
Album:	USA: Meet the Beatles! Capitol ST 2047
	UK: A Collection of Beatles Oldies, Parlophone PCS 7016
Released:	USA: Jan 1964 UK: Dec 1966
Gold:	USA: February 3, 1964

IF I FELL

Written by:	Lennon/McCartney
Single #:	USA: Capitol 5235
Released:	USA: July 1964
Weeks on chart:	USA: 9
Produced by:	George Martin
EP:	UK: A Hard Day's Night I, Parlophone GEP 8920, Nov 1964
Album:	USA: A Hard Day's Night United Artists Uas 6366
	Something New Capitol ST 2108
	UK: A Hard Day's Night Parlophone PCS 3058

Released: USA: June 1964
July 1964
UK: July 1964
Gold: USA: August 24, 1964
Arrangements: CH
Cover versions:
Chet Atkins, Terry Baxter Orchestra, The Beatles, Petty Botkin Jr., The Brothers Four, Cafe Creme, Lou Christie, Renee Claude, Don Cooper, Sonny Curtis, The Hollyridge Strings, Les Baronets, The Johnny Mann Singers, George Martin & His Orchestra, Gerry Mulligan, New Hilltop Singers, The Other Company, Peter & Gordon, Peters & Lee, Philip & Vanessa, Pozo Seco Singers, Joe Reisman & His Orchestra, The Rollers, Robin Sanderson, Keely Smith, Sound Alike, The Suntones, Gabor Szabo, George Van Eps

IF I NEEDED SOMEONE

Written by: George Harrison
Produced by: George Martin
Album: USA: "Yesterday"... and Today
Capitol ST 2553
UK: Rubber Soul
Parlophone PCS 3075
Released: USA: June 1966 UK: Dec 1965
Gold: USA: July 8, 1966
Additional
Musicians: John & Paul, Back-up vocals
Cover versions:
The Beatles, Bit A Sweet, The Cryan Shames, George Harrison, The Hollies, The Kingsmen, Hugh Masakela, The Naked Truth, The Other Company, The Rollers, Sound Alike, The Stained Glass, Stingrays of Newburgh, Street, Livingston Taylor

I'LL BE BACK

Written by: Lennon/McCartney
Produced by: George Martin
Album: USA: Beatles '65
Capitol ST 2228
UK: A Hard Day's Night
Parlophone PCS 3058
Released: USA: Dec 1964 UK: July 1964
Gold: USA: December 31, 1964
Additional
Musicians: Paul & George, Back-up vocals
Cover versions:
Herb Alpert & The Tiajuana Brass, Baroque Ensemble, The Beatles, The Big Ben Banjo Band, The Buckinghams, Charles River Valley Boys, James Cohoon Lindsay Band, The Hollyridge Strings, Johnny Mann Singers, Lincoln Mayorga, Wes Montgomery, Roger Nichols, Cliff Richard, Joshua Rifkin, Peter Schickele & Orchestra, The Tremeloes, Emily Yancy

I'LL CRY INSTEAD

Written by: Lennon/McCartney
Single #: USA: Capitol 5234
Released: USA: July 1964
Weeks on chart: USA: 7
Produced by: George Martin
EP: UK: A Hard Day's Night II,
Parlophone GEP 8924, Nov 1964
Album: USA: A Hard Day's Night
United Artists Uas 6366
Something New
Capitol ST 2108
UK: A Hard Day's Night
Parlophone PCS 3058
Released: USA: June 1964
July 1964
UK: July 1964
Gold: USA: August 24, 1964
Cover versions:
Chet Atkins, Baroque Ensemble, The Beatles, Charles River Valley Boys, Gary Chester, Joe Cocker, The Hollyridge Strings, Jerry Inman, The Meryside Kammermusik, Lester Lanin, George Martin & Orchestra, Jimmy Payne, The Rainbow Press, Joshua Rifkin, Billy Lee Riley, Johnny Rivers, The Windjammers

I'LL FOLLOW THE SUN

Written by: Lennon/McCartney
Produced by: George Martin
EP: UK: Beatles for Sale II,
Parlophone GEP 8938, June 1965
Album: USA: Beatles '65
Capitol ST 2228
UK: Beatles for Sale, Parlophone
PCS 3062
Released: USA: Dec 1964 UK: Dec 1964
Gold: USA: December 31, 1964
Cover versions:
Chet Atkins, The Beatles, The Brothers Four, The Floyd Cramer Piano, Hollyridge Strings, Roger Kellaway

I'LL GET YOU

Written by: Lennon/McCartney
Single #: USA: Swan 4152
UK: Parlophone R5055
Released: USA: Sept 1963 UK: Aug 1963
Produced by: George Martin
Album: USA: The Beatles Second
Album, Capitol ST 2080
UK: Beatles Rarities
Released: USA: April 1964
Gold: USA: April 13, 1964
Cover versions:
The Beatles, The Big Ben Banjo Band, Liverpool Sound, The Merseyboys, Leon Young

I'M A LOSER

Written by: Lennon/McCartney
Produced by: George Martin
EP: USA: 4 By The Beatles, Capitol
R 5365, Feb 1965
UK: Beatles for Sale, Parlophone
GEP 8931, April 1965
Album: USA: Beatles '65
Capitol ST 2228
UK: Beatles for Sale
Parlophone PCS 3062
Released: USA: Dec 1964 UK: Dec 1964
Gold: USA: December 31, 1964
Additional
Musicians: Paul, Back-up vocals
Cover versions:
The Beatles, The Big Ben Banjo Band, Cafe Creme, Marianne Faithful, Vince Guaraldi & Bola Sete, The Hollyridge Strings, Doug Kershaw, The Other Company, The Rollers, Sound Alike, Tufano & Giammarese

I'M DOWN

Written by: Lennon/McCartney
Single #: USA: Capitol 5476
UK: Parlophone R5305
Released: USA: July 1965 UK: July 1965
Produced by: George Martin
Additional
Musicians: John, Hammond Organ
Cover versions:
The Beatles, La Seine, The Wailers

I'M HAPPY JUST TO DANCE WITH YOU

Written by: Lennon/McCartney
Single #: USA: Capitol 5234
Released: USA: July 1964
Weeks on chart: USA: 1
Produced by: George Martin
Album: USA: A Hard Day's Night
United Artists Uas 6366
Something New
Capitol ST 2108
UK: A Hard Day's Night
Parlophone PCS 3058
Released: USA: June 1964
July 1964
UK: July 1964
Gold: USA: August 24, 1964
Cover versions:
The Beatles, The Big Ben Banjo Band, The Cyrkle, Bob Hammer Band, The Hollyridge Strings, Lester Lanin, Andre Lauzon, Maureen McGovern, The Johnny Mann Singers, George Martin & His Orchestra, Anne Murray

I'M LOOKING THROUGH YOU

Written by: Lennon/McCartney
Produced by: George Martin
Album: USA: Rubber Soul
Capitol ST 2442
UK: Rubber Soul
Parlophone PCS 3075
Released: USA: Dec 1965 UK: Dec 1965
Gold: USA: December 24, 1965
Additional
Musicians: Ringo, Hammond Organ; John,
Back-up vocals
Cover versions:
Jack Bailey, The Beatles, Chance Eden, Lester Lanin, Dale Miller, The Music Company

I'M ONLY SLEEPING

Written by: Lennon/McCartney
Produced by: George Martin
Album: USA: "Yesterday"... and Today
Capitol ST 2553
UK: Revolver
Parlophone PCS 7009
Released: USA: June 1965 UK: Aug 1966
Gold: USA: July 8, 1966
Additional
Musicians: Paul & George, Back-up vocals
Cover versions:
The Beatles, Lobo, George Martin

IN MY LIFE

Written by: Lennon/McCartney
Produced by: George Martin
Album: USA: Rubber Soul
Capitol ST 2442
UK: Rubber Soul
Parlophone PCS 3075
Released: USA: Dec 1965 UK: Dec 1965
Gold: USA: December 24, 1965
Additional
Musicians: George Martin, piano; Paul,
back-up vocals
Arrangements: JB, CH
Cover versions:
The Beatles, Leon Bibb, The Candy Rock Fountain, Judy Collins, The Dillards, Jose Feliciano, Astrud Gilberto, Francois Glorieux, Marty Gold Orchestra, Joel Grey, Roni Hill, Lena Horne & Gabor Szabo, Jackie & Roy, Miriam Makeba, Keith Moon, The Music Company, Marc Neely, Oliver, Pozo Seco, Kaye Stevens, Carol Stromme, Karen Wyman

IT WON'T BE LONG

Written by: Lennon/McCartney
Produced by: George Martin
Album: USA: Meet the Beatles!
Capitol ST 2047
UK: With the Beatles
Parlophone PCS 3045
Released: USA: Jan 1964 UK: Nov 1963
Gold: USA: February 3, 1964
Cover versions:
The Beatles, The Big Ben Banjo Band, Clefs of Lavender Hill, Lester Lanin, Bob Leaper and his Band, Don Leaper, Les Baronets, Les Lionceaux, The Merseyboys, Jack Nitzche, Bonnie Pruden, Quick

IT'S ONLY LOVE

Written by: Lennon/McCartney
Produced by: George Martin
EP: UK: Yesterday, Parlophone GEP
8948, March 1966
Album: USA: Rubber Soul
Capitol ST 2442
UK: Help!
Parlophone PCS 3071
Released: USA: Dec 1965 UK: Aug 1965
Gold: USA: December 24, 1965
Additional
Musicians: Paul, Back-up vocals
Arrangements: JB, CH
Cover versions:
The Beatles, Bryan Ferry, Lester Lanin, The Music Company

HELP!

WORDS & MUSIC BY JOHN LENNON & PAUL McCARTNEY

THE BEATLES

A WALTER SHENSON SUBAFILMS Production

UNITED ARTISTS

produced by **WALTER SHENSON**   screenplay by **MARC BEHM & CHARLES WOOD**   story by **MARC BEHM**   directed by **RICHARD LEST**

MACLEN MUSIC, Inc.

04399

I'VE JUST SEEN A FACE

Written by:	Lennon/McCartney
Produced by:	George Martin
Album:	USA: Rubber Soul Capitol ST 2442 UK: Help! Parlophone PCS 3071
Released:	USA: Dec 1965 UK: Aug 1965
Gold:	USA: December 24, 1965

Cover versions:
Steve Bateman, The Beatles, Bonnie Bramlett, Charles River Valley Boys, Jordan Christopher, Charlie Cline, Hank Crawford, The Dillards, Free Beer, Arlo Guthrie, The Hollyridge Strings, Jerry Inman, Lester Lanin, Dickey Lee, Magne Tronics Combo, The Music Company, The Other Company, The Rollers, Sound Alike, Gabor Szabo, Ward Six, Wings

KANSAS CITY/HEY HEY HEY HEY

Written by:	Jerry Leiber-Mike Stoller/Richard Penniman
Single #:	USA: Capitol Starline 6066
Released:	USA: Oct 1965
Produced by:	George Martin
Album:	USA: Beatles VI Capitol ST 2358 UK: Beatles for Sale Parlophone PCS 3062
Released:	USA: June 1965 UK: Dec 1964
Gold:	USA: July 1, 1965
Additional Musicians:	John & George, Back-up vocals

Cover versions:
The Beatles, Dave Baby Cortez, Little Richard, Ten Years After

LITTLE CHILD

Written by:	Lennon/McCartney
Produced by:	George Martin
Album:	USA: Meet the Beatles! Capitol ST 2047 UK: With the Beatles Parlophone PCS 3045
Released:	USA: Jan 1964 UK: Nov 1963
Gold:	USA: February 3, 1964
Additional Musicians:	Paul, Piano; John, Harmonica

Cover versions:
Beatlemania, The Beatles, The Big Ben Banjo Band, Sonny Curtis, Henry Duval, George Martin & His Orchestra

LONG TALL SALLY

Written by:	Enotris Johnson-Richard Penniman-Robert Blackwell
Produced by:	George Martin
EP:	UK: Long Tall Sally, Parlophone GEP 8913, June 1964
Album:	USA: The Beatles' Second Album, Capitol ST 2080
Released:	USA: April 1964
Gold:	USA: April 13, 1964

LOVE ME DO

Written by:	Lennon/McCartney
Single #:	USA: Tollie 9008 UK: Parlophone R4949
Released:	USA: April 1964 UK: Oct 1962
Weeks on chart:	USA: 14 UK: 18
Produced by:	George Martin
EP:	UK: The Beatles' Hits, Parlophone GEP 8880, September 1963
Album:	USA: Introducing the Beatles Vee Jay VJLP 1062 The Early Beatles Capitol ST 2309 UK: Please Please Me Parlophone PCS 3042
Released:	USA: July 1963 March 1965 UK: March 1963
Additional Musicians:	Ringo, Tambourine; Andy White, Drums; George, Back-up vocals

MATCHBOX

Written by:	Carl Perkins
Single #:	USA: Capitol 5255
Released:	USA: Aug 1964
Weeks on chart:	USA: 8
Produced by:	George Martin
EP:	UK: Long Tall Sally, Parlophone GEP 8913, June 1964
Album:	USA: Something New Capitol ST 2108
Released:	USA: July 1964
Gold:	USA: August 24, 1964

MICHELLE

Written by:	Lennon/McCartney
Awards:	Million performance song: December 1969 Most performed pop song: 1966, 1967, 1968 Grammy: 1966 "Song of the year"
Produced by:	George Martin
EP:	UK: Nowhere Man, Parlophone GEP 8952, July 1966
Album:	USA: Rubber Soul Capitol ST 2442 UK: Rubber Soul Parlophone PCS 3075
Released:	USA: Dec 1965 UK: Dec 1965
Gold:	USA: December 24, 1965
Additional Musicians:	John & George, Back-up vocals
Arrangements:	MB, JB, CB, OR, CH

Cover versions:
Jeff Afdem & Springfield Flute, All Star Pop Orchestra, Laurindo Almeida, Ed Ames, Nancy Ames, Ray Anthony, Chet Atkins, Average Disco Band, The Bachelors, Ena Baga, Bands of the Irish Guards, Eddie Barclay & Orchestra, Count Basie & His Orchestra, Les Baxter, Terry Baxter Orchestra & Chorus, Beatlemania, The Beatles, Paul Beauregard, Big Band Moog, The Big Ben Banjo Band, Nat Bigwan, Stanley Black, Bob & Phil & Orchestra, Bobby & Buddy, Willie Bobo, Booker T & The MG's, Maurice Bouvin, The Brazilian Echoes, Briarcliff Strings Voices, Jack Brokensha, The Brothers Four, Brunnerdale Concert Choir, Bud Brisbois, Burbank Philharmonic, Charlie Byrd, John Cacavas, Cafe Creme, Ace Cannon, Lee Castle, George Cates, Frank Chacksfield, Sam Chalpin, The Chords, Arnie Chycoski, Claude Ciari, Richard Cocciante, The Coffee Set, Columbia Musical Treasury, Columbia Starlight Orchestra, Ray Conniff, Lawrence Cook, Pete Cooley, Henry Cuesta, The Current Event, King Curtis, Danny & Richard, David & Jonathan, John Davidson, The Dukes of Dixieland, Jimmy Dorsey, John Eaton, Les & Larry Elgart, Enoch Light & The Light Brigade, Esso Trinidad Steel Band, The Percy Faith Strings, Ferrante & Teicher, Arthur Fiedler & The Boston Pops, Shep Fields & Orchestra, Fiesta Brass, 50 Guitars, 50 Mixed Voices, Horst Fischer & Werner Mull, Buddy Fite, The Four Freshmen, The Four Tops, Fraser High Vocal Department, The Free Design, Tommy Garrett, John Gary, George Gates, Daniel Giraud, Francois Glorieux, Marty Gold Orchestra, The Golden Strings, Bobby Goldsboro, Earl Grant, The Tony Hatch Orchestra, Eddie Higgins, Nino & Pulaski Highwaymen, Xaviera Hollander, The Hollyridge Strings, Huntingtons, Dick Hyman, Harry James, Jan & Dean, Jack Jones, Jonah Jones, Georges Jouvin & Orchestra, Sammy Kaye & Orchestra, John Keating & Orchestra, Stan Kenton, Peter King Chorale, Wayne King, Kings Road, Rudi Knabl, Andre Kostelanetz & Orchestra, Lester Lanin, Maurice Larcange, Yusef Lateef, Lennon Sisters, Les Atomes, The Lettermen, Hank Levine Singers & Orchestra, David Lloyd & Orchestra, Lochestre Du Festival In, The Londonderry Aires, Longines Symphonette, Rufus Lomley, Los Hnos Castro, Norman Luboff Choir, David McCallum, Gary McFarland, Bill McGuffie, Gordon Macrae, Magne Tronics Combo, Malta High School Band, Henry Mancini, Mantovani & Orchestra, Jeffrey & Ronald Marlowe, George Martin, Ray Martin & Orchestra, Johnny Mathis, Peter Matz Quad Spetac, Paul Mauriat Orchestra, Billy May, Tony Mergel, Buddy Merrill, The Mexicali Singers, Midnight String Quartet, Michelle, Vincent Morocco Orchestra, Martin Mull, Music City Twin Pianos, The Music Company, The Musicmakers, Jack Nathan & Orchestra, Oliver Nelson, Peter Nero, Wayne Newton, Bud Noble, The Now Generation, The Octet West, 101 Strings, The Outsiders, Overlanders, Larry Page, Steve Perry, Andre Previn, G. Puente & C. Atkins, Pancho Purcell, Pancho Purcell & Bambuco, Boots Randolph, Johnny Reimar, The Relations, Howard Roberts, Eric Rogers, Diana Ross & The Supremes, Ginette Sage, The Sandpipers, The Senate, Doc Severinson, Bud Shank, George Shearing, The Singers Unlimited, Johnny Smith, David Snell, Sound Alikes, Sound Orchestral J. Pears, The Spokesman, Cyril Stapleton, Cyril Stapleton Choir & Orch., Starlight Woodwinds, Billy Strange, Ray Terrace, Top of the Poppers, George & Rod Tremblay, The Trumpet Men, University of Denver Jazz Band, Rudy Vallee, George Van Eps, Billy Vaughn, Sarah Vaughn, The Ventures, Bobby Vinton on Saxophone, The Waikikis, Dick Watson, Mark Weinstein, Andy Williams, Eddie Williams & Orchestra, Stan Worth, Klaus Wunderlich, The Young Americans

MISERY

Written by:	Lennon/McCartney
Single #:	USA: Capitol Starline 6065
Released:	USA: Oct 1965
Produced by:	George Martin
EP:	USA: The Beatles, Vee Jay VEP 1-903, March 1964 UK: The Beatles #1, Parlophone GEP 8883, November 1963
Album:	USA: Introducing the Beatles Vee Jay VJLP 1062 UK: Please Please Me PCS 3042
Released:	USA: July 1963 UK: March 1963

MR. MOONLIGHT

Written by:	Roy Lee Johnson
Produced by:	George Martin
EP:	USA: 4 By The Beatles, Capitol R5365, Feb 1965
Album:	USA: Beatles '65 Capitol ST 2228 UK: Beatles for Sale Parlophone PCS 3062
Released:	USA: Dec 1964 UK: Dec 1964
Gold:	USA: December 31, 1964
Additional Musicians:	Paul, Hammond Organ; George, African Drum

MONEY (THAT'S WHAT I WANT)

Written by:	Berry Gordy Jr.,-Janie Bradford
Produced by:	George Martin
EP:	UK: All My Loving, Parlophone GEP 8891, February 1964
Album:	USA: The Beatles' Second Album Capitol ST 2080 UK: With the Beatles Parlophone PCS 3045
Released:	USA: April 1964 UK: Nov 1963
Gold:	USA: April 13, 1964
Additional Musicians:	George Martin, Piano; George & Paul, Back-up vocals

THE NIGHT BEFORE

Written by:	Lennon/McCartney
Produced by:	George Martin
Album:	USA: Help! Capitol SMAS 2386 UK: Help! Parlophone PCS 3071
Released:	USA: Aug 1965 UK: Aug 1965
Gold:	USA: August 23, 1965
Additional Musicians:	John, Electric piano; George & John, Back-up vocals

Cover versions:
The Beatles, Cafe Creme, James Cahoon Lindsay Band, The Hollyridge Strings, Herbie Mann, George Martin & Orchestra, The Other Company, The Rollers, Sound Alike

NO REPLY

Written by:	Lennon/McCartney
Produced by:	George Martin
EP:	UK: Beatles For Sale, Parlophone GEP 8931, April 1965
Album:	USA: Beatles '65 Capitol ST 2228 UK: Beatles For Sale Parlophone PCS 3062
Released:	USA: Dec 1964 UK: Dec 1964
Gold:	USA: December 31, 1964
Additional Musicians:	Paul & George, Back-up vocals

Cover versions:
The Beatles, The Big Ben Banjo Band, James Cahoon Lindsay Band, The Gophers, The Hollyridge Strings, James Last, James Last Band, The Last Words, George Martin, The Rollers, Sound Alike

NORWEGIAN WOOD

Written by:	Lennon/McCartney
Awards:	Million performance song: December 1979
Produced by:	George Martin
Album:	USA: Rubber Soul Capitol ST 2442 UK: Rubber Soul Parlophone PCS 3075
Released:	USA: Dec 1965 UK: Dec 1965
Gold:	USA: December 24, 1965
Additional Musicians:	George, Sitar; Paul, Back-up vocals
Arrangements:	MB, JB, CB, SOR, CH

Cover versions:
Bangor Flying Circus, Count Basie, Terry Baxter Orchestra & Chorus, The Beatles, The Big Ben Banjo Band, Perry Botkin Jr. & Orchestra, The Brothers Four, Gary Burton, Charlie Byrd, Frank Chacksfield, Charles River Valley Boys, Richard Christensen, Charlie Cline, Colosseum, Alan Copeland, Charles & Roger Cowan, Bob Dorough, Peter Duchin & Orchestra, George Edwards, Enoch Light & The Light Brigade, The Percy Faith Strings, Jose Feliciano, The Folkswingers, The Frugal Sound, Terry Gibbs, Francois Glorieux, Marty Gold Orchestra, Tony Hatch Orchestra, Ted Heath, The Hollyridge Strings, The Paul Horn Quintet, The Hourglass, Brian Hyland, The J J Band, Jack & Mike with Bluegrass, Jackie & Roy, Jalopy Five, Bobby Jameson, Jan & Dean, Waylon Jennings, John Keating & Orchestra, Verrill Keene, The Kimberlys, The Kingston Trio, Moe Koffman, LA Smog, Lester Lanin, McFarland & Szabo, Dave McKenna, Marion McPartland, Lincoln Majorga, Henry Mancini, Herbie Mann, Frank Marino & Mahogany, Hugh Masakela, Mason & Dixon, Peter Matz Quad Spectac, Sergio Mendes, Sergio Mendes & Brazil 66, Roy Meriwether Trio, Buddy Merrill, Hugo Montenegro, The Music Company, Mystic Moods Orchestra, Nashville Fiddles, The New Bag, New World Electronic Cham, Nina & Frederik, Nth Texas State University Lab., John Pike, Don Randi & Quest, Joe Reisman & His Orchestra, Buddy Rich, Gene Russell Trio, Bud Shank, Silhouettes, Ira Sullivan, Trombones Unlimited, The Underground All Stars, Peter Walker

NOT A SECOND TIME

Written by:	Lennon/McCartney
Produced by:	George Martin
Album:	USA: Meet the Beatles! Capitol ST 2047 UK: With the Beatles Parlophone PCS 3045
Released:	USA: Jan 1964 UK: Nov 1963
Gold:	USA: February 3, 1964
Additional Musicians:	George Martin, Piano

Cover versions:
The Beatles, Lester Lanin, Robert Palmer

NOWHERE MAN

Written by:	Lennon/McCartney
Single #:	USA: Capitol 5587

Released:	USA: February 1966
Gold:	USA: April 1, 1966
Awards:	Most performed pop song: 1966
Weeks on chart:	USA: 9
Produced by:	George Martin
EP:	UK: Nowhere Man, Parlophone GEP 8952, July 1966
Album:	USA: "Yesterday"... and Today Capitol ST 2553 UK: Rubber Soul Parlophone PCS 3075
Released:	USA: June 1966 UK: Dec 1965
Gold:	USA: July 8, 1966
Additional Musicians:	Paul & George, Back-up vocals

Cover versions:
Beatlemania, The Beatles, The Bee Gees, Big Ben Banjo Band, The Brothers Four, Vicki Carr, Chris Connor, Dino, Desi & Billy, Les & Larry Elgart, The Extortions, Francois Glorieux, The Gophers, Guitars Unlimited, Jimmie Haskell, The Hollyridge Strings, Gershon Kingsley, Lester Lanin, Ken Lazarus, Liverpool 5, Jeff Lynne, Magne Tronics Combo, The Odyssey Singers, The Other Company, Joe Pass Guitar & Voices, The Rollers, Stan Ruffin, Sound Alike, The Sound-a-likes, Cyril Stapleton, The Waikikis

PAPERBACK WRITER

Written by:	Lennon/McCartney
Single #:	USA: Capitol 5651 UK: Parlophone R5452
Released:	USA: May 1966 UK: June 1966
Gold:	USA: July 14, 1966
Awards:	Most performed pop song: 1966
Weeks on chart:	USA: 10 UK: 11
Album:	USA: Hey Jude Apple SW 385/SO 385 UK: A Collection of Beatle Oldies, Parlophone PCS 7016
Released:	USA: Feb 1970 UK: Dec 1966
Additional Musicians:	George & John, Back-up vocals

Cover versions:
Terry Baxter Orchestra & Chorus, The Beatles, The Big Ben Banjo Band, Cafe Creme, Charles River Valley Boys, Frank Cooper & Orchestra, The Cowsills, Floyd Cramer, RB Greaves, Gershon Kingsley, James Last Band, Mike Melvoin, The Other Company, Herb Penderson, Powers of Blue, Kenny Rogers & 1st Edition, The Rollers, Sound Alike, The Young Gyants

PLEASE MR. POSTMAN

Written by:	William Garrett, Robert Bateman, Georgia Dobbins, Brian Holland and Freddie Gorman
Produced by:	George Martin
EP:	USA: Four By The Beatles, Capitol EAP 2121, May 1964
Album:	USA: The Beatles' Second Album Capitol ST 2080 UK: With The Beatles Parlophone PCS 3045
Released:	USA: April 1964 UK: Nov 1963
Gold:	USA: April 13, 1964
Additional Musicians:	Paul & George, Back-up vocals

PLEASE PLEASE ME

Written by:	Lennon/McCartney
Single #:	USA: Vee Jay VJ498 UK: Parlophone R4983
Released:	USA: Feb 1963 UK: Jan 1963
Weeks on chart:	USA: 13 UK: 18
Produced by:	George Martin
EP:	UK: The Beatles' Hits, Parlophone GEP 8880, September 1963
Album:	USA: The Early Beatles Capitol ST 2309 UK: Please Please Me Parlophone PCS 3042
Released:	USA: March 1965 UK: March 1963
Additional Musicians:	George, Back-up vocals

P.S. I LOVE YOU

Written by:	Lennon/McCartney
Single #:	USA: Tollie 9008 UK: Parlophone R4949
Released:	USA: April 1964 UK: Oct 1962
Weeks on chart:	USA: 8
Produced by:	George Martin
EP:	UK: All My Loving, Parlophone GEP 8891, Feb 1964
Album:	USA: Introducing The Beatles Vee Jay VJLP 1062 The Early Beatles Capitol ST 2309 UK: Please Please Me Parlophone PCS 3042
Released:	USA: July 1963 March 1965 UK: March 1963

RAIN

Written by:	Lennon/McCartney
Single #:	USA: Capitol 5651 UK: Parlophone R5452
Released:	USA: May 1966 UK: June 1966
Weeks on chart:	USA: 7
Produced by:	George Martin
Album:	USA: Hey Jude Apple SW 385/SO 385
Released:	USA: Feb 1970
Gold:	USA: March 6, 1970
Additional Musicians:	Paul & George, Back-up vocals

Cover versions:
Abilene Christian College, The Beatles, Denhy Belline & Rich Kids, The Big Ben Banjo Band, Keith Carradine, Petula Clark, The Gants, Humble Pie, Kapt Kopter & Twirly Bird, Mary McCaslin, Steve Marcus, Todd Rundgren, Peter Schickele & Orchestra, The Sunshine Company

ROCK AND ROLL MUSIC

Written by:	Chuck Berry
Produced by:	George Martin
EP:	UK: Beatles for Sale, Parlophone GEP 8931, April 1965
Album:	USA: Beatles '65 Capitol ST 2228 UK: Beatles for Sale Parlophone PCS 3062
Released:	USA: Dec 1964 UK: Dec 1964
Gold:	USA: December 31, 1964
Additional Musicians:	John, Paul and George Martin on the same piano

ROLL OVER BEETHOVEN

Written by:	Chuck Berry
Single #:	USA: Capitol Starline 6065
Released:	USA: Oct 1965
Weeks on chart:	USA: 4
Produced by:	George Martin
EP:	USA: Four By The Beatles, Capitol EAP 2121, May 1964
Album:	USA: The Beatles' Second Album Capitol ST 2080 UK: With The Beatles Parlophone PCS 3045
Released:	USA: April 1964 UK: Nov 1963
Gold:	USA: April 13, 1964

RUN FOR YOUR LIFE

Written by:	Lennon/McCartney
Produced by:	George Martin
Album:	USA: Rubber Soul Capitol ST 2442 UK: Rubber Soul Parlophone PCS 3075
Released:	USA: Dec 1965 UK: Dec 1965
Gold:	USA: December 24, 1965
Additional Musicians:	Paul & George, Back-up vocals

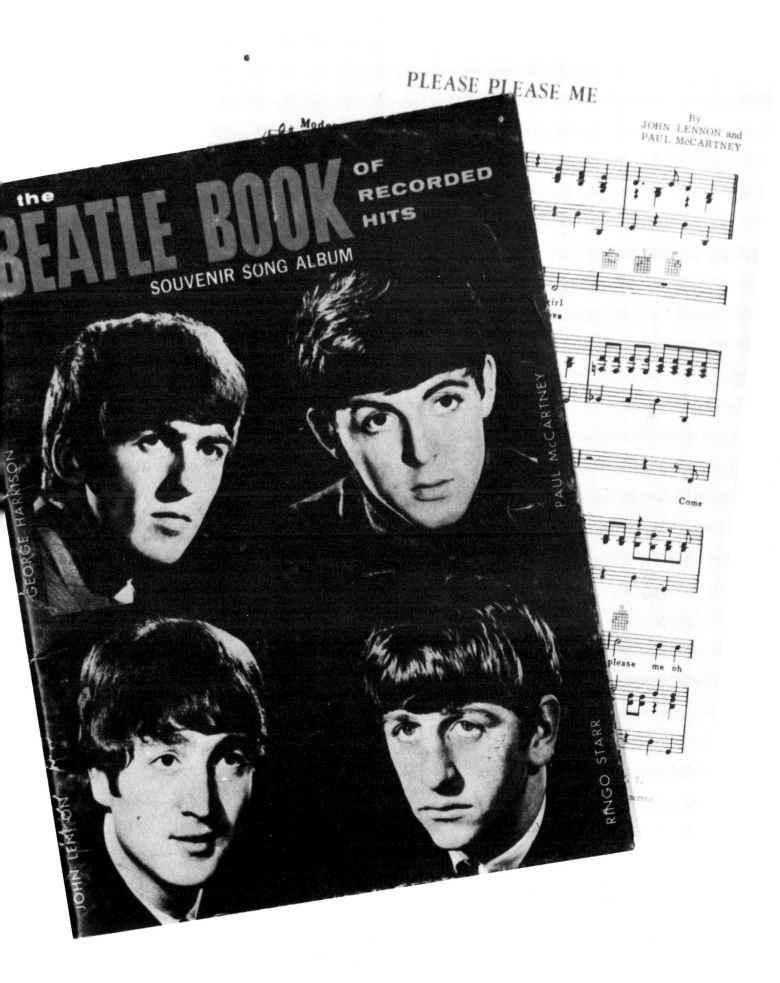

Cover versions:
Richard Anthony, The Beatles, Paul Delaney, Pancho Gonzales, The Goodtimes, The Harbor Lites, The Immigrants, Kentucky Express, Lester Lanin, Gary Lewis & The Playboys, The Music Company, The Other Company, The Pair, The Pair Extraordinaire, The Raw Meat, Johnny Rivers, The Rollers, Nancy Sinatra, Sound Alike, Tarney/Spencer Band, The Transatlantics

SHE LOVES YOU

Written by:	Lennon/McCartney
Single #:	USA: Swan 4152
	UK: Parlophone R5055
Released:	USA: Sept 1963 UK: Aug 1963
Weeks on chart:	USA: 15 UK: 33
Produced by:	George Martin
EP:	UK: The Beatles' Million Sellers, Parlophone GEP 8946, December 1965
Album:	USA: The Beatles' Second Album Capitol ST 2080
	UK: A Collection of Beatle Oldies, Parlophone PCS 7016
Released:	USA: April 1964 UK: Dec 1966
Gold:	USA: April 13, 1964

SHE'S A WOMAN

Written by:	Lennon/McCartney
Single #:	USA: Capitol 5327
	UK: Parlophone R5200
Released:	USA: Nov 1964 UK: 1964
Awards:	Most performed pop song: 1964
Weeks on chart:	USA: 9
Produced by:	George Martin
Album:	USA: Beatles '65 Capitol ST 2228
	UK: Beatles Rarities
Released:	USA: Dec 1964
Gold:	USA: December 31, 1964
Additional Musicians:	Paul, Piano

Cover versions:
Chet Atkins, The Beatles, Jeff Beck, The Big Ben Banjo Band, Cafe Creme, Frank Chacksfield, George Chakiris, The Challengers, Charles River Valley Boys, Sammy Davis & Count Basie, The Decibels, Jose Feliciano, Johnny Hallyday, Noel Harrison, Jimmie Haskell, The Hollyridge Strings, Jalopy Five, Lester Lanin, Charles Lloyd, The Northwest Company, The Power Pack, Arthur Prysock, The Surfaris

SLOW DOWN

Written by:	Larry Williams
Single #:	USA: Capitol 5255
Released:	USA: Aug 1964
Weeks on chart:	USA: 7
Produced by:	George Martin
EP:	UK: Long Tall Sally, Parlophone GEP 8913, June 1964
Album:	USA: Something New Capitol ST 2108
Released:	USA: July 1964
Gold:	USA: August 24, 1964

Cover versions:
The Beatles, Shaun Cassidy, Crow, Gerry & The Pacemakers, Brian Hyland, Jam, Alvin Lee, Sandy Nelson, Night Hawks, Hal Serra, Larry Williams

A TASTE OF HONEY

Written by:	Rick Marlow-Bobby Scott
Produced by:	George Martin
EP:	USA: The Beatles, Vee Jay VJEP 1-903, March 1964
	UK: Twist and Shout, Parlophone GEP 8882, July 1963
Album:	USA: Introducing The Beatles Vee Jay VJLP 1062
	The Early Beatles Capitol ST 2309
	UK: Please Please Me Parlophone PCS 3042
Released:	USA: July 1963
	March 1965
	UK: March 1963

TELL ME WHAT YOU SEE

Written by:	Lennon/McCartney
Produced by:	George Martin
Album:	USA: Beatles VI Capitol ST 2358
	UK: Help! Parlophone PCS 3071
Released:	USA: June 1965 UK: Aug 1965
Gold:	USA: July 1, 1965
Additional Musicians:	Paul, Electric Piano

Cover versions:
The Beatles, George Martin & His Orchestra

TELL ME WHY

Written by:	Lennon/McCartney
Produced by:	George Martin
Album:	USA: A Hard Day's Night United Artists Uas 6366
	Something New Capitol ST 2108
	UK: A Hard Day's Night Parlophone PCS 3058
Released:	USA: June 1964
	July 1964
	UK: July 1964
Gold:	USA: August 24, 1964

Cover versions:
Terry Baxter Orchestra & Chorus, The Beach Boys, The Beatles, The Big Ben Banjo Band, Cafe Creme, Les Lionceaux, George Martin & His Orchestra, Billy Lee Riley

THANK YOU GIRL

Written by:	Lennon/McCartney
Single #:	USA: Vee Jay VJ522
	UK: Parlophone R5015
Released:	USA: March 1963 UK: April 1963
Weeks on chart:	USA: 7
Produced by:	George Martin
EP:	UK: The Beatles' Hits, Parlophone GEP 8880, September 1963
Album:	USA: The Beatles' Second Album Capitol ST 2080
Released:	USA: April 1964
Gold:	USA: April 13, 1964

THERE'S A PLACE

Written by:	Lennon/McCartney
Single #:	USA: Tollie 9001
Released:	USA: March 1964
Weeks on chart:	USA: 1
Produced by:	George Martin
EP:	UK: Twist and Shout, Parlophone GEP 8882, July 1963
Album:	UK: Please Please Me Parlophone PCS 3042
Released:	UK: March 1963

THINGS WE SAID TODAY

Written by:	Lennon/McCartney
Single #:	UK: Parlophone R5160
Released:	UK: July 1964
Produced by:	George Martin
EP:	UK: A Hard Day's Night I, Parlophone GEP 8924, Nov 1964
Album:	USA: Something New Capitol ST 2108
	UK: A Hard Day's Night Parlophone PC 3058
Released:	USA: July 1964 UK: July 1964
Gold:	USA: August 24, 1964

Cover versions:
Chet Atkins, Band of the Irish Guards, Baroque Ensemble, The Beatles, The Big Ben Banjo Band, Sonny Curtis, Jackie DeShannon, The Bob Hammer Band, Woody Herman, The Hollyridge Strings, Meryside Kammermusik, Mary McCaslin, The Johnny Mann Singers, The Nightwalkers, The Pleasure Fair, Sir Walter Raleigh, The Ravens, Joshua Rifkin, Dick Rivers, The Sandpipers, Peter Schickele & Orchestra, The Sentries, Sneakers, String Driven Thing

THINK FOR YOURSELF

Written by:	George Harrison
Produced by:	George Martin
Album:	USA: Rubber Soul Capitol ST 2442
	UK: Rubber Soul Parlophone PCS 3075
Released:	USA: Dec 1965 UK: Dec 1965
Gold:	USA: December 24, 1965
Additional Musicians:	Paul, Fuzz Bass; George, Tambourine, John & Paul, Back-up vocals

Cover versions:
The Beatles, George Harrison, The Music Company

THIS BOY (RINGO'S THEME)

Written by:	Lennon/McCartney
Single #:	UK: Parlophone R5084
Released:	UK: Nov 1963
Produced by:	George Martin
EP:	USA: Four By The Beatles, Capitol EAP 2121, May 1964
Album:	USA: Meet The Beatles! Capitol ST 2047
Released:	USA: Jan 1964
Gold:	USA: February 3, 1964

Cover versions:
Jeff Afdem, Jeff Afdem & Spring Flute, Terry Baxter Orchestra & Chorus, The Beatles, The Big Ben Banjo Band, Gilles Brown, Columbia Musical Treasury Orchestra, Sonny Curtis, Max Harris & His Orchestra, Lester Lanin, Bob Leaper, Don Leaper, Robert Lee, Les Lionceaux, Johnny Mann Singers, George Martin & His Orchestra, BillyLee Riley, Bruce Roberts, Keely Smith, The Swinging Blue Jeans, Roger Webb & His Trio, Si Zentner & His Orchestra

TICKET TO RIDE

Written by:	Lennon/McCartney
Single #:	USA: Capitol 5407
	UK: Parlophone R5265
Released:	USA: April 1965 UK: April 1965
Awards:	Most performed pop song: 1965
Weeks on chart:	USA: 11 UK: 12
Produced by:	George Martin
Album:	USA: Help! Capitol SMAS 2386
	UK: Help! Parlophone PCS 3071
Released:	USA: Aug 1965 UK: 1965
Gold:	USA: August 23, 1965
Additional Musicians:	Paul, Lead guitar; Paul, Back-up vocals
Arrangements:	MB, JB, CH

Cover versions:
The Bantams, Baroque Ensemble, Terry Baxter Orchestra & Chorus, The Beatles, The Beautiful People, Madame Catherine Berberian, The Big Ben Banjo Band, Ambrose Brazelton, Cafe Creme, Tutti Camarata, Glen Campbell, The Carpenters, Frank Chacksfield, The Changing Tyde, Charles River Valley Boys, The Dick Crest Orchestra, English Muffin, The 5th Dimension, GH Presents, Dick Glasser, Francois Glorieux, The Hollyridge Strings, The In Sect, Meryside Kammermusik, Johnny Keating, Lester Lanin, Liverpool 5, George Martin & His Orchestra, Rudy Martin, Mystic Moods, The New Seekers, The Other Company, The Purple Haze, Queen Anne's Lace, Joshua Rifkin, Dick Rivers, The Rollers, Hal Serra, The Shakers, Sound Alikes, Cyril Stapleton Choir & Orchestra, Ron Steele, Billy Strange, Billy Stranson, Sydney Thompson & His Orchestra, Vanilla Fudge, Wee Willie Walker, Mary Wells

TILL THERE WAS YOU

Written by:	Meredith Willson
Produced by:	George Martin
Album:	USA: Meet The Beatles! Capitol ST 2047
	UK: With the Beatles Parlophone PCS 3045

Released:	USA: Jan 1964 *UK:* Nov 1963
Gold:	USA: February 3, 1964
Additional Musicians:	Paul, Electric Bass; John & George, Acoustic Guitars; Ringo, Bongos

TWIST AND SHOUT

Written by:	Bert Russell-Phil Medley
Single #:	USA: Tollie 9001
	UK: Parlophone R6016
Released:	USA: March 1964 *UK:* July 1976
Weeks on chart:	USA: 11
Produced by:	George Martin
EP:	UK: Twist and Shout, Parlophone GEP 8882, July 1963
Album:	USA: Introducing The Beatles Vee Jay VJLP 1062
	The Early Beatles Capitol ST 2309
	UK: Please Please Me Parlophone PCS 3042
Released:	USA: July 1963
	March 1965
	UK: March 1963
Additional Musicians:	Paul & George, Back-up vocals

WAIT

Written by:	Lennon/McCartney
Produced by:	George Martin
Album:	USA: Rubber Soul Capitol St 2442
	UK: Rubber Soul Parlophone PCS 3075
Released:	USA: Dec 1965 *UK:* Dec 1965
Gold:	USA: December 24, 1965

Cover versions:
The Beatles, Lester Lanin, The Music Company, Frankie Vaughn

WE CAN WORK IT OUT

Written by:	Lennon/McCartney
Single #:	USA: Capitol 5555
	UK: Parlophone R5389
Released:	USA: Dec 1965 *UK:* Dec 1965
Gold:	USA: January 6, 1966
Awards:	Most performed pop song: 1965 Other: 1965, Highest Certified British Sales (Ivor Novello Awards)
Weeks on chart:	USA: 12 *UK:* 12
Produced by:	George Martin
Album:	USA: "Yesterday"... and Today Capitol ST 2553
	UK: A Collection of Beatle Oldies, Parlophone PCS 7016
Released:	USA: June 1966 *UK:* Dec 1966
Gold:	USA: July 8, 1966
Additional Musicians:	John, Harmonium; John, Back-up vocals

Cover versions:
American Pick Hits Band, Richard Anthony, Astromusical House of Cap., Michael Barnes, Terry Baxter Orchestra & Chorus, The Beatles, The Brothers Four, Maxine Brown, George Burns, Cafe Creme, Petula Clark, J. Lawrence Cook, James Darren, Deep Purple, Dillards, Exile, Family Guitar, The Fantastic Four, Fever Tree, Four Seasons, The Gophers, Dave Hall, Mike Harrison, The Hollyridge Strings, Humble Pie, Jerry Inman, The Jalopy Five, Jamie & The J Silvia Singers, Randy James, Kaseneta Katz Super Cirkus, Kate Kasenete Singing Orchestra, Lester Lanin, Liverpool 5, Johnny Mathis, Peter Matz, Melanie, The MGM Singing Strings, The Naked Truth, Johnny Nash, Orchestra of Capricorn, The Other Company, Pick Hit Artists, The Rollers, Sam & Dave, Joe Scott, Johnny Simon, Valerie Simpson, Sound Alikes, Leslie Uggams, Caterina Valente, Dionne Warwicke, Stevie Wonder, Wild Honey Singers, Stan Worth

WHAT GOES ON

Written by:	Lennon/McCartney/Richard Starkey
Single #:	USA: Capitol 5587
Released:	USA: Feb 1966
Weeks on chart:	USA: 2
Produced by:	George Martin
Album:	USA: "Yesterday"... and Today Capitol ST 2553
	UK: Rubber Soul Parlophone PCS 3075
Released:	USA: June 1966 *UK:* Dec 1965
Gold:	USA: July 8, 1966
Additional Musicians:	Paul & John, Back-up vocals

Cover versions:
The Beatles, Charles River Valley Boys, Orphan

WHAT YOU'RE DOING

Written by:	Lennon/McCartney
Produced by:	George Martin
Album:	USA: Beatles VI Capitol ST 2358
	UK: Beatles for Sale Parlophone PCS 3062
Released:	USA: June 1965 *UK:* Dec 1964
Gold:	USA: July 1, 1965

Cover versions:
The Beatles, Terri Fisher, Lester Lanin

WHEN I GET HOME

Written by:	Lennon/McCartney
Produced by:	George Martin
EP:	UK: A Hard Day's Night, Parlophone GEP 8924, November 1964
Album:	USA: Something New Capitol ST 2108
	UK: A Hard Day's Night Parlophone PCS 3058
Released:	USA: July 1964 *UK:* July 1964
Gold:	USA: August 24, 1964
Additional Musicians:	Paul & George, Back-up vocals

Cover versions:
The Back Alley, The Beatles, Brotherhood, Bob Hammer, Bob Hammer Band, Lester Lanin, The Rustix, Space

THE WORD

Written by:	Lennon/McCartney
Produced by:	George Martin
Album:	USA: Rubber Soul Capitol ST 2442
	UK: Rubber Soul Parlophone PCS 3075
Released:	USA: Dec 1965 *UK:* Dec 1965
Gold:	USA: December 24, 1965
Additional Musicians:	Paul, Piano; George Martin, Harmonium

Cover versions:
The Harvey Averne Dozen, The Beatles, The Big Ben Banjo Band, The Carnival, Jackie & Roy, Lester Lanin, Gary McFarland, The Music Company, Don Sebesky & Jazz Rock S, Gabor Szabo

WORDS OF LOVE

Written by:	Buddy Holly
Produced by:	George Martin
EP:	UK: Beatles for Sale II, Parlophone GEP 8938, June 1965
Album:	USA: Beatles VI Capitol ST 2358
	UK: Beatles for Sale Parlophone PCS 3062
Released:	USA: June 1965 *UK:* Dec 1964
Gold:	USA: July 1, 1965
Additional Musicians:	Ringo, Packing Case

YES IT IS

Written by:	Lennon/McCartney
Single #:	USA: Capitol 5407
	UK: Parlophone R5265
Released:	USA: April 1965 *UK:* April 1965
Weeks on chart:	USA: 4
Produced by:	George Martin
Album:	USA: Beatles VI Capitol ST 2358
Released:	USA: June 1965
Gold:	USA: July 1, 1965

Cover versions:
The Beatles, Charles River Valley Boys, The In Sect

YESTERDAY

Written by:	Lennon/McCartney
Single #:	USA: Capitol 5498
	UK: Parlophone R6013
Released:	USA: Sept 1965 *UK:* Feb 1976
Gold:	USA: October 20, 1965
Awards:	Million performance song: March 1968
	Most performed pop song: 1965, 1966, 1968, 1969, 1970, 1971, 1972, 1973
	Other: Outstanding Song of 1965, U.K. (Ivor Novello Awards)
Weeks on chart:	USA: 11 *UK:* 7
Produced by:	George Martin
EP:	UK: Yesterday, Parlophone GEP 8948, March 1966
Album:	USA: "Yesterday"... and Today Capitol ST 2553
	UK: Help! Parlophone PCS 3071
Released:	USA: June 1966 *UK:* Aug 1965
Gold:	USA: July 8, 1966
Additional Musicians:	Paul, Acoustic Guitar; String Quartet. John, George and Ringo did not participate.
Arrangements:	MB, JB, CB, OR, CH

Cover versions:
Ronnie Aldrich, The All Star Pop Orchestra, Bob Allen, Robert Allen, Amanda Ambrose, American Pick Hit Singers, Ed Ames, Nancy Ames, Vicki Anderson, Ray Anthony, P.P. Arnold, Asbda Conv Tattan High School, Chet Atkins, Hughes Aufray, Leon Austin, Sil Austin, Ena Baga, Band of the Irish Guards, Bar-Kays, Count Basie, Terry Baxter Orchestra & Chorus, Roger Bean & His Orchestra, Beatlemania, The Beatles, Beau Brummels, Beau Brummels 66, Yves Beausoleil, Jim Benzmiller, Madame Catherine Berberian, Harold Betters, Leon Bibb, The Big Ben Banjo Band, Cilla Black, Howard Blake & His Combo, Blues Magoos, Willie Bobo, Maurice Boivin, Luiz Bonfa, Pat Boone, Harry Boz, Bravada Brass, The Brazilian Echoes, The Brothers Four, James Brown, Jim Ed Brown, Puncho Brown, Ruth Brown, The Brian Browne Trio, Miss Bruce, Tony Bruno, Anita Bryant, Browing Bryant, Ray Bryant, Wilma Green, Wilma Burgess, Ann Burton, Paul Buskirk, Jerry Butler, Charlie Byrd, John Cacavas Orchestra, Cafe Creme, Al Caiola, Molly Camp, Ace Cannon, Thumbs Carllile, The Carmel Strings, Carstairs, Lee Castle & Jimmy Dorsey, Carmen Cavallaro Camp, Frank Chacksfield, David Chambeau Orchestra, Ray Charles Singers, Don Cherry, The Chords, Arnie Chycosky, John Coates Jr., Jack Cockerly, Nat King Cole, Columbia Musical Treasury, Mt. Combo, Perry Como, Ray Conniff, Lawrence Cook, Cesar Cost Y Orq de Gust, Floyd Cramer, Crazy Otto, Jack Crossan, Xavier Cugat & His Orchestra, Current Event, Vic Dana, David & Jonathan, Mel Davis, Little Jimmy Dempsey, The Destitutes, The Dillards, Dino, Desi & Billy, Francois Dompierre, Doodletown Pipers, Val Doonican, Steve Douglas, Dr. John, Lee Dresser, Roy Drusky, John Duffy, Patty Duke, Ron Eliran, Ray Ellis, Enchanted Organ Plays, David Essex, Eyes of Blue, Percy Faith, Marianne Faithful, Robert Farnon & Tony Coe, Jose Feliciano, Marcello Ferial, Ferrante & Teicher, George Feyer, Arthur Fiedler & Boston Pops, Jerry Fielding, Horst & Fischer Werner Mull, Eddie Fisher, Buddy Fite, Ella Fitzgerald, Shelby Flint, Tennessee Ernie Ford, Pete Fountain, Four King Sisters, The 4 Renegades, Sergio Franchi, Connie

Francis, Friends of the Family, Julian Gallo & Carol Cole, June Gardner, Erroll Garner, Glen Garrison, John Gary, Marvin Gaye, Jackie Gleason, Francois Glorieux, The Gnats, Marty Gold Orchestra, The Golden Strings, Bobby Goldsboro, Benny Goodman, The Gophers, Harry Goz, Earl Grant, Max Greger, Roosevelt Grier, The Groovers, Dick Grove & His Orchestra, Vince Guaraldi, Johnny Guarnieri, Mrs. G F Hanna, Jack Hansen & His Orchestra, The Hawaiian Surfers, Leon Haywood, Tom Hazelton & Gene Cisze, Head Shop, The Hesitations, Lucien Hetu, Monk Higgins, Hines, Hines & Dad, Al Hirt, Don Ho & The Aliis, The Hollyridge Strings, Hollywood Brass, George Holmes, The Horsehairs, Frank Hubell & Stompers, Craig Hundley Trio, Stan Hunter & Sonny Fortune, Dick Hyman, Impressions, Jerry Inman, Burl Ives, Jackie & Ron, Jackie & Roy, Willie Jackson, Jalopy Five, Jamaican All Stars, Jamie & J Silvia, Jan & Dean, Horst Jankowski, Fran Jeffries, Dick Jensen, The Alex Johns Trio, Jack Jones, Linda Jones, Tom Jones, Katz Kasenetz Singing Orchestral, Alan Keaton, Bill Kenny, Stan Kenton, Barney Kessel, The Kimberlys, The King Family, Wayne King & His Orchestra, Rudi Knabl, Hildegard Knef, Gladys Knight & The Pips, Andre Kostelanetz, Patti Labelle, Patti Labelle & The Bluebelles, Pierre Lalonde, Hoagy Lands, Lester Lanin, Timothy Laskey, James Last, Latin Dimension, Brenda Lee, Michelle Lee, Raymond Lefevre Orchestra, Michel Legrand, Les Strand, The Lettermen, Barbara Lewis, The Jerry Lewis Singers, Leroy Lewis, Liberace, Carlos Lico, Mark Lindsay, Liverpool 5, David Lloyd & Orchestra, Guy Lombardo, London Philharmonic Orchestra, London Sound 70 Orchestra, Longines Symphonette, Trini Lopez, Los Indios Tabajaras, Los Mustang, Michel Louvain, Norman Luboff Choir, Pat Lundy, Arthur Lyman, Ed Lyman, Gloria Lynne, David McCallum, Les McCann Ltd., Dick McClish Quintet, Gordon Macrae, Barry McGuire, Kenneth McKellar, Dave McKenna, Ellix McLintock, Father Colmba McManus, Magne Tronics Combo, Henry Mancini, Herbie Mann, Johnny Mann Singers, Mantovani & (Mantovani Society), Mariachi Mexico 70, Jeffrey & Ronald Marlowe, Dewey Martin & Medicine Band, Ray Martin & Orchestra, Al Martino, Maryvale High School Chorus, Johnny Mathis, Peter Matz, Curtis Mayfield, Bill Medley, George Merdichian, Tony Mergel, Buddy Merrill, The Merrymen, Midnight String Quartet, Molly Camp, Moments, Matt Monro, Monterey String Ensemble, Chris Montez, Wes Montgomery, Jane Morgan, Lee Morgan, Tony Mottola, Mountain Dew Brass, Werner Muller Un Sein Or, Mat Munro, Jerry Murad's Harmonicats, Music City Orchestra, George Nardello, Nashville Country Strings, Jack Nathan & His Orchestra, Oliver Nelson, Willie Nelson, Peter Nero, The New Classic Singers, The Newcomers, The New Dance Band, David Newman, Wayne Newton, The Nova Baroque Ensemble, The Now Generation, Anita O'Day, 101 Strings & Joe Adams, The Orchestra of Pisces, Tony Osborne Orchestra, The Other Company, Crazy Otto, Marty Paich, Paris Sisters, Freda Payne, Pedal Steel Guitar, Steve Perry, Oscar Peterson, Philadelphia Orchestra, Pic & Bill, Frank Pourcell & Orchestra, Patty Pravo, Elvis Presley, Ray Price, Arthur Prysock, Pucho, G. Puente & C. Atkins, Tito Puente La Lupe, The Quartette Tres Bien, Susan Rafey, The Rainy Day Orchestra, The Rainy Day Singers, Don Randi Trio, Boots Randolph, Sue Raney, Lou Rawls, Raymond & Eddie, Otis Redding, Jimmy Reesor, Herbert Rehbein, The Relations, Diane Renay, Ben Richardello & Orchestra, Ron Richardello & Orchestra, Nelson Riddle, Marty Robbins, Smokey Robinson & The Miracles, Ralph Robles, Jen Rogers, The Rollers, The Romantic Strings, Charles Ross Reggae Combo, Diana Ross & The Supremes, Nini Rossi, Andy Russell, Ginette Sage, The Sandpipers, The Scarborough Strings, Peter Schofield & Canadia, Scots Guard on Tour, Bruce Scott, The Seekers, Jeannie Seely, The Senate, Pierre Senecal, Bud Shank, Roland Shaw Orchestra & Chorus, George Shearing, Don Shirley Trio, Bunny Sigler, The Silkie, Sylvia Sims, Frank Sinatra, Singers Unlimited, Jimmy Smith, Johnny Smith, Kate Smith, The Smothers Brothers, Sound Alike, The Sounds of Tiajuana, Billie Jo Spears, Spirit, Cyril Stapleton & Orchestra, Starlight Woodwinds, Stone Mountain

Boys, Enso Stuarti, The Ed Sullivan Singers, Supremes, Bob Swanson & Company, Karl Swoboda, Sylvers II, Gabor Szabo, The Templeton Twins, The Temptations, the Keith Textor Singers, Carla Thomas, George Thomas Quartet 67, Threads of Glory, Ozzie Torrens, The Toys, Treble Teens Choir, Georges et Rod Tremblay, Jerry Tuttle, Jerry Vale, George Van Eps, Theo Vaness, Sarah Vaughn, Tom Vaughn, The Ventures, Jackie Vernon, The Versatile Impressions, The Village Stompers, The Waikikis, Timothy Walker, Dionne Warwick, Weli Community Chorus, Lawrence Welk, Marcy Wells, Dick Wellstood, Jimmy Wilkerson, Allen Williams, Andy Williams, Roger Williams, Chris Williamson, Gerald Wilson Orchestra, Nancy Wilson, Kai Winding, Hugo Winterhalter, The Womenfolk, The Woodstock Singers, Stan Worth, J.J. Worthington, Klaus Wunderlich, Tammy Wynette, Barry Young, The Young Gyants, Young Holt Trio, Zacharias-Provocative Strings

YOU CAN'T DO THAT

Written by:	Lennon/McCartney
Single #:	USA: Capitol 5150
	UK: Parlophone R5114
Released:	USA: March 1964
	UK: March 1964
Weeks on chart:	USA: 4
Produced by:	George Martin
Album:	USA: The Beatles' Second Album
	Capitol ST 2080
	UK: A Hard Day's Night
	Parlophone PCS 3058
Released:	USA: April 1964 UK: July 1964
Gold:	USA: April 13, 1964
Additional Musicians:	George, 12-String Guitar

Cover versions:
The Beatles, The Big Ben Banjo Band, Tony Bruno, Ian Gomm, Johnny & The Hurricanes, Kurt & Noah, Lester Lanin, New Adventures, Nilsson, The Rollers, Sound Alikes, The Standells

YOU LIKE ME TOO MUCH

Written by:	George Harrison
Produced by:	George Martin
EP:	UK: Yesterday, Parlophone GEP 8948, March 1966
Album:	USA: Beatles VI
	Capitol ST 2358
	UK: Help!
	Parlophone PCS 3071
Released:	USA: June 1965 UK: Aug 1965
Gold:	USA: July 1, 1965
Additional Musicians:	John, Electric Piano; Paul and George Martin, Steinway Piano

Cover versions:
The Beatles, The Challengers, The Waikikis

YOU REALLY GOT A HOLD ON ME

Written by:	William "Smokey" Robinson
Produced by:	George Martin
Album:	USA: The Beatles Second Album
	Capitol ST 2080
Released:	USA: April 1964
Gold:	USA: April 13, 1964
Additional Musicians:	George Martin, Piano

YOU WON'T SEE ME

Written by:	Lennon/McCartney
Produced by:	George Martin
EP:	UK: Nowhere Man, Parlophone GEP 8952, July 1966
Album:	USA: Rubber Soul
	Capitol ST 2442
	UK: Rubber Soul
	Parlophone PCS 3075
Released:	USA: Dec 1965 UK: Dec 1965
Gold:	USA: December 24, 1965
Additional Musicians:	Paul, Piano; Mal Evans, Hammond Organ

Cover versions:
American Pick Hit Artists, Atlanta Connection, The Beatles, Ben Benay, Harvey Brooks, Cafe Creme, The Godz, Andrea Hansen, Ramona Hutton, Anne Murray, The Music Company, The Oxfords, Pick Hit Artists, Ernie Ranglin, The Realistics, Richard Ruskin, Sound Alikes, Gabor Szabo, The Tom Fools, Ian Whitcomb & Somebody's

YOU'RE GOING TO LOSE THAT GIRL

Written by:	Lennon/McCartney
Produced by:	George Martin
Album:	USA: Help!
	Capitol SMAS 2386
	UK: Help!
	Parlophone PCS 3071
Released:	USA: Aug 1965 UK: Aug 1965
Gold:	USA: August 23, 1965

Cover versions:
Baroque Ensemble, Terry Baxter Orchestra & Chorus, The Beatles, Cafe Creme, The Cryan Shames, The Escorts, Five Band Electrical Band, The Green Giants, Meryside Kammermusik, George Martin & His Orchestra, Joshua Rifkin, The Villagers

YOU'VE GOT TO HIDE YOUR LOVE AWAY

Written by:	Lennon/McCartney
Produced by:	George Martin
Album:	USA: Help!
	Capitol SMAS 2386
	UK: Help!
	Parlophone PCS 3071
Released:	USA: Aug 1965 UK: Aug 1965
Gold:	USA: August 23, 1965
Additional Musicians:	Flute playing

Cover versions:
Baroque Ensemble, Terry Baxter Orchestra & Chorus, The Beach Boys, The Beatles, Beau Brummels, Beau Brummels 66, Ben Benay, Madame Catherine Berberian, Floyd Cramer, Dino, Desi & Billy, Percy Faith, Percy Faith & His Orchestra, Francois Glorieux, The Gophers, The Hollyridge Strings, Jan & Dean, Waylon Jennings & Waylors, Meryside Kammermusik, Lester Lanin, Les Excentriques, Gary Lewis & The Playboys, Roger Lorendo, Barry McGuire, Magne Tronics Combo, George Martin & His Orchestra, Eddy Mitchell, Pozo Seco Singer, Joshua Rifkin, Tim Rose, Silkie, Sound Alike, The Spokesman, Sweet Smoke

ACROSS THE UNIVERSE

Written by:	Lennon/McCartney
Produced by:	George Martin
Album:	USA: Let It Be
	Red Apple 34001
	UK: Let It Be
	Apple PXS1/Apple PCS 7096
Released:	USA: May 1970
	UK: May 1970/Nov 1970
Gold:	USA: May 26, 1970
Additional	
Musicians:	John, Lead Guitar; Paul, Piano; John & George Martin, Organ; Lizzie Bravo & Gayleen Pease, Back-up vocals.
Arrangements:	CH

Cover versions:
The Beatles, Cilla Black, David Bowie, Lightmyth, Barbara Love, Rod McKuen and the Stanyan Strings, Portable Flower Factory, Sounds Galactic, Story Theatre

ALL TOGETHER NOW

Written by:	Lennon/McCartney
Produced by:	George Martin
Album:	USA: Yellow Submarine
	Apple SW 153
	UK: Yellow Submarine
	Apple PCS 7070
Released:	USA: Jan 1969 UK: Jan 1969
Gold:	USA: February 5, 1969
Arrangements:	CB

Cover versions:
The Beatles, C Number Five, Joy Unlimited, James Last, Sezo

ALL YOU NEED IS LOVE

Written by:	Lennon/McCartney
Single #:	USA: Capitol 5964
	UK: Parlophone R5620
Released:	USA: July 1967 UK: July 1967
Gold:	USA: September 11, 1967
Awards:	Most performed pop song: 1975
Weeks on chart:	USA: 11 UK: 13
Produced by:	George Martin
EP:	UK: Yellow Submarine, Apple PCS 7070, January 1969
Album:	USA: Magical Mystery Tour Capitol SM 2835
	UK: Magical Mystery Tour Parlophone PCTC 255
Released:	USA: Nov 1967 UK: Dec 1976
Gold:	USA: December 15, 1967
Album:	USA: Yellow Submarine Apple SW 153
Released:	USA: Jan 1969
Gold:	USA: February 5, 1969
Additional	
Musicians:	Mick Jagger, Gary Leeds, Keith Richard, Marianne Faithful, Jane Asher, Patti Boyd, Keith Moon, Graham Nash, Chorus; Studio Orchestra
Arrangements:	CH

Cover versions:
Terry Baxter, Beatlemania, The Beatles, Ray Bloch Singers, Cafe Creme, Calvary Twill, Don Costa, Peter Covent Band, Ferrante & Teicher, Fifth Dimension, Freedom Sounds, Frannie Golde, Anita Harris, The Hollyridge Strings, Jalopy Five, Henry Jerome, Anita Kerr Singers, Lester Lanin, Liverpool 5, 101 Strings, Osmond Brothers, Tony Osborne, Norman Percival, Percussion Ltd., Hal Serra, Bill Sheperd Orchestra, Sound Alikes, Studio Musicians, Bob Thiele, Three Brass Buttons, Unknown

BABY YOU'RE A RICH MAN

Written by:	Lennon/McCartney
Single #:	USA: Capitol 5964
	UK: Parlophone R5620
Released:	USA: July 1967 UK: July 1967
Weeks on chart:	USA: 5
Produced by:	George Martin
Album:	USA: Magical Mystery Tour Capitol SMAL 2835
	UK: Magical Mystery Tour Parlophone PCTC 255
Released:	USA: Nov 1967 UK: Dec 1976
Gold:	USA: December 15, 1967

Cover versions:
The Beatles, The Hollyridge Strings, The Living Guitars

BACK IN THE U.S.S.R.

Written by:	Lennon/McCartney
Single #:	UK: Parlophone R 6016
Released:	UK: July 1976
Produced by:	George Martin
Album:	USA: The Beatles Apple SWBO 101
	UK: The Beatles Apple PCS 7067/8
Released:	USA: Nov 1968 UK: Nov 1968
Gold:	USA: December 6, 1968
Additional	
Musicians:	Paul, Lead Guitar; George, Bass Guitar; John, Six-String Bass

Cover versions:
Average Disco Band, The Beatles, Cafe Creme, Cakewalk to the Cup, California Poppy Pickers, Chubby Checker, John Fred, The Gophers, Ramsey Lewis, The Other Company, Jimmy Powell, The Rollers

BALLAD OF JOHN AND YOKO

Written by:	Lennon/McCartney
Single #:	USA: Apple 2531
	UK: Apple R5786
Released:	USA: June 1969 UK: May 1969
Gold:	USA: July 16, 1969
Weeks on chart:	USA: 9 UK: 14
Produced by:	George Martin
Album:	USA: Hey Jude Apple SW 385/SO 385
Released:	USA: Feb 1970
Gold:	USA: March 6, 1970
Additional	
Musicians:	John, Guitar; Paul, Drums, Piano, Back-up vocals; George & Ringo not present

Cover versions:
Ron Anthony, The Beatles, Vinnie Bell, California Poppy Pickers, James Last, Los Norte Americanos, Magne-Tronics Combo, Mike Melvoin, The Percey Faith Singers, The Spare Change

BECAUSE

Written by:	Lennon/McCartney
Produced by:	George Martin
Album:	USA: Abbey Road Apple SO 383
	UK: Abbey Road Apple PCS 7088
Released:	USA: Oct 1969 UK: Sept 1969
Gold:	USA: October 27, 1969

Cover versions:
Ronnie Aldrich, The Beatles, George Benson, Booker T & The M.G.'s, Cafe Creme, Alice Cooper, Lynsey De Paul, Stan Getz, London Pops Orchestra, Gary McFarland, Magne-Tronics Combo, New Christy Minstrels, The Odyssey Singers, The Percy Faith Strings, Isabelle Pierre, Stan Ruffin, Shirley Scott, Doc Severinsen, John Williams

BEING FOR THE BENEFIT OF MR. KITE

Written by:	Lennon/McCartney
Produced by:	George Martin
Album:	USA: Sergeant Pepper's Lonely Hearts Club Band, Capitol SMAS 2653
	UK: Sergeant Pepper's Lonely Hearts Club Band, Parlophone PCS 7027
Released:	USA: June 1967 UK: June 1967
Gold:	USA: June 15, 1967
Additional	
Musicians:	John, Main Organ; George Martin, Harmony Organ; Mal Evans, Bass Harmonica

Cover versions:
The Beatles, Maurice Gibb, Peter Frampton, The Odyssey Singers, Stan Ruffin

BIRTHDAY

Written by:	Lennon/McCartney
Produced by:	George Martin
Album:	USA: The Beatles Apple SWBO 01
	UK: The Beatles Apple PCS 7067/8
Released:	USA: Nov 1968 UK: Nov 1968
Gold:	USA: December 6, 1968
Additional	
Musicians:	George, Tambourine; Paul, Piano; Yoko Ono & Patti Harrison, Back-up vocals
Arrangements:	CH

Cover versions:
The Beatles, Cafe Creme, Lee Castle, La Famille La Combe, Los Yaki, Pablo Beltran Ruiz, Underground Sunshine

BLACKBIRD

Written by:	Lennon/McCartney
Produced by:	George Martin
Album:	USA: The Beatles Apple SWBO 101
	UK: The Beatles Apple PCS 7067/8
Released:	USA: Nov 1968 UK: Nov 1968
Gold:	USA: December 6, 1968
Arrangements:	JB, CH

Cover versions:
Chet Atkins, Terry Baxter, The Beatles, Harpers
Bizarre, Bossa Rio, Clingers, Dion, Bob Duros,
Laura Greene, Dick Hyman, The Jazz Crusaders,
Laredo, Lincoln Mayorga, Ramsey Lewis, Los
Yaki, Mary McCaslin, Danny McCulloch, Pedal
Steel Guitar Album, Power and Light, Billy
Preston, Punch, Kenny Rankin, Rubber Band,
Sandler and Young, Sisters Love, Sounds of our
Times, Sylvester, Bob Theile Emergency,
Unknown, Dave Valentin, Wings

BLUE JAY WAY

Written by:	George Harrison
Produced by:	George Martin
EP:	UK: Magical Mystery Tour, Parlophone SMMT 112, December 1967
Album:	USA: Magical Mystery Tour Capitol SMAL 2835
	UK: Magical Mystery Tour Parlophone PCTC 255
	USA: Nov 1967 UK: Dec 1976
Gold:	USA: December 15, 1964
Additional Musicians:	Paul, Back-up vocals

Cover versions:
The Beatles, Bud Shank, Lord Sitar

CARRY THAT WEIGHT

Written by:	Lennon/McCartney
Produced by:	George Martin
Album:	USA: Abbey Road Apple SO 383
	UK: Abbey Road Apple PCS 7088
Released:	USA: Oct 1969 UK: Sept 1969
Gold:	USA: October 27, 1969
Arrangements:	CH, MB

Cover versions:
Terry Baxter, The Beatles, The Bee Gees, Bola
Sete, Booker T & The M.G.'s, Francis Lai, Carmen
McRae, Mod, English Muffin, Mystic Moods
Orchestra, The Odyssey Singers, Stan Ruffin, Doc
Severinsen, Sound Alike, Trash

COME TOGETHER

Written by:	Lennon/McCartney
Single #:	USA: Apple 2654
	UK: Apple R5814
Released:	USA: Oct 1969 UK: Oct 1969
Gold:	USA: October 27, 1969
Awards:	Most performed pop song: 1970
Weeks on chart:	USA: 16
Produced by:	George Martin
Album:	USA: Abbey Road Apple SO 383
	UK: Abbey Road Apple PCS 7088
Released:	USA: Oct 1969 UK: Sept 1969
Gold:	USA: October 27, 1969
Arrangements:	JB

Cover versions:
Aerosmith, Charlie Barnet & Orchestra, Count
Basie, Terry Baxter, The Beatles, George Benson,
John Bishop, Willie Bobo, Booker T & The M.G.'s,
Brothers Johnson, Odell Brown, Charlie Byrd, Cafe
Creme, The Care Package, James Cast, Frank
Chacksfield, Chairman of the Board, Decibels,
Claude Denjean, The Detroit Underground,
George Duke, Family Guitar, Funky Junction,
Gladys Knight & The Pips, Guitars Unlimited, The
Handicappers, Richard Groove Holmes, Richard
Holmes & E. Watts, The Ice Man's Band, The
Jalopy Five, Syc Johnson, Harrison Kennedy, Ben
E. King, The Love Childs, Herbie Mann, Mike Curb
Congregation, Tony Mottola, New Generation,
Odyssey, Norrie Paramour, The Phoenix
Authority, Relations, Diana Ross, Gary Ruffin,
Stan Ruffin, Doc Severinsen, Ben Sidran, Sound
A-Like, Hans Stayner, The Supremes, Ike & Tina
Turner, David T. Walker, Dionne Warwicke, Mary
Wells, Stan Worth

THE CONTINUING STORY OF BUNGALOW BILL

Written by:	Lennon/McCartney
Produced by:	George Martin
Album:	USA: The Beatles Apple SWBO 101
	UK: The Beatles Apple SWBO 101
Released:	USA: Nov 1968 UK: Nov 1968
Gold:	USA: December 6, 1968
Additional Musicians:	John, Organ; Chris Thomas, Mellotron; Yoko Ono, Back-up vocals

Cover versions:
The Beatles, Christian-Getro, Los Yaki

CRY BABY CRY

Written by:	Lennon/McCartney
Produced by:	George Martin
Album:	USA: The Beatles Apple SWBO 101
	UK: The Beatles Apple PCS 7067/8
Released:	USA: Nov 1968 UK: Nov 1968
Gold:	USA: December 6, 1968
Additional Musicians:	John, Guitar, Piano & Organ

Cover versions:
The Beatles, Commander Cody, Inner Dialogue,
Ramsey Lewis

A DAY IN THE LIFE

Written by:	Lennon/McCartney
Produced by:	George Martin
Album:	USA: Sergeant Pepper's Lonely Hearts Club Band, Capitol SMAS 2653
	UK: Sergeant Pepper's Lonely Hearts Club Band, Parlophone PCS 7027
Released:	USA: June 1967 UK: June 1967
Gold:	USA: June 15, 1967
Additional Musicians:	Mal Evans, Alarm Clock; 41 Piece Orchestra Conducted by Paul

Cover versions:
Brian Auger, Terry Baxter, The Beatles, Bobbi
Boyle, Eric Burdon & War, Cafe Creme, Jimmy
Caravan, Danny Cox, Jose Feliciano, Barry Gibb
& Bee Gees, Grant Green, The Hollyridge Strings,
Peter Knight, Les Demerle, Lighthouse, London
Symphony Orchestra, Wes Montgomery, The
Odyssey Singers, Recording Love Habit, Stan
Ruffin, Joe Scott, Sound A-Likes, Gabor Szabo,
Tartaglia, Ken Thorne, Frankie Valli, War

DEAR PRUDENCE

Written by:	Lennon/McCartney
Produced by:	George Martin
Album:	USA: The Beatles Apple SWBO 101
	UK: The Beatles Apple PCS 7067/8
Released:	USA: Nov 1968 UK: Nov 1968
Gold:	USA: December 6, 1968
Additional Musicians:	Paul, Piano & Flugelhorn; John & Mal Evans, Tambourine

Cover versions:
The Beatles, Danny Cox, Cecilla, Neil Darrow,
The Five Stairsteps, Imitations, Katfish, Ramsey
Lewis, Kenny Rankin, Sound Foundation, Gabor
Szabo, Don Walker, The Leslie West Band, Wild
Honey Singers

DIG A PONY

Written by:	Lennon/McCartney
Produced by:	Phil Spector
Album:	USA: Let It Be Red Apple 34001
	UK: Let It Be Apple PXS1/Apple PCS 7096
Released:	USA: May 1970
	UK: May 1970/Nov 1970
Gold:	USA: May 26, 1970
Cover versions:	The Beatles

DIG IT

Written by:	Lennon/McCartney
Produced by:	Phil Spector
Album:	USA: Let It Be Red Apple 34001
	UK: Let It Be Apple PXS1/Apple PCS 7096
Released:	USA: May 1970
	UK: May 1970/Nov 1970
Gold:	USA: May 26, 1970
Cover versions:	The Beatles

DON'T LET ME DOWN

Written by:	Lennon/McCartney
Single #:	USA: Apple 2490
	UK: Apple R5777
Released:	USA: May 1969 UK: April 1969
Weeks on chart:	USA: 4
Produced by:	George Martin
Album:	USA: Hey Jude Apple SW 385/SO 385
Released:	USA: Feb 1970
Gold:	USA: March 6, 1970
Additional Musicians:	Paul, Back-up vocals

Cover versions:
The Beatles, Cafe Creme, Randy Crawford,
Dillard & Clark, Fraser & Debolt, Donald Height,
Ben E. King, Claudine Longet, Nicole & Frederic,
Billy Preston, Phoebe Snow, The Spare Change,
Underground Sunshine

DON'T PASS ME BY

Written by:	Richard Starkey
Produced by:	George Martin
Album:	USA: The Beatles Apple SWBO 101
	UK: The Beatles Apple PCS 7067/8
Released:	USA: Nov 1968 UK: Nov 1968
Gold:	USA: December 6, 1968
Additional Musicians:	Ringo, Piano

ELEANOR RIGBY

Written by:	Lennon/McCartney
Single #:	USA: Capitol 5715
	UK: Parlophone R5489
Released:	USA: Aug 1966 UK: Aug 1966
Awards:	Million performance song: June 1974
	Most performed pop song: 1968, 1970
	Grammy: 1966 "Best Contemporary Pop Solo Vocal Performance—Paul McCartney"
Weeks on chart:	USA: 8 UK: 13
Produced by:	George Martin
Album:	USA: Revolver Capitol ST 2576
	UK: Revolver Parlophone PCS 7009
Released:	USA: Aug 1966 UK: Aug 1966
Gold:	USA: August 22, 1966
Additional Musicians:	4 violins, 2 violas & 2 cellos
Arrangements:	CH, SOR, CB, JB, MB

Cover versions:
Paul Anka, P. P. Arnold, Average Disco Band, Joan Baez, Ena Baga, Baroque Inevitable, Count Basie, Terry Baxter, Beatlemania, The Beatles, Vincent Bell, Tony Bennett, Madame Catherine Berberia, Big Maybelle, Anna Black, Blonde On Blonde, Bloodrock, Booker T & The M.G.'s, Bossa Rio, Boston Pop Orchestra, Perry Botkin Jr., The Brass Choir, Brass Impact, Ambrose Brazelton, Buckwheat, Cafe Creme, Jackie Cain & Roy Kral, Jimmy Caravan & His Trio, Walter Carlos, Larry Carlton, Lee Castle, Carmen Cavallaro, Gene Chandler, Ray Charles, Wayne Cochran, Bill Comeau, The Contrasts, Sonny Criss, Crusaders, Michael Dees, Dr. Demento, John Denver, 18th Century Concepts, El Chicano, Enoch Light, Esperato, Lee Evans, Percy Faith Strings, Arthur Fiedler & The Boston Pops Orchestra, The Four Tops, Charlie Fox, Aretha Franklin, The Free Design, The Free-Men, Jonna Gault, Bobbie Gentry, Francois Glorieux, Goliath, Marty Gold, Morton Gould, Annie Green, Vince Guaraldi, Gene Harris, Richie Havens, Herbie Helbig, Denny Hinman, Al Hirt, The Hollyridge Strings, The Hollywood Strings, The Horsehairs, Craig Hundley Trio, Dick Hyman, Ides of March, Horst Jankowski, Jazz Crusaders, JP Stevens High School, Ken & Beverly, Anita Kerr Singers, Morgana King, Warren King, Gershon Kingsley, Chim Kothari, Cleo Laine & John William, James Last Band, Latin Dimension, Arnie Lawrence, Le Grand Orchestre Mauria, Les Strand, Liverpool 5, Living Jazz, Living Marimbas, London Pop Orchestra, Longines Symphonette, Lord Sitar, Rufus Lumley, Tony McCaulay, Magne-Tronics Combo, Marion McPartland, Mariachi Mexico, Jeffrey & Ron Marlowe, George Martin & His Orchestra, Johnny Mathis, Paul Mauriat, Mike Melvoin, Midwest Directors Orchestra, Jackie Mittoo, Wes Montgomery, Nana Mouskouri, Mark Murphy, Allis Murray, The Mystic Moods Orchestra, George Nardello, New Apocalypse, New World Electronic Ensemble, The Nite-Liters, 101 Strings, Trudy Pitts, Pure Food & Drug Act, Queen City Show Band, Frank Rand, Don Randi Trio, Rare Earth, Red, White, and Blue Grass Band, Diana Ross & The Supremes, Rostalt Schaefer, Chim Rothari, Erik Saint-Laurent, The Senate, Hal Serra, George Shearing, Side Effect, The Singers Unlimited, Lonnie Smith, The Standells, Bobby Taylor, Teegarden & Van Winkle, Temptations, Joe Torres, Unknown, Frankie Valli, Vanilla Fudge, The Ventures, Viv Tirado, Baron Von Ohlen Quartet, Waikikis, We Five, Doodles Weaver, Julius Wechter, Klauss Weiss Orchestra, Kim Weston, Pat Williams, Jackie Wilson, Kai Winding, Wing & A Prayer Fife & Drum Corp., Stan Worth, Felipe Yanez, Young Holt Unlimited

THE END

Written by:	Lennon/McCartney
Produced by:	George Martin
Album:	USA: Abbey Road
	Apple SO 383
	UK: Abbey Road
	Apple PCS 7088
Released:	USA: Oct 1969 UK: Sept 1969
Gold:	USA: October 27, 1969

Cover versions:
The Beatles, Belport Rock Jazz Ensemble, George Benson, Booker T & The M.G.'s, The Everly Brothers, Gap Mangione, London Symphony Orchestra, Doc Severinsen

EVERYBODY'S GOT SOMETHING TO HIDE EXCEPT ME AND MY MONKEY

Written by:	Lennon/McCartney
Produced by:	George Martin
Album:	USA: The Beatles
	Apple SWBO 101
	UK: The Beatles
	Apple PCS 7067/8
Released:	USA: Nov 1968 UK: Nov 1968
Gold:	USA: December 6, 1968

Cover versions:
The Beatles, Fats Domino, Ramsey Lewis, Orchestra Harlow

FIXING A HOLE

Written by:	Lennon/McCartney
Produced by:	George Martin
Album:	USA: Sergeant Pepper's Lonely Hearts Club Band, Capitol SMAS 2653
	UK: Sergeant Pepper's Lonely Hearts Club Band, Parlophone PCS 7027
Released:	USA: June 1967 UK: June 1967
Gold:	USA: June 15, 1967

Cover versions:
The Beatles, George Burns, Jackie Cain & Roy Kral, Sydney Fox, Johnson & Drake, Little Joe, The Odyssey Singers, Stan Ruffin

FLYING

Written by:	Lennon/McCartney/Harrison/Starkey
Produced by:	George Martin
EP:	UK: Magical Mystery Tour, Parlophone SMMT 1/2, December 1967
Album:	USA: Magical Mystery Tour Capitol SMAL 2835
	UK: Magical Mystery Tour Parlophone PCTC 255
Released:	USA: Nov 1967 UK: Dec 1976
Gold:	USA: December 15, 1967
Additional Musicians:	John, Mellotron; John, Paul, George & Ringo, Chanting

Cover versions:
The Beatles, Herbie Mann, Bud Shank, Sounds Nice

THE FOOL ON THE HILL

Written by:	Lennon/McCartney
Awards:	1968-9, Certificate of Honor, U.K. (Ivor Novello Awards)
Produced by:	George Martin
EP:	UK: Magical Mystery Tour, Parlophone SMMT 1/2, Dec 1967
Album:	USA: Magical Mystery Tour Capitol SMAL 2835
	UK: Magical Mystery Tour Parlophone PCTC 255
Released:	USA: Nov 1967 UK: Dec 1976
Gold:	USA: December 15, 1967
Additional Musicians:	Paul, Piano, Flute & Recorder; George & John, Harmonicas
Arrangements:	MB, JB, OR, CH

Cover versions:
Ampex International Pop Orchestra, Dorothy Ashby, Chucho Avellanet, Count Basie, Shirley Bassey, Terry Baxter Orchestra & Chorus, The Beatles, Beatlemania, Acker Bilk, Boston Pops Orchestra, The Brass Menagerie, Button Down Brass, Cafe Creme, Lana Cantrell, Lee Castle & Jimmy Dorsey, Frank Chucksfield, Joe Chapman & Orchestra, Petula Clark, Columbia Musical Treasury, J.L. Cook, Xavier Cugat, Ray Davies, John Duffy, Rick Ely, Enoch Light, Current Event, Fernando Escandon, Percy Faith Singers, Maynard Ferguson, Arthur Fiedler & Boston Pops Orchestra, Eddie Fisher, The Four Tops, Aretha Franklin, G Stellard, Bobby Gentry, Francois Glorieux, Marty Gold Orchestra, Barry Goldberg, Bette Graham & Ken Jeffers, Groovin' Strongs, Rune Gustafsson, The Hollyridge Strings, Lena Horne, Gabor Szabo, Impressions, Jankowski Singers, Pepe Jaramillo, Roslyn Kind, King's Road, King's Singers, Andre Kostelanetz & Orchestra, Mike Leander & His Orchestra, Les Miladys, Ramsey Lewis, Little Joe, Living Brass, Living Jazz, London Festival Orchestra, Longines Symphonette, Lynn Vera, Mario Said, Curtis Mayfield, Sergio Mendes & Brazil '66, MCR Studio Productions, Joe Morello, Orchestra of Aquarius, Anita Ortez, John Pike, Queen Anne's Lace, Helen Reddy, Joe Reisman & His Orchestra, Robertha, Dick Rosmini, Rostal and Schaefer, Jean Pierre Sabar, Santo & Johnny, Mario Said, Bud Shank, George Shearing, The Singers Unlimited, Sound Alike, Sounds of Our Times, Cyril Stapleton, G.

Stellard, Ray Stevens, Stone The Crows, The Sultan Street Nine, Alan Tew Orchestra, Keith Texter & Friends, Jackie Thompson, Libby Titus, Today's People, Jerry Toth Orchestra, Jackie Trent & Tony Hatch, Stanley Turrentine, Caterina Valente Edmundo, Louis Van Dyke, Billy Vaughn Singers, Versatile Impressions, Lovelace Watkins, Dick Watson, Joni Wild

FOR NO ONE

Written by:	Lennon/McCartney
Produced by:	George Martin
Album:	USA: Revolver
	Capitol ST 2576
	UK: Revolver
	Parlophone PCS 7009
Released:	USA: Aug 1966 UK: Aug 1966
Gold:	USA: August 22, 1966
Additional Musicians:	Paul, Piano; Alan Civil, Horn

Cover versions:
Chet Atkins, The Beatles, Theo Bikel, Cilla Black, Bottle Hill, Cafe Creme, Charles River Valley Boys, Floyd Cramer, Wayne Gibson, Emmylou Harris, Herbie Helbig, The Letterman, Maceo & All The Kings Men, Mike Melvoin, Dale Miller, Liza Minelli, Octopus 4, Don Randi Trio, Ron Reece, Tony & Terri & Pirates

FOR YOU BLUE

Written by:	George Harrison
Single #:	USA: Apple 2832
Released:	USA: May 1970
Weeks on chart:	USA: 4
Produced by:	Phil Spector
Album:	USA: Let It Be
	Red Apple 34001
	UK: Let It Be
	Apple PXS1/Apple PCS 7096
Released:	USA: May 1970
	UK: May 1970/Nov 1970
Gold:	USA: May 26, 1970
Additional Musicians:	George, Acoustic Guitar; John, Steel Guitar; Paul, Piano

GET BACK

Written by:	Lennon/McCartney
Single #:	USA: Apple 2490
	UK: Apple R5777
Released:	USA: May 1969 UK: April 1969
Gold:	USA: May 19, 1969
Awards:	Most performed pop song: 1969 Other: 1969, Highest Certified British Sales (Ivor Novello Awards)
Weeks on chart:	USA: 12 UK: 17
Produced by:	Phil Spector
Album:	USA: Let It Be
	Red Apple 34001
	UK: Let It Be
	Apple PXS1/Apple PCS 7096
Released:	USA: May 1970
	UK: May 1970/Nov 1970
Gold:	USA: May 26, 1970
Additional Musicians:	Billy Preston, Organ; John, Lead Guitar; George, Rhythm Guitar
Arrangements:	MB, JB,

Cover versions:
Beatlemania, The Beatles, Cafe Creme, Jessi Colter, Al Green, Jimmy McGriff, The Odyssey Singers, The Other Company, Elvis Presley, Billy Preston, Garry Ruffin, Stan Ruffin, Mongo Santamaria, The Sound Alikes, Rod Stewart, The Top Of The Poppers, Ike & Tina Turner

GETTING BETTER

Written by:	Lennon/McCartney
Produced by:	George Martin
Album:	USA: Sergeant Pepper's Lonely Hearts Club Band, Capitol SMAS 2653
	UK: Sergeant Pepper's Lonely Hearts Club Band, Parlophone PCS 7027
Released:	USA: June 1967 UK: June 1967
Gold:	USA: June 15, 1967

Cover versions:
The Beatles, The Five Stairsteps, Peter Frampton, Steve Hillage, Peter Knight, Music Machine, Odyssey, The Other Company, Rollers, Rubberband, Stan Ruffin, The Sound Alikes, Status Quo

GLASS ONION

Written by:	Lennon/McCartney
Produced by:	George Martin
Album:	USA: The Beatles Apple SWBO 101
	UK: The Beatles Apple PCS 7067/8
Released:	USA: Nov 1968 UK: Nov 1968
Gold:	USA: December 6, 1968

Cover versions:
The Beatles, Arif Mardin

GOLDEN SLUMBERS

Written by:	Lennon/McCartney
Produced by:	George Martin
Album:	USA: Abbey Road Apple SO 383
	UK: Abbey Road Apple PCS 7088
Released:	USA: Oct 1969 UK: Sept 1969
Gold:	USA: October 27, 1969

Cover versions:
The Bee Gees, George Benson, John Blair, Bola Sete, Booker T & The M.G.'s, Cafe Creme, Crusaders, John Denver, Peter Frampton, Imitations, Jazz Crusaders, Bonnie Koloc, Ramsey Lewis, Claudine Longet, Warren Marley, Mystic Moods Orchestra, The Odyssey Singers, Lou Rawls, Stan Ruffin, Sound Alikes, Trash

GOOD DAY SUNSHINE

Written by:	Lennon/McCartney
Produced by:	George Martin
Album:	USA: Revolver Capitol ST 2576
	UK: Revolver Parlophone PCS 7009
Released:	USA: Aug 1966 UK: Aug 1966
Gold:	USA: August 22, 1966
Additional Musicians:	George Martin, Piano
Arrangements:	CH,

Cover versions:
The Arbors, Astromusical House of Leo, Barooga Bandit, Terry Baxter Orchestra, David Budin, Cafe Creme, Charles River Valley Boys, Linda Divine, Don and the Goodtimes, Four King Cousins, The Hollyridge Strings, Jimmy James & The Vagabonds, Liberation Stage Band, Claudine Longet, Gloria Loring, Lulu, Magne Tronics Combo, Renee Martel, George Martin, P. Little & T. Overstreet, Don Randi Trio, Roy Redmond, Tremeloes, Lee Webber, The Zoo

GOOD MORNING GOOD MORNING

Written by:	Lennon/McCartney
Produced by:	George Martin
Album:	USA: Sergeant Pepper's Lonely Hearts Club Band, Capitol SMAS 2653
	UK: Sergeant Pepper's Lonely Hearts Club Band, Parlophone PCS 7027
Released:	USA: June 1967 UK: June 1967
Gold:	USA: June 15, 1967
Additional Musicians:	With Sounds Inc.

Cover versions:
The Beatles, Peter Frampton, Paul Micholas, Music Machine, The Odyssey Singers, Sound-A-Like

GOOD NIGHT

Written by:	Lennon/McCartney
Produced by:	George Martin
Album:	USA: The Beatles Apple SWBO 101
	UK: The Beatles Apple PCS 7067/8
Released:	USA: Nov 1968 UK: Nov 1968
Gold:	USA: December 6, 1968
Additional Musicians:	Thirty Piece Orchestra

Cover versions:
The Beatles, Marty Gold Orchestra, Ramsey Lewis, Vera Lynn, Betty Madigan, Mabel Mercer & Bobby Short, John Pike, Robin Sanderson, Cyril Stapleton Orchestra, Barbara Streisand, John Andrews Tartaglia, Sydney Thompson & His Orchestra

GOT TO GET YOU INTO MY LIFE

Written by:	Lennon/McCartney
Single #:	USA: Capitol 4274
Released:	USA: May 1976
Awards:	Million performance song: June 1978
	Most performed pop song: 1970, 1978
Weeks on chart:	USA: 16
Produced by:	George Martin
Album:	USA: Revolver Capitol ST 2576
	UK: Revolver Parlophone PCS 7009
Released:	USA: Aug 1966 UK: Aug 1966
Gold:	USA: August 22, 1966
Additional Musicians:	Ian Hammer, Les Condon & Eddie Thornton, Trumpets; Alan Branscombe & Peter Coe, Tenor
Arrangements:	MB, JB, CH

Cover versions:
Arbors, Baby Dolls, Bagatelle, Chet Baker & Strings, Banda Macho, Beatlemania, The Beatles, Cliff Bennett, Blood, Sweat & Tears, Ambrose Brazelton, Cafe Creme, Frank Chacksfield, Chris Clark, Stuart Crosby, Steve Davies, Dino, Desi & Billy, Disciple, Earth, Wind & Fire, Elk Grove H.S. Jazz Band, John Fred & Playboys, Ella Fitzgerald, Four Tops, The Gophers, Johnny Hallyday, Hands of Time, Jimmy Helms, Thelma Houston, Morgana King, Little Joe, Carmen McRae, George Martin, Marilyn Michaels, New World Electronic Ensemble, Odyssey, The Other Company, Power Pack, Don Randi Trio, Lou Rawls, The Rollers, Rubberband, Stan Ruffin, Sonny & Cher, Soul Cure, Sound Alikes, The Sound Effects, Stitch In Tyme, Jackie Trent, Bobbi Wilsyn

HAPPINESS IS A WARM GUN

Written by:	Lennon/McCartney
Produced by:	George Martin
Album:	USA: The Beatles Apple SWBO 101
	UK: The Beatles Apple PCS 7067/8
Released:	USA: Nov 1968 UK: Nov 1968
Gold:	USA: December 6, 1968

Cover versions:
The Beatles, Bobby Bryant

HELLO GOODBYE

Written by:	Lennon/McCartney
Single #:	USA: Capitol 2056
	UK: Parlophone R5655
Released:	USA: Nov 1967 UK: Nov 1967
Awards:	Most performed pop song: 1968
Weeks on chart:	USA: 11 UK: 12
Produced by:	George Martin
Album:	USA: Magical Mystery Tour Capitol SMAL 2835
	UK: Magical Mystery Tour Parlophone PCTC 255
Released:	USA: Nov 1967 UK: Dec 1976
Gold:	USA: December 15, 1967
Additional Musicians:	Paul, Piano; Ringo, Maracas
Arrangements:	OR

Cover versions:
Baroque Brass, Terry Baxter Orchestra & Chorus, The Beatles, Cafe Creme, Peter Covent, James Darren, Enoch Light, Frank Ferrer, Francois Glorieux, The Hollyridge Strings, Ted Hunter, Intrigantes, Kings Road, Les 409, Liverpool Five, Longines Symphonette, Marble Arch Music Association, Mariano Moreno, James Moody, Santo & Johnny, Bud Shank, Soulful Strings, Sound Alikes, Super Rock, Anthony Swete, Vanilla Fudge

HELTER SKELTER

Written by:	Lennon/McCartney
Single #:	USA: Capitol 4274
Released:	USA: May 1976
Produced by:	George Martin
Album:	USA: The Beatles Apple SWBO 101
	UK: The Beatles Apple PCS 7067/8
Released:	USA: Nov 1968 UK: Nov 1968
Gold:	USA: December 6, 1968
Additional Musicians:	Mal Evans, Trumpet; John, Sax

Cover versions:
The Beatles, Diamond Reo, Don Harrison, Siouxsie And The Banshees

HER MAJESTY

Written by:	Lennon/McCartney
Produced by:	George Martin
Album:	USA: Abbey Road Apple SO 383
	UK: Abbey Road Apple PCS 7088
Released:	USA: Oct 1969 UK: Sept 1969
Gold:	USA: October 27, 1969

Cover versions:
The Beatles, Charlie Byrd

HERE COMES THE SUN

Written by:	George Harrison
Produced by:	George Martin
Album:	USA: Abbey Road Apple SO 383
	UK: Abbey Road Apple PCS 7088
Released:	USA: Oct 1969 UK: Sept 1969
Gold:	USA: October 27, 1969
Additional Musicians:	George, Synthesizer

HERE THERE AND EVERYWHERE

Written by:	Lennon/McCartney
Awards:	Million performance song: June 1976
Produced by:	George Martin
Album:	USA: Revolver Capitol ST 2576
	UK: Revolver Parlophone PCS 7009
Released:	USA: Aug 1966 UK: Aug 1966
Gold:	USA: August 22, 1966
Arrangements:	MB, JB, CB, CH

Cover versions:
Chet Atkins Guitar, Ena Baga, Baja Marimba Band, Chet Baker & Strings, Baker Street Philharmonic, Count Basie, Terry Baxter & Orchestra, The Beatles, Tony Bennett, Catherine Berberian, Gene Bertoncini, Leon Bibb, Ruby Braff-George Barnes, Caleb Brooks, Carmen Cavallaro, Charles River Valley Boys, Dean Christopher & Orchestra, Petula Clark, Perry Como, Alan Copeland, Jim Crowley, Bill Deal & The Rhondels, Episode Six, Percy Faith Strings, Jose Feliciano, Pete Fountain, Four King Counsin The Fourmost, Bobby Gentry, Astrud Gilberto, Jackie Gleason, Francois Glorieux, Golden Guitar Magic, Greg Hamon, The Hard Times, Joe Harnel Emmylou Harris, Herbie Helbig, Bonnie Herman, Jerry Inman, Jay & The Americans, Jennifer,

Manny Kellem and Orchestra, Pete King & Orchestra, Kole & Param, Mike Leander & Orchestra, The Lettermen, Liberace, Charles Lloyd Quartet, Kenny Loggins, London Festival Orchestra, Claudine Longet, Gloria Lynn, Gary McFarland, Rod McKuen, Carmen McRae, Magne Tronics Combo, Jeffrey and Ronald Marlowe, Hugh Masekela, Johnny Mathis, Peter Matz, Mike Melvoin, Lindy Michaels, Marilyn Michaels, Matt Monro, Mystic Moods Orchestra, The Mustang, New World Electronic, Orchestra of Gemini, Overton Berry Trio, Bobby Pierce, John Pike, Bucky Pizzarelli, Don Randi Trio, Christopher Robbins, Richard Ruskin, Bobby Scott, Doc Severinsen, George Shearing, The Singers Unlimited, Kate Smith, Dick Smothers, Sounds Orchestra, Tommy Stark, Enzo Stuarti, Sydney Thompson, Rose Mary Tierney, Libby Titus, Stanley Turrentine, Waikikis, Billy Edd Wheeler, Andy Williams, Kai Winding, Stan Worth, Young American

HEY BULLDOG

Written by:	Lennon/McCartney
Produced by:	George Martin
Album:	USA: Yellow Submarine
	Apple SW 153
	UK: Yellow Submarine
	Apple PCS 7070
Released:	USA: Jan 1969 UK: Jan 1969
Gold:	USA: February 5, 1969

Cover versions:
Jay Barry, The Beatles, Boxer, Coachmen, Bill Deal & The Rhondels, Fanny, The Gods, Jim Schoenfeld

HEY JUDE

Written by:	Lennon/McCartney
Single #:	USA: Apple 2276
	UK: Apple R5722
Released:	USA: Aug 1968 UK: Aug 1968
Gold:	USA: September 13, 1968
Awards:	Million performance song: September 1970
	Most performed pop song: 1968, 1969, 1970
	Other: 1968, Highest Certified British Sales (Ivor Novello Awards)
Weeks on chart:	USA: 19 UK: 16
Produced by:	George Martin
Album:	USA: Hey Jude
	Apple SW 385/SO 385
Released:	USA: February 1970
Gold:	USA: March 6, 1970
Additional Musicians:	40 Piece Orchestra; John & George, Back-up vocals
Arrangements:	MB, JB, OR, CH

Cover versions:
Jeff Afdem, Ronnie Aldrich, Lorez Alexandria, Duane Allman, Claudius Alzner, Ampex International Pops Orchestra, Area Code 615, Artistry in Sound, Assagai, Chet Atkins, Sil Austin, Ena Baga, Bar-Kays, Mariachi Barroco, Count Basie, Phil Baugh, Terry Baxter & Orchestra, The Beatles, Vincent Bell, Beatlemania, Belport Rock Jazz Ensemble, Bill & His Pop Guitar, Bill Black's Combo, Ray Bloch Singers & Orchestra, Mike Bloomfield & Al Kooper, Bugs Bower Chorus & Orchestra, The Brothers Johnson, Chris Bruhn & Orchestra, Ray Bryant, The Burbank Philharmonic, Charlie Byrd, Cafe Creme, Ace Cannon, Captain Milk, Jimmy Caravan, Caravelli, Vangie Carmichael, Lee Castle & J. Dorsey Orchestra, Frank Chacksfield, Ray Charles Singers, The Chords, Petula Clark, Wayne Cochran & The CC Riders, Dennis Coffey Trio, Jesse Colter, Ray Conniff Singers, J.L. Cook, Pete Cooley, Copper Plated Integrated, Cesar Costa, Don Costa, Danny Cox, Bing Crosby, Mike Curb Congregation, Godfrey Daniel, Francois Dassise & M. Pagl, David, Rusty Dean, Mick Decaro, Nick Decaro & Orchestra, Little Jimmy Dempsey, Lee Dresser, John Duffy, Dukes of Dixieland, Electric Concept Orchestra, Enoch Light, Esperanza Encantada, The Everly Brothers, The Fabulous Counts, Tanya Falan, Jose Feliciano, Maynard Ferguson, Arthur Fiedler & Boston Pops Orch., Ella Fitzgerald, Floating Bridge, Four Freshman, Paul Frees & Poster People, Gene Gertoncini, Dick

Glasser, Francois Glorieux, Marty Gold Orchestra, Barry Goldberg, The Gophers, Teresa Graves, The Group, The Happy Day Youth Choir, Hara S Big Band, John Hartford, Tony Hatch & Satin Brass, Richard Hayman Walter Sea, Hear & Now, Ted Heath, Jimmy Helms, Hollyridge Strings, Hypnotic Harps, Il Milionari, Imitations, Willis Jackson, Jalopy Five, The Jazz Crusaders, Tom Jones, Remy Jouvence, Emmett Kelly Jr. Singers, Stan Kenton, King Curtis, Kings Road, John Klemmer, Terry Knight, James Last, Yusef Lateef, Le 25eme Regiment, The Lettermen, Liberation Street Band, The Little Big Horns, Liverpool 5, Living Strings, Living Voices, Edu Lobo, The Lollipop Tree, London Festival Orchestra, Longines Symphonette, Al Lopaka, Los Mustang, Los Norte Americanos, Los Vaqueros Del Rastro, Jon Loss & Orchestra, Arthur Lynn, Julie Lynn, Freddie McCoy, Magne Tronics Combo, Steve Marcus, Jeffrey & Ronald Marlowe, Massachusetts Delegation, Paul Mauriat, Bill Medley, Jo Ment, The Mercy, Ron Mesing, Dale Miller, Glenn Miller Orchestra, The Moog Machine, Jane Morgan, Tony Mottola, Peter Nero, The New Christy Minstrels, The New Hope, The Now Generation, 101 Strings, Orchestra 70, The Orchestra of Virgo, The Berry Overton Trio, Larry Page Orchestra, Parade of Hits Album, Stu Phillips, Wilson Pickett, Frank Pourcel, G.H. Prentiss, Elvis Presley, Lloyd Price, Boots Randolph, Raw Spitt, Regimental Band & Pipes, Joe Reisman & Orchestra, Nydia Card Ricardo Roy, Rolfo Richardson, Ripple Blast Singers, Roadshow Entertainers, Smokey Robinson & The Miracles, The Rollers, Edmundo Ros & Orchestra, David Rose, Diana Ross & The Supremes, Royal Regiment, The Royal Teens Rubberband, The Saxaphone Circus, Earl Scruggs, The Senate, Sequoia Jr. High School, Donald Seward, Shango, Mike Sharpe, George Shearing, Silk, Sing in Boulder, Hal Singer, O.C. Smith, Society of Seven, Sonny & Cher, Sound Alikes, The Sound Symposium, Sounds of Our Times, Cyril Stapleton, Steel Images, Ron Steele, Ray Stevens, The Ed Sullivan Singers, The Tams, The Templeton Twins, The Temptations, Tuesday's Children, Stanley Turrentine, The Underground Electronics, The Underground Guitar, Frank Valdor, Nate Vecchio, The Ventures, Fernand Verstraete, Vikings VI, Waldo De Los Rios & Orchestra, Jr. Walker & The All Stars, Mister Bill Wallys, Dionne Warwick, Lawrence Welk, Ricky West, Clerence Wheeler & The Enforcers, Brian Williams, Pat Williams, Roger Williams, Stan Worth, Klaus Wunderlich, Hozan Yamamoto Nobuo Hara, Lonnie Youngblood, The Young Lovers, Florian Zaback, Harry Zonk

HONEY PIE

Written by:	Lennon/McCartney
Produced by:	George Martin
Album:	UK: The Beatles
	Apple PCS 7067/8
Released:	UK: Nov 1968
Additional Musicians:	Paul, Piano; John, Lead Guitar; George, Bass
Arrangements:	OR

Cover versions:
Richard Alden & Orchestra, The Beatles, Cafe Creme, Earl of Cricklewood, Skitch Henderson, Cliff Jones, Gary Lawrence, Jack Sheldon, Barbara Streisand, Brian Williams

I AM THE WALRUS

Written by:	Lennon/McCartney
Single #:	USA: Capitol 2056
	UK: Parlophone R5655
Released:	USA: Nov 1967 UK: Nov 1967
Weeks on chart:	USA: 4
Produced by:	George Martin
EP:	UK: Magical Mystery Tour, Parlophone SMMT 1/2, December 1967
Album:	USA: Magical Mystery Tour Capitol SMAL 2835
	UK: Magical Mystery Tour Parlophone PCTC 255
Released:	USA: Nov 1967 UK: Dec 1976
Gold:	USA: December 15, 1967
Arrangements:	OR

Cover versions:
Beatlemania, The Beatles, Cafe Creme, Crack the Sky, Hollyridge Strings, Les Demerle, Lord Sitar, Freddie McCoy, George Martin, Leo Sayer, Bud Shank, John Andrews, Tartaglia, Spooky Tooth

I ME MINE

Written by:	George Harrison
Produced by:	Phil Spector
Album:	USA: Let It Be
	Red Apple 34001
	UK: Let It Be
	Apple PXS1/Apple PCS 7096
Released:	USA: May 1970
	UK: May 1970/Nov 1970
Gold:	USA: May 26, 1970

I WANT TO TELL YOU

Written by:	George Harrison
Produced by:	George Martin
Album:	USA: Revolver
	Capitol ST 2576
	UK: Revolver
	Parlophone PCS 7009
Released:	USA: Aug 1966 UK: Aug 1966
Gold:	USA: August 22, 1966
Additional Musicians:	Paul, Piano

Cover versions:
The Beatles, Mike Melvoin, Ted Nugent, Don Randi Trio

I WANT YOU (SHE'S SO HEAVY)

Written by:	Lennon/McCartney
Produced by:	George Martin
Album:	USA: Abbey Road
	Apple SO 383
	UK: Abbey Road
	Apple PCS 7088
Released:	USA: Oct 1969 UK: Sept 1969
Gold:	USA: October 27, 1969
Additional Musicians:	John, Lead Guitar

Cover versions:
The Assembled Multitude, Average Disco Band, The Beatles, The Bee Gees, George Benson, Booker T & The M.G.'s, Cafe Creme, Catfish Hodge, Eddie Hazel, Sammy Kaye & His Orchestra, Music Machine, The Odyssey Singers, Dianne Steinberg

I WILL

Written by:	Lennon/McCartney
Produced by:	George Martin
Album:	USA: The Beatles
	Apple SWBO 101
	UK: The Beatles
	Apple PCS 7067/8
Released:	USA: Nov 1968 UK: Nov 1968
Gold:	USA: December 6, 1968

Cover versions:
Terry Baxter Orchestra & Chorus, The Beatles, Tim Curry, Hal Frazier, Francois Glorieux, Heaven Bound & T Scotti, La Tropa Loca, Hugh Masekela, Melissa, Robin Sanderson, Tom Scott, Tony Scott, Bob Thiele Emergency

I'M SO TIRED

Written by:	Lennon/McCartney
Produced by:	George Martin
Album:	USA: The Beatles
	Apple SWBO 101
	UK: The Beatles
	Apple PCS 7067/8
Released:	USA: Nov 1968 UK: Nov 1968
Gold:	USA: December 6, 1968

Cover versions:
The Beatles, Susan Carter

THE INNER LIGHT

Written by:	George Harrison
Single #:	USA: Capitol 2138
	UK: Parlophone R5675
Released:	USA: March 1968 UK: March 1968
Weeks on chart:	USA: 1
Produced by:	George Martin
Additional Musicians:	Indian Musicians on all instruments; John & Paul, Back-up vocals

Cover versions:
The Beatles, Jimmy McGriff & Jr. Parker, The Soulful Strings

IT'S ALL TOO MUCH

Written by:	George Harrison
Produced by:	George Martin
Album:	USA: Yellow Submarine Apple SW 153
	UK: Yellow Submarine Apple PCS 7070
Released:	USA: Jan 1969 UK: Jan 1969
Gold:	USA: February 5, 1969

Cover versions:
The Beatles, Steve Hillage, Journey, Monday Rain

I'VE GOT A FEELING

Written by:	Lennon/McCartney
Produced by:	Phil Spector
Album:	USA: Let It Be Red Apple 34001
	UK: Let It Be Apple PXS1/Apple PCS 7096
Released:	USA: May 1970 UK: May 1970/Nov 1970
Gold:	USA: May 26, 1970

Cover versions:
The Beatles, Fifth Dimension, KGB

JULIA

Written by:	Lennon/McCartney
Single #:	USA: Capitol 4347
Released:	USA: Nov 1976
Produced by:	George Martin
Album:	USA: The Beatles Apple SWBO 101
	UK: The Beatles Apple PCS 7067/8
Released:	USA: Nov 1968 UK: Nov 1968
Gold:	USA: December 6, 1968
Additional Musicians:	John, Lead Acoustic Guitar

Cover versions:
The Beatles, Charlie Byrd, Cafe Creme, Christian-Getro, Ramsey Lewis, The New Hope, Tom Scott, Bob Thiele Emergency

LADY MADONNA

Written by:	Lennon/McCartney
Single #:	USA: Capitol 2138
	UK: Parlophone R5675
Released:	USA: March 1968 UK: March 1968
Gold:	USA: April 8, 1968
Weeks on chart:	USA: 11 UK: 8
Produced by:	George Martin
Album:	USA: Hey Jude Apple SW 385/SO 385
Released:	USA: Feb 1970
Gold:	USA: March 6, 1970
Additional Musicians:	Paul, Piano; Ronnie Scott, Harry Klein, Bill Porey & Bill Jackman, Sax; John & George, Back-up vocals
Arrangements:	MB, JB, OR

Cover versions:
Chet Atkins, Area Code 615, Tomey Banks & Judy Singh, Terry Baxter Orchestra & Chorus, Beatlemania, The Beatles, Big Frog, Andre Blot, Booker T & The M.G.'s, David Briggs, Bruce, Larry Butler, Cafe Creme, Jackie Cain & Roy Kral, Terry Canady & Rudy Perez, Charlie's Children, The Chords, Dean Christopher & Orchestra, Columbia Musical Treasury, The Distant Galaxy, Fats Domino, John Duffy, Family Guitar, Jose Feliciano, The Four Freshmen, Francois Glorieux, The Gophers, Richie Havens, The Hesitations, Mieko Hirota, Imitations, Integrity Orchestra, Andre Kostelantz, James Last Orchestra, Ramsey Lewis, Liverpool 5, London Festival Orchestra, Longines Symphonette, Los Johnny Jets, Los Mustang, Mariachi Mexico '70, Paul Mauriat Orchestra, Harry Middlebrooks Musical Ensemble, Melba Moore, Cam Mullins, Natural Gass, Orchestra of Capricorn, The Other Company, Buck Owens, Junior Parker, Potliquor, Gary Puckett & The Union Gap, The Rollers, Richard Ruskin, Will Schaefer Band, The Soulful Strings, Sound Alikes, Swamp Dogg, Peter Thomas & Orchestra, Cal Tjader, The Top Notchers, Trombones Unlimited, Kenny White, Lenny White, Wings, Klaus Wunderlich, Young-Holt Unlimited

LET IT BE

Written by:	Lennon/McCartney
Single #:	USA: Apple 2764
	UK: Apple R5833
Released:	USA: March 1970 UK: March 1970
Gold:	USA: March 17, 1970
Awards:	Million performance song: December 1972
	Most performed pop song: 1970, 1971
Weeks on chart:	USA: 14 UK: 10
Produced by:	Phil Spector
Album:	USA: Let It Be Red Apple 34001
	UK: Let It Be Apple PXS1/Apple PCS 7096
Released:	USA: May 1970 UK: May 1970/Nov 1970
Gold:	USA: May 26, 1970
Additional Musicians:	Billy Preston, Organ; John, Bass; Paul, Piano
Arrangements:	MB, JB, CH

Cover versions:
Ronnie Aldrich, Monty Alexander, Graeme Allwright, Joan Baez, Terry Baxter Orchestra & Chorus, Beatlemania, The Beatles, Belport Rock Jazz Ensemble, Bill Black's Combo, Ray Bryant, Bugs Bower Chorus & Orchestra, The Bully Boys Band, Cafe Creme, Ace Cannon, Clarence Carter, Leonard Caston, Carmen Cavallaro, Ray Charles, Chartbusters, Chevy Chase, Coldwater Folk, William Collins Jr., Ray Conniff Singers, Floyd Cramer, Stuart Crosby, Mike Curb Congregation, Current Event, King Curtis, Liz Damon's Orient Express, Godfrey Daniel, John Davidson, Chris De Burgh, The Decibels, John Denver, Little Jimmy Dorsey, Dion, Enoch Light & The Light Brigade, Esperanza Encantada, Percy Faith, Jose Feliciano, Ferrante & Teicher, Arthur Fiedler & The Boston Pops, Tennessee Ernie Ford, The Four Score Pianos, Aretha Franklin, Don Fraser Orchestra, Paul Frees & Poster People, Francois Glorieux, The God Squad, Bonnie Guitar, Guitars Unlimited, Bobby Hatfield, Ted Heath, Jane & Bob Henley, Tessie Hill, Hollyridge Strings, Jan Howard, Imperials, Jalopy Five, Jimmy Joyce Family, The Kimberlys, King James Version, Kings Road, Danny Kirwan, Gladys Knight & The Pips, Andre Kostelanetz, James Last, Hubert Laws, Ken Lazarus, Claudia Lennear, Liverpool 5, Living Guitars, Living Voices, London Philharmonic Orchestra, Longines Symphonette, Los 3 Diamontes, Julie Lynn, Magne Tronics Combo, Mar Keys, Rudy Martin, Nana Moskouri, Barbara Mason, Peter Matz Quadrophonic, Paul Mauriat, Bill Medley, Mike Melvoin, Michael 7, Nashville Guitars, Larry Norman, The Now Generation, Orchestra & Chorus Les Humphri, The Originals, The Other Company, Paris Opera Orchestra, Peacemakers, Persuasions, Harland Powell, Billy Preston, Earl Robinson, Nicole Rieu, Rev. Cleophus Robinson, The Rollers, Rouvaun, Sandler & Young, Oscar Santana, Leo Sayer, Shirley Scott, Earl & Randy Scruggs, Gary & Randy Scruggs, Bud Shank, Henry Shed, Rhonda Silver, The Singalong Genises, The Sisters & Brothers, Harold Smith Magestic Singers, Soul Stirrers, Sound Alikes, The Tennessee Guitars, The Top of the Poppers, Tribe, Ike & Tina Turner, Union Station Singers, Univ. of Bridgeport Jazz, Jerry Vale, Billy Vaughn, The Venture, Victory Chorale Ensemble, Jerry Walsh, Spanky Wilson, Bill Withers, Stan Worth, George Wright, Klaus Wunderlich, The Young Lovers

LONG LONG LONG

Written by:	George Harrison
Produced by:	George Martin
Album:	USA: The Beatles Apple SWBO 101
	UK: The Beatles Apple PCS 7067/8
Released:	USA: Nov 1968 UK: Nov 1968
Gold:	USA: December 6, 1968
Additional Musicians:	Paul, Hammond Organ; George Acoustic Guitar

THE LONG AND WINDING ROAD

Written by:	Lennon/McCartney
Single #:	USA: Apple 2832
Released:	USA: May 1970
Awards:	Million performance song: December 1975
	Most performed pop song: 1970
Weeks on chart:	USA: 10
Produced by:	Phil Spector
Album:	USA: Let It Be Red Apple 34001
	UK: Let It Be Apple PXS1/Apple PCS 7096
Released:	USA: May 1970 UK: May 1970/Nov 1970
Gold:	USA: May 26, 1970
Additional Musicians:	Strings, Voices, Harp & Drums, overdubbed; John, Bass; Paul, Piano
Arrangements:	MB, CB, SOR, CH

Cover versions:
Ronnie Aldrich, Terry Baxter Orchestra & Chorus, Beatlemania, The Beatles, Leon Bibb, Charlie Brown, Julie Budd, Cafe Creme, Ray Charles, Cher, Chris Connor, Mike Curb Congregation, Frank Fanelli, The Four Score Pianos, The Four Tops, Peter Frampton, Aretha Franklin, Donny Gerrard, Francois Glorieux, Hollyridge Strings, Leroy Holmes Orchestra & Chorus, Cissy Houston, Willis Jackson, Clyde King, Kings Road, Gladys Knight & The Pips, Andre Kostelanetz, Julius LaRosa, Peggy Lee, Liberace, Mark Lindsay, Living Strings, Living Trio, Living Voices, Magne Tronics Combo, Mantovani & Orchestra, Mariachi Mexico '70, Johnny Mathis, Bill Medley, Midnight String Quartet, Melba Moore, New Birth, Wayne Newton, Olivia Newton-John, Odyssey, The Odyssey Singers, Stu Phillips, The Pop Machine, Frank Pourcel, Kenny Rogers & The First Edition, Diana Ross, Stan Ruffin, Sal Salvador, The Sandpipers, Leo Sayer, Bob Shank & Alivar Singer, Rhonda Silver, Jerry Smith, Sonny & Cher Sound Alikes, The Top of the Poppers, Andy Williams, Nancy Wilson, Wings, Hugo Winterhalter, Karen Wyman, The Young World

LOVE YOU TO

Written by:	George Harrison
Produced by:	George Martin
Album:	USA: Revolver Capitol ST 2576
	UK: Revolver Parlophone PCS 7009
Released:	USA: Aug 1966 UK: Aug 1966
Gold:	USA: August 22, 1966
Additional Musicians:	Anil Bagwat, Tabla

Cover versions:
The Beatles, Don Randi Trio

LOVELY RITA

Written by:	Lennon/McCartney
Produced by:	George Martin
Album:	USA: Sergeant Pepper's Lonely Hearts Club Band, Capitol SMAS 2653
	UK: Sergeant Pepper's Lonely Hearts Club Band, Parlophone PCS 7027
Released:	USA: June 1967 UK: June 1967
Gold:	USA: June 15, 1967

Cover versions:
The Beatles, Fats Domino, Peter Knight, Les Merseys, Roy Wood

LUCY IN THE SKY WITH DIAMONDS

Written by:	Lennon/McCartney
Produced by:	George Martin
Album:	USA: Sergeant Pepper's Lonely Hearts Club Band, Capitol SMAS 2653
	UK: Sergeant Pepper's Lonely Hearts Club Band, Parlophone PCS 7027
Released:	USA: June 1967 UK: June 1967
Gold:	USA: June 15, 1967
Arrangements:	MB, CH

Cover versions:
American Pick Hits Artists, Atlanta Connection, Terry Baxter Orchestra & Chorus, Beatles, John Blair, Cafe Creme, Natalie Cole, Enoch Light, Percy Faith Strings, The Free Spirits, Francois Glorieux, Marty Gold Orchestra, Pancho Gonzalez, Noel Harrison, Richard Hayman & Orchestra, Elton John, John Keating, Alan Keaton, Kings Road, Peter Knight, Le 25eme Regiment, London Symphony Orchestra, Alan Lorber Orchestra, Hugo Montenegro, Music Machine, Odyssey, The Odyssey Singers, Arthur Offen, 101 Strings, The Other Company, The Realistics, Stan Ruffin, The John Schroeder Orchestra, William Shatner, Sound Alikes, Dianne Steinberg, Al Stewart's Brass, Gabor Szabo & California Cream

MAGGIE MAE

Written by:	Lennon/McCartney/Harrison/Starkey
Produced by:	Phil Spector
Album:	USA: Let It Be Red Apple 34001
	UK: Let It Be Apple PXS1/Apple PCS 7096
Released:	USA: May 1970
	UK: May 1970/Nov 1970
Gold:	USA: May 26, 1970

MAGICAL MYSTERY TOUR

Written by:	Lennon/McCartney
Weeks on chart:	UK: 12
Produced by:	George Martin
EP:	UK: Magical Mystery Tour, Parlophone SMMT 1/2, December 1967
Album:	USA: Magical Mystery Tour Capitol SMAL 2835
	UK: Magical Mystery Tour Parlophone PCTC 255
Released:	USA: Nov 1967 UK: Dec 1967
Gold:	USA: December 15, 1967

Cover versions:
Ambrosia, Terry Baxter, Beatlemania, The Beatles, The Hollyridge Strings

MARTHA MY DEAR

Written by:	Lennon/McCartney
Produced by:	George Martin
Album:	USA: The Beatles Apple SWBO 101
	UK: The Beatles Apple PCS 7067/8
Released:	USA: Nov 1968 UK: Nov 1968
Gold:	USA: December 6, 1968
Additional Musicians:	Paul, Piano

Cover versions:
Herb Alpert & The Tijuana Brass, The Beatles, Crystal Ball, Wendel Horne, Craig Hundley Trio, Ambrose Slade

MAXWELL'S SILVER HAMMER

Written by:	Lennon/McCartney
Produced by:	George Martin
Album:	USA: Abbey Road Apple SO 383
	UK: Abbey Road Apple PCS 7088
Released:	USA: Oct 1969 UK: Sept 1969
Gold:	USA: October 27, 1969
Additional Musicians:	George, Synthesizer & Acoustic Guitar; Ringo, Anvil
Arrangements:	MB, JB, OR, CH

Cover versions:
The Beatles, The Bells, Current Event, Format, GH Presents, Good Ship Lollipop, George Howe & Carl Davis, Sammy Kaye & His Orchestra, Frankie Laine, Les S T P, The London Pops Orchestra, Steve Martin & Chorus, Music Machine, The Odyssey Singers, Rostal and Schaefer, Rubber Band, Stan Ruffin, Dick Schory, Jack Wild

MOTHER NATURE'S SON

Written by:	Lennon/McCartney
Produced by:	George Martin
Album:	USA: The Beatles Apple SWBO 101
	UK: The Beatles Apple PCS 7067/8
Released:	USA: Nov 1968 UK: Nov 1968
Gold:	USA: December 6, 1968
Additional Musicians:	Paul, Acoustic Guitar; Horns; John, George & Ringo not present

Cover versions:
Terry Baxter Orchestra & Chorus, The Beatles, Theo Bikel, Lynn Blessing, John Denver, Ramsey Lewis, Nilsson, Staten Brothers Band

MEAN MR. MUSTARD

Written by:	Lennon/McCartney
Produced by:	George Martin
Album:	UK: Abbey Road Apple PCS 7088
Released:	UK: Sept 1969

Cover versions:
The Beatles, Booker T & The M.G.'s, Frankie Howerd, Terry Knight, The Odyssey Singers, Stan Ruffin, The Third Tree

OB-LA-DI-OB-LA-DA

Written by:	Lennon/McCartney
Single #:	USA: Capitol 4347
Released:	USA: Nov 1976
Awards:	Million performance song: September 1974
	Most performed pop song: 1969, U.S. and U.K.
Weeks on chart:	USA: 6
Album:	USA: The Beatles Apple SWBO 101
	UK: The Beatles Apple PCS 7067/8
Released:	USA: Nov 1968 UK: Nov 1968
Gold:	USA: December 6, 1968
Arrangements:	MB, JB, OR, CH

Cover versions:
Herb Alpert & Tijuana Brass, Average Disco Band, Ena Baga, Joss Baselli, Terry Baxter Orchestra & Chorus, The Beatles, Bill & His Pop Guitar, Bill Black's Combo, Joyce Bond, Boston Pops Orchestra, Ambrose Brazelton, Otto Bredl & Jiggs Whigha, Mel Brown, Cafe Creme, Lee Castle & Jimmy Dorsey, Frank Chacksfield, The Collingwood Trio, Arthur Conley, Ray Conniff, Don Costa, Xavier Cugat, Floyd Cramer, Jack Crossan, Current Event, Dallas, John Davidson, Nick De Caro & Orchestra, Luis Alberto Del Parana, Roberto Delgado & Orchestra, Paul Desmond, The Dirty Old Men, Bob Dorough,

Enoch Light & The Light Brigade, Farmer Fritz, Danny Fisher, Four Freshmen, The Globe Show, Francois Glorieux, Joel Grey, Guitars Unlimited, Jack Hennig, Dick Hyman, I Dik Dik, I Ribelli, Georges Jouvin, Anita Kerr Singers, Lester Lanin & Orchestra, James Last Orchestra, Ken Lazarus, Living Strings, Los Junior Squad, Los Moonlights, Los Mustang, Los Norte Americanos, Waldo de Los Rios & Orchestra, Los Yacomas, Rob McConnell, Herbie Mann, Manuel, Mariachi Mexico '70, The Marmalade, Jeffrey & Ronald Marlowe, Multi-Sound Orchestra, Alica Mazur, Mercy, Paul Nero, Peter Nero, Orchestra Di Franco Cassano, Louis Prima & Sam Butera, Jean Pierre Sabar, Alan Black Schackner, Hal Serra, Chris Shakespeare Globe 5, Shango, Victor Silvester & Orchestra, Sound Alikes, Arthur Spin, Cyril Stapleton & Orchestra, Alan Thicke, Sydney Thompson & Orchestra, The Today People, TWA Braw Lads, Dana Valery, Fernand Verstraete, Bobby Vinton, Washington Jr. High School Band, Henry Watterson Expressway, Horst Wende & Accordion Band, Jack Wild, Klaus Wunderlich, Patrick Zabe,

OCTOPUS'S GARDEN

Written by:	Richard Starkey
Produced by:	George Martin
Album:	USA: Abbey Road Apple SO 383
	UK: Abbey Road Apple PCS 7088
Released:	USA: Oct 1969 UK: Sept 1969
Gold:	USA: October 27, 1969

OH! DARLING

Written by:	Lennon/McCartney
Produced by:	George Martin
Album:	USA: Abbey Road Apple SO 383
	UK: Abbey Road Apple PCS 7088
Released:	USA: Oct 1969 UK: Sept 1969
Gold:	USA: October 27, 1969
Arrangements:	CH

OLD BROWN SHOE

Written by:	George Harrison
Single #:	USA: Apple 2531
	UK: Apple R5786
Released:	USA: June 1969 UK: May 1969
Produced by:	George Martin
Album:	USA: Hey Jude Apple SW 385/SO 385
Released:	USA: Feb 1970
Gold:	USA: March 6, 1970
Additional Musicians:	Paul & John, Back-up vocals

ONE AFTER 909

Written by:	Lennon/McCartney
Produced by:	Phil Spector
Album:	USA: Let It Be Red Apple 34001
	UK: Let It Be Apple PXS1/Apple PCS 7096
Released:	USA: May 1970
	UK: May 1970/Nov 1970
Gold:	USA: May 26, 1970

Cover versions:
The Beatles, Helen Reddy

ONLY A NORTHERN SONG

Written by:	George Harrison
Produced by:	George Martin
Album:	USA: Yellow Submarine Apple SW 153
	UK: Yellow Submarine Apple PCS 7070
Released:	USA: Jan 1969 UK: Jan 1969
Gold:	USA: February 5, 1969

Cover versions:
The Beatles

PENNY LANE

Written by:	Lennon/McCartney
Single #:	USA: Capitol 5810
	UK: Parlophone R5570
Released:	USA: Feb 1967 UK: Feb 1967
Gold:	USA: March 20, 1967
Awards:	Million performance song: June 1977
	Most performed pop song: 1967
Weeks on chart:	USA: 10 UK: 11
Produced by:	George Martin
Album:	USA: Magical Mystery Tour Capitol SMAL 2835
	UK: Magical Mystery Tour Parlophone PCTC 255
Released:	USA: Nov 1967 UK: Dec 1967
Gold:	USA: December 15, 1964
Additional Musicians:	Paul & George Martin, Pianos; John, Conga Drums; Frank Clarke, String Bass; David Mason, Sped-up Piccolo B Flat Trumpet; Philip Jones, Trumpet Solo
Arrangements:	CB, SOR, CH

Cover versions:
The Baskerville Hounds, Count Basie, Terry Baxter Orchestra & Chorus, Beatlemania, The Beatles, Ray Bloch Singers, Boston Pops Orchestra, Laurie Bower Singers, Cafe Creme, Lee Castle & Jim Dorsey, The Chords, Columbia Musical Treasury Orchestra, Lawrence Cook, Peter Covent Band, Milton DeLugg, 18th Century Concepts, Electronic Concept Orchestra, Enoch Light & The Light Brigade, Arthur Fiedler & Boston Pops, The Four Score Pianos, Francois Glorieux, Marty Gold Orchestra, Good Vibrations, Anita Harris, The Hollyridge Strings, Jalopy Five, Les Sinners, Liverpool 5, David McCallum, Mariachi Mexico 70, Paul Mauriat Orchestra, Tony Mottola, The Now Generation, 101 Strings, Bill Page, Frank Pourcel, Kenny Rankin, Sound Alikes, Sinners, Sydney Thompson & Orchestra, Kai Winding, Stan Worth, Klaus Wunderlich

PIGGIES

Written by:	George Harrison
Produced by:	George Martin
Album:	USA: The Beatles Apple SWBO 101
	UK: The Beatles Apple PCS 7067/8
Released:	USA: Nov 1968 UK: Nov 1968
Gold:	USA: December 6, 1968
Additional Musicians:	Chris Thomas, Harpsichord; Ringo, Tambourine

POLYTHENE PAM

Written by:	Lennon/McCartney
Produced by:	George Martin
Album:	UK: Abbey Road Apple PCS 7088
Released:	UK: Sept 1969

Cover versions:
The Beatles, The Bee Gees, Bola Sete, Booker T & The M.G.'s, McClemore Avenue, Music Machine, The Odyssey Singers, Stan Ruffin, Roy Wood

REVOLUTION

Written by:	Lennon/McCartney
Single #:	USA: Apple 2276
	UK: Apple R5722
Released:	USA: Aug 1968 UK: Aug 1968
Weeks on chart:	USA: 11
Produced by:	George Martin
Album:	USA: The Beatles Apple SWBO 101
	UK: The Beatles Apple PCS 7067/8
Released:	USA: Nov 1968 UK: Nov 1968
Album:	Hey Jude, Apple SW 385/SO 385
Released:	USA: Feb 1970
Gold:	USA: December 6, 1968
Arrangements:	OR

Cover versions:
Beatlemania, The Beatles, The Brothers Four, Cafe Creme, The Chords, Columbia Musical Treasury Orch., Copper Plated Integrated, Richard Hayman & W Sear, Head Shop, Jalopy Five, Kings Road, Wilbert Longmire, The Other Company, M. Pagliaro, The Rollers, Rubberband, Santo & Johnny, Silk, Sound Alike, The Top of the Poppers, The Wild Thing

ROCKY RACCOON

Written by:	Lennon/McCartney
Produced by:	George Martin
Album:	USA: The Beatles Apple SWBO 101
	UK: The Beatles Apple PCS 7067/8
Released:	USA: Nov 1968 UK: Nov 1968
Gold:	USA: December 6, 1968
Additional Musicians:	Paul, Acoustic Guitar; John, Harmonium; George Martin, Piano
Arrangements:	MB

Cover versions:
Terry Baxter Orchestra & Chorus, The Beatles, The Jules Blattner Group, Cafe Creme, The Driving Beat, Andy Fairweather Low, Benny Goodman, Richie Havens, Lena Horne & Gabor Szabo, Ramsey Lewis, Bruce Westcott, Hank Wickham, Hank & Lewie Wickham

SAVOY TRUFFLE

Written by:	George Harrison
Produced by:	George Martin
Album:	USA: The Beatles Apple SWBO 101
	UK: The Beatles Apple PCS 7067/8
Released:	USA: Nov 1968 UK: Nov 1968
Gold:	USA: December 6, 1968

SEXY SADIE

Written by:	Lennon/McCartney
Produced by:	George Martin
Album:	USA: The Beatles Apple SWBO 101
	UK: The Beatles Apple PCS 7067/8
Released:	USA: Nov 1968 UK: Nov 1968
Gold:	USA: December 6, 1968
Additional Musicians:	Paul, Piano; John, Acoustic Guitar

Cover versions:
The Beatles, Cafe Creme, Ramsey Lewis

SGT. PEPPER'S LONELY HEARTS CLUB BAND

Written by:	Lennon/McCartney
Weeks on chart:	USA: 7
Produced by:	George Martin
Album:	USA: Sergeant Pepper's Lonely Hearts Club Band, Capitol SMAS 2653
	UK: Sergeant Pepper's Lonely Hearts Club Band, Parlophone PCS 7027
Released:	USA: June 1967 UK: June 1967
Gold:	USA: June 15, 1967
Arrangements:	MB, JB, CB, CH

Cover versions:
Terry Baxter Orchestra & Chorus, The Beatles, The Bee Gees, Paul Nichol, Brian Browne, The Bubble Gum Machine, Cafe Creme, Cast, Bill Cosby, Peter Frampton, The Bee Gees, Heavy Balloon Band, Jimi Hendrix, The Hollyridge Strings, Kid Stuff Repertory Company, Peter Knight, Andre Kostelanetz, Los Mustang, Peter Matz, George Martin & his Orchestra, Music Machine, Odyssey, The Other Company, The Rollers, Stan Ruffin, Salsoul Orchestra, Hal Serra, Sound Alike, The Sound-a-likes

SHE CAME IN THROUGH THE BATHROOM WINDOW

Written by:	Lennon/McCartney
Produced by:	George Martin
Album:	USA: Abbey Road Apple SO 383
	UK: Abbey Road Apple PCS 7088
Released:	USA: Oct 1969 UK: Sept 1969
Gold:	USA: October 27, 1969

Cover versions:
The Beatles, The Bee Gees, Bola Sete, Booker T & M.G.'s, Joe Cocker, Jose Feliciano, Peter Frampton, The Bee Gees, Bert Kaempfert & James Last, James Last, The Odyssey Singers, Stan Ruffin, Doc Severinsen, The Sound-a-likes, Ray Stevens, Ike & Tina Turner, The Youngbloods

SHE SAID SHE SAID

Written by:	Lennon/McCartney
Produced by:	George Martin
Album:	USA: Revolver Capitol ST 2576
	UK: Revolver Parlophone PCS 7009
Released:	USA: Aug 1966 UK: Aug 1966
Gold:	USA: August 22, 1966

Cover versions:
The Beatles, Hedge & Donna, Lone Star, George Martin, The Neighborhood, Tom Newman, Rainbow Canyon, Don Randi Trio, The Zoo

SHE'S LEAVING HOME

Written by:	Lennon/McCartney
Produced by:	George Martin
Album:	USA: Sergeant Pepper's Lonely Hearts Club Band, Capitol SMAS 2653
	UK: Sergeant Pepper's Lonely Hearts Club Band, Parlophone PCS 7027
Released:	USA: June 1967 UK: June 1967
Gold:	USA: June 15, 1967
Additional Musicians:	Strings arranged by Mike Leander
Arrangements:	JB

Cover versions:
Terry Baxter Orchestra & Chorus, The Beatles, The Bee Gees, Jay Macinto, Leon Bibb, Barnaby Bye, Cafe Creme, Lana Cantrell, Stuart Crosby, David & Jonathan, David Essex, Bryan Ferry, The Four Freshmen, Joel Grey, Richie Havens, The Hollyridge Strings, Al Jarreau, Peter Knight, Knight Sounds, London Pops Orchestra, Kathy McCord, Music Machine, Lincoln Mayorga, The Odyssey Singers, Esther & Abi Ofarim, Tony Osborne & His Orchestra, Rubberband, Tom Scott & California Dreamer, Roland Shaw Orchestra & Chorus, Louie Shelton, Big Jim Sullivan, Syreeta, Cal Tjader, Mel Torme, Julius Wechter & Baja Marimba Band

SOMETHING

Written by:	George Harrison
Single #:	USA: Apple 2654
	UK: Apple R5814
Released:	USA: Oct 1969 UK: Oct 1969
Gold:	USA: October 27, 1969
Weeks on chart:	USA: 16 UK: 12
Produced by:	George Martin
Album:	USA: Abbey Road Apple SO 383
	UK: Abbey Road Apple PCS 7088
Released:	USA: Oct 1969 UK: Sept 1969
Gold:	USA: October 27, 1969

STRAWBERRY FIELDS FOREVER

Written by:	Lennon/McCartney
Single #:	USA: Capitol 5810
	UK: Parlophone R5570
Released:	USA: Feb 1967 UK: Feb 1967
Weeks on chart:	USA: 9 UK: 11
Produced by:	George Martin
Album:	USA: Magical Mystery Tour Capitol SMAL 2835
	UK: Magical Mystery Tour Parlophone PCTC 255
Released:	USA: Nov 1967 UK: Dec 1967
Gold:	USA: December 15, 1967
Additional Musicians:	Paul & George, Timpani & Bongos; Mal Evans, Tambourine; Alto Trumpet, Electric Drum Track, Flutes, Cellos, Harpsichord & Brass
Arrangements:	SOR, CH

Cover versions:
Astromusical House of Sag., Terry Baxter Orchestra & Chorus, Beatlemania, The Beatles, Cafe Creme, Sandy Farina, Peter Gabriel, Anita Harris, Noel Harrison, Richie Havens, The Hollyridge Strings, Life, Liverpool 5, London Festival Orchestra, David McCallum, New World Electronic Cham, Odetta, Odyssey, The Odyssey Singers, Orchestra of Sagittarius, Poco Sezo, Stan Ruffin, Todd Rundgren, Sound-a-like, Stardrive, Libby Titus, Tomorrow, The Ventures, Keith West

SUN KING

Written by:	Lennon/McCartney
Produced by:	George Martin
Album:	UK: Abbey Road Apple PCS 7088
Released:	UK: Sept 1969
Additional Musicians:	John, Maracas; Paul, Harmonium; Ringo, Bongos; George Martin, Organ

Cover versions:
The Beatles, The Bee Gees, Booker T & The M.G.'s, Percy Faith, Doc Severinsen, Roy Wood

TAXMAN

Written by:	George Harrison
Produced by:	George Martin
Album:	USA: Revolver Capitol ST 2576
	UK: Revolver Parlophone PCS 7009
Released:	USA: Aug 1966 UK: Aug 1966
Gold:	USA: August 22, 1966

Cover versions:
The Beatles, Black Oak Arkansas, Cafe Creme, George Harrison, The Hollyridge Strings, Magne Tronics Combo, The Music Machine, Junior Parker, Don Randi Trio

TOMORROW NEVER KNOWS

Written by:	Lennon/McCartney
Produced by:	George Martin
Album:	USA: Revolver Capitol ST 2576
	UK: Revolver Parlophone PCS 7009
Released:	USA: Aug 1966 UK: Aug 1966
Gold:	USA: August 22, 1966
Additional Musicians:	Sound effects arranged by Paul

Cover versions:
The Beatles, Morgana King, Phil Manzanara, Steve Marcus, Junior Parker, Don Randi Trio

TWO OF US

Written by:	Lennon/McCartney
Produced by:	Phil Spector
Album:	USA: Let It Be Red Apple 34001
	UK: Let It Be Apple PXS1/Apple PCS 7096
Released:	USA: May 1970
	UK: May 1970/Nov 1970

Gold:	USA: May 26, 1970

Cover versions:
The Beatles, Denny Doherty, Marie Jane, MT Combo, Rare Earth, Shake, R Dean Taylor

WHEN I'M SIXTY FOUR

Written by:	Lennon/McCartney
Produced by:	George Martin
Album:	USA: Sergeant Pepper's Lonely Hearts Club Band, Capitol SMAS 2653
	UK: Sergeant Pepper's Lonely Hearts Club Band, Parlophone PCS 7027
Released:	USA: June 1967 UK: June 1967
Gold:	USA: June 15, 1967
Arrangements:	MB, CB, OR, CH

Cover versions:
Archie & Edith, Average Disco Band, Kenny Ball & His Jazzmen, Terry Baxter Orchestra & Chorus, The Beatles, Artie Butler, Cafe Creme, Renne Claude, Gene Cotton, Bernard Cribbins, Rhett Davis, Joel Dennis, John Denver, Walter Erickson, George Fame, GH Presents Beatles, Francois Glorieux, Dave Graley, Noel Harrison, The Hollyridge Strings, Holt (Rinehart & Winston) Music Dept., Honky Tonk Herman, Frankie Howard, Sandy Farina, Peter Knight, Claudine Longet, Los Norte Americanos, Magne Tronics Combo, Keith Moon, Phyllis Newman, The Odyssey Singers, Stan Ruffin, Cyril Stapleton & Choir, Strawberry Street Singers, Sydney Thompson & His Orchestra, Leo Wijnkamp, Jack Wild, Wild Honey Singers, Your Father's Moustache

WHILE MY GUITAR GENTLY WEEPS

Written by:	George Harrison
Produced by:	George Martin
Album:	USA: The Beatles Apple SWBO 101
	UK: The Beatles Apple PCS 7067/8
Released:	USA: Nov 1968 UK: Nov 1968
Gold:	USA: December 6, 1968
Additional Musicians:	Eric Clapton, Lead Guitar

WHY DON'T WE DO IT IN THE ROAD

Written by:	Lennon/McCartney
Produced by:	George Martin
Album:	USA: The Beatles Apple SWBO 101
	UK: The Beatles Apple PCS 7067/8
Released:	USA: Nov 1968 UK: Nov 1968
Gold:	USA: December 6, 1968
Additional Musicians:	Paul, Guitar, Piano, Bass and Drum

Cover versions:
The Beatles, California Poppy Pickers, The Children, Haircuts & Impossibles, James Cahoon Lindsay Band, Midnight Movers, Mudd

WILD HONEY PIE

Written by:	Lennon/McCartney
Produced by:	George Martin
Album:	USA: The Beatles Apple SWBO 101
	UK: The Beatles Apple PCS 7067/8
Released:	USA: Nov 1968 UK: Nov 1968
Gold:	USA: December 6, 1968
Additional Musicians:	Paul, Guitar, Bass, Drums

Cover versions:
The Beatles

WITH A LITTLE HELP FROM MY FRIENDS

Written by:	Lennon/McCartney
Weeks on chart:	USA: 7
Produced by:	George Martin
Album:	USA: Sergeant Pepper's Lonely Hearts Club Band, Capitol SMAS 2653
	UK: Sergeant Pepper's Lonely Hearts Club Band, Parlophone PCS 7027
Released:	USA: June 1967 UK: June 1967
Gold:	USA: June 15, 1967
Arrangements:	MB, JB, CB, SOR, CH

Cover versions:
A Musical Trip, Herb Alpert & The Tijuana Brass, Ena Baga, Joss Baselli, Count Basie, Terry Baxter Orchestra & Chorus, The Beatles, The Board of Regents, Bola Sete, Boston Pops Orchestra, Joe Brown, George Burns, Cafe Creme, Larry Carlton, Chris Clark, The Clebanoff Strings, Joe Cocker, Steve Cropper, Homer Dennison Night Strings, Lu Elliott, Enoch Light, The Fabulous Farquahr, Wilton Felder, The Mickie Finn Group, Peter Frampton, The Bee Gees, GH Presents Beatles, Francois Glorieux, George Gruntz, Tony Hatch Orchestra, Richie Havens, I Beans, Jay Jackson & Heads Up, The Jaggers, Jazz Rock Symposium, Jackson Knight Revue, Peter Knight, James Last Orchestra, Latin Vibrations, Donald Lautrec, Betty Lavette, Steve Lawrence & Eydie Gorme, Les Merseys, Los Mustang, Arthur Lyman, Jeff Lynne, Rod McKuen, Sergio Mendes & Brazil 66, Eddie Miller, Pete Fountain, Glenn Miller Orchestra, Patti Miller, Dom Minasi, Len Mink, Tony Mottola, Music Machine, New Chartbusters 9, Roger Nichols, Odyssey, The Odyssey Singers, The Other Company, Jean Luc Ponty, Nat Raider, Sue Raney, Kenny Rankin, The Rollers, Biff Rose, Dick Rosmini, Stan Ruffin, Tommy Sands, Freddie Scott, Earl Scruggs, Mike Sharpe, Jack Sheldon, Cyril Stapleton Choir & Orchestra, Barbra Streisand, The Sound-a-likes, Ike & Tina Turner, Uncle Bill, The Undisputed Truth, University of Bridgeport Jazz, David T. Walker, The Young Idea

WITHIN YOU WITHOUT YOU

Written by:	George Harrison
Produced by:	George Martin
Album:	USA: Sergeant Pepper's Lonely Hearts Club Band, Capitol SMAS 2653
	UK: Sergeant Pepper's Lonely Hearts Club Band, Parlophone PCS 7027
Released:	USA: June 1967 UK: June 1967
Gold:	USA: June 15, 1967
Additional Musicians:	George and Indian musicians. Paul, John and Ringo did not participate.

Cover versions:
The Beatles, The Clebanoff Strings, Peter Knight, David Liebman, The Alan Lorber Orchestra, Richard Ruskin, The Soulful Strings, Big Jim Sullivan, Tartaglia

YELLOW SUBMARINE

Written by:	Lennon/McCartney
Single #:	USA: Capitol 5715
	UK: Parlophone R5489
Released:	USA: Aug 1966 UK: Aug 1966
Gold:	USA: September 12, 1966
Awards:	Most performed pop song: 1966 Other: 1966, Highest Certified British Sales (Ivor Novello Awards)
Weeks on chart:	USA: 9 UK: 13
Produced by:	George Martin
Album:	USA: Revolver Capitol ST 2576
	UK: Revolver Parlophone PCS 7009
Released:	USA: Aug 1966 UK: Aug 1966
Gold:	USA: August 22, 1966
Album:	USA: Yellow Submarine Apple SW 153
	UK: Yellow Submarine Apple PCS 7070

Released: USA: Jan 1969 UK: Jan 1969
Additional
Musicians: John, Blowing bubbles; George, swirling water in a bucket; Chorus: Mal Evans, Neil Aspinal, Patty Harrison, George Martin, Geoffrey Emerick, Studio staff.
Arrangements: MB, CB, OR, CH
Cover versions:
Aboite Jr. High Chorus, The Baroque, Baroque Inevitable, Terry Baxter Orchestra & Chorus, The Beatles, Madame Catherine Berberian, Milton Berle, Boston Pops Orch., Cafe Creme, California Poppy Pickers, Ace Cannon, Lee Castle & Jimmy Dorsey, Leonard Caston, Charles River Valley Boys, Maurice Chevalier, The Chords, Columbia Musical Treasury Orch., Ray Conniff, Cricketones Chorus & Orchestra, Enoch Light & The Light Brigade, Ferrante & Teicher, Arthur Fiedler & Boston Pops, John Foster & Sons Ltd., Galaxy Kiddie Chorus & Orchestra, GH Presents Beatles, Will Glahe, Francois Glorieux, Happy Time Children's Chorus, Ted Heath Orchestra, Al Hirt, The Hollyridge Strings, Rod Hunter, Irwin the Dynamic Duck, Jalopy Five, Peter Knight, James Last Band, Les Baronets, Les Compagnons Dela Chans, Les Nouveaux Baronets, Hank Levine Singers & Orchestra, Los Mustang, Magne Tronics Combo, Henry Mancini, Mariachi Mexico 70, George Martin & His Orchestra, Vaughn Meader, Mrs. Elvira Miller, The Muppets, The Music Makers, The Now Generation, Peter Pan Orchestra & Chorus, Pickwick Children's Chorus, Don Randi Trio, Revelation, Joe Scott, The Senate, The Stardust Voices, The Tattoos, Tingling Mother's

Circus, United States Double Quartet & Token, Dick Watson, Watts 103rd St. Rhythm Band, Richard Wolfe Children, Stan Worth

YER BLUES

Written by: Lennon/McCartney
Produced by: George Martin
Album: USA: The Beatles
Apple SWBO 101
UK: The Beatles
Apple PCS 7067/8
Released: USA: Nov 1968 UK: Nov 1968
Gold: USA: December 6, 1968
Cover versions:
The Beatles, The Plastic Ono Band

YOU KNOW MY NAME (LOOK UP THE NUMBER)

Written by: Lennon/McCartney
Single #: USA: Apple 2764
UK: Apple R5883
Released: USA: March 1970
UK: March 1970
Produced by: George Martin
Additional
Musicians: Brian Jones, Saxophone; Mal Evans, Background vocals
Cover versions:
The Beatles

YOU NEVER GIVE ME YOUR MONEY

Written by: Lennon/McCartney

Produced by: George Martin
Album: USA: Abbey Road
Apple SO 383
UK: Abbey Road
Apple PCS 7088
Released: USA: Oct 1969 UK: Sept 1969
Gold: USA: October 27, 1969
Cover versions:
Terry Baxter Orchestra & Chorus, The Beatles, George Benson, Booker T & The M.G.'s, Broken Arrow, Cafe Creme, Stuart Crosby, Wil Malone & Lou Reizner, Herbie Mann, Dale Miller, Music Machine, Paul Nicholas, Dianne Ste., The Odyssey Singers

YOUR MOTHER SHOULD KNOW

Written by: Lennon/McCartney
Produced by: George Martin
EP: UK: Magical Mystery Tour, Parlophone SMMT 1/2, December 1967
Album: USA: Magical Mystery Tour Capitol SMAL 2835
UK: Magical Mystery Tour Parlophone PCTC 255
Released: USA: Nov 1967 UK: Dec 1967
Gold: USA: December 15, 1967
Arrangements: CH
Cover versions:
A Musical Trip, The Beatles, George Burns, Lana Cantrell, The Hollyridge Strings, Jeremy Hunter, Damita Jo, Les Merseys, Marble Arch Music Assn. A Musical Trip, Phyllis Newman, Ivor Raymonde, Raymonde Singers, Bud Shank

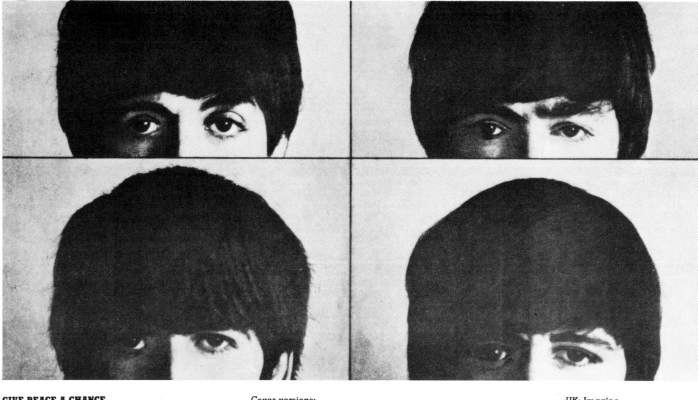

GIVE PEACE A CHANCE

Written by: John Lennon
Single #: USA: Apple 1809 UK: Apple 13
Released: USA: July 1969 UK: July 1969
Weeks on chart: USA: 9 UK: 13
Produced by: John Lennon and Yoko Ono
Album: The Plastic Ono Band - Live Peace in Toronto
USA: Apple SW 3362
UK: Apple CORE 2001
Released: USA: Dec 1969 UK: Dec 1969
Additional
Musicians: Plastic Ono Band; with Timothy Leary; Canadian Radna Krisna Temple; Derek Taylor; Murray the K; Tommy Smothers; Rabbi Feinburg
Arrangements: CH, MB

Cover versions:
Louis Armstrong, The Beatles, Chorus With Orchestra, Mike Curb Congregation, The Everly Brothers, Hot Chocolate Band, Jazz Crusaders, La Compagnie, James Last Band, Ken Lazarus, Mitch Miller & The Gang, Movie Soundtrack, Plastic Ono Band, Strawberry Statement Cast, Wondrous Joy Clouds

IMAGINE

Written by: John Lennon
Single #: USA: Apple 1840
UK: Apple R6009
Released: USA: Oct 1971 UK: Nov 1975
Weeks on chart: USA: 9 UK: 11
Produced by: John Lennon, Yoko Ono, Phil Spector
Album: USA: Imagine
Apple SW 3379

UK: Imagine
Apple PA S 10004
Released: USA: Oct 1971 UK: Sept 1971
Gold: USA: October 1, 1971
Additional
Musicians: John Lennon Plastic Ono Band with the Flux Fiddlers; John, Pianos; Klaus Voorman, Bass; Andy White, Drums
Arrangements: CH, OR
Cover versions:
Ronnie Aldrich, Average White Band, Joan Baez, Ted Baxter, Terry Baxter Orchestra, Ray Conniff, Hank Crawford, Gerri Granger, Klaus Weiss Orchestra, John Lennon, Enoch Light, Mariachi Mexico, Nana Mouskouri, Mae McKenna, Ben McPeek, Houston Person, Frank Pourcel, Diana Ross, Merl Sanders, Ray Sanders, Earl J. Sorrento, Gonzalo Valdovinos, Sarah Vaughn, Roger Whittaker, Stan Worth

EIGHT DAYS A WEEK/EARLY CHART HISTORY

The Beatles, as a group, have sold more than 60 million records in North America and a total of nearly 100 million records around the globe, probably more than any other group in history. The individual members have sold even more as solo artists and with other groups.

The Beatles recorded 102 songs just in the years 1962 to 1966. In Britain these appeared on 8 LPs (including the anthology), 12 EPs and 13 singles. The very same selections were repackaged for the American consumer into 11 albums, 4 EPs and 20 singles. No two records in the two sets feature the same contents.

In England, Beatles singles spent 386 weeks on the charts. They had 23 Top Ten hits; 17 No. 1 hits; and were at the No. 1 spot for 64 weeks — 16 of those weeks were in 1963.

In the United States, the Beatles singles were in the No. 1 spot for 59 weeks, and their albums were at No. 1 for 119 weeks. They had 20 No. 1 songs on the "Hot 100"; Elvis Presley is right behind them with 14.

In September, 1962, George Martin signed the Beatles to EMI's Parlophone Records and produced their recordings, including the first single, "Love Me Do"/ "P.S. I Love You." On November 26, the second single "Please Please Me" was recorded.

On February 16, 1963, "Please Please Me" became the Beatles' first No. 1 hit in England, eventually selling over a million copies. The Beatles made pop music history by topping Britain's bestselling record charts with singles and albums in December 1963. In mid-December, their singles were Nos. 1 and 2; EPs were 1, 2, and 3; albums 1 and 2 — all at the same time, an unprecedented achievement in record history. On December 29, at 12:50 p.m., WMCA radio station in New York City broadcasted the first Beatles song in the United States ("I Want To Hold Your Hand").

From February 18 through March 31, 1964, Beatles' singles in the United States grossed 17.5 million dollars. During the month of February, the Beatles accounted for 60% of all singles sold in America.

"She Loves You" sold over 1.5 million in Britain alone by January 1964 (finally 1,527,000) and a further 3 million by March 1964 on the Swan label in the United States, where it was No. 1 for two weeks. The global sales of the record are estimated at well over 5 million.

"I Want To Hold Your Hand" held the British record for an advance sale of 950,000 (November 1963) up to that time. It sold over 1.5 million in Britain by mid-January 1964 (finally 1,509,000) and was a No. 1 chart entry in its first week. The single was Capitol's fastest breaking single ever. As later reported by Ian Dove in *Billboard*, Capitol shipped 694,000 during the first week, with 294,000 copies just for New York City. "I Want To Hold Your Hand" eventually sold 3,400,000 copies by the end of March 1964. The first American Beatles record, *Meet The Beatles*, sold even more, with a total of 3,650,000 by the same date.

"Can't Buy Me Love" hit the HOT 100 at position No. 27 on March 28, 1964. Capitol claimed sales of 940,225 on the very first day — the highest spot anyone could remember. 2,100,000 copies were pressed — the record to date for the biggest advance sale of any single — and they needed more! Over 1 million copies were pressed in England, and by the first week of release it sold 1,226,000 copies.

At the end of March, the Beatles had ten singles in the charts and they occupied the *first five* positions. "Can't Buy Me Love" was at No. 1; "Twist and Shout" at No. 2; "She Loves You" at No. 3; "I Want To Hold Your Hand" at No. 4; "Please Please Me" at No. 5; plus tunes at positions 16, 44, 49, 69, 78, 84, 88 on the Top 100 chart. In Canada they occupied nine places in the Top 10.

By the end of 1970, the Beatles tally of million sellers was:

25 singles	**USA**
1 EP	**USA**
19 LPs	**USA**
7 singles	**Britain**
1 LP	**Britain**
2 singles	**Combined USA/Britain**
2 EPs	**Global**
2 singles	**Global**
Total	**59**

In 1976 in England, every Beatles single was re-released as well as "Yesterday" (never before released there as a single) and all 23 of them jumped onto the Top 100 national charts. In the United States in June, 1976, Capitol released *Rock 'n' Roll Music* — a double album repackaging 28 rocking Beatles tunes — backed by the largest and most extensive marketing campaign in the label's history. More than 500,000 copies were shipped the day of release and the record was immediately certified Gold by the Recording Industry Association of America (R.I.A.A.). Four days later the album sold more than a million copies and was certified Platinum.

In 1978, the National Hall of Fame's Top Ten most popular tunes were determined by Drake-Chenault after a monumental poll of listeners to their consulted radio stations across the United States. The Beatles topped the list with "Hey Jude" at No. 1, and "Yesterday" at No. 4.

BEATLES GRAMMY AWARDS

1964

"A Hard Day's Night"	*Best performance by a vocal group*
The Beatles	*Best new artist*

1966

"Michelle"	*Song of the Year*
"Eleanor Rigby"	*Best Contemporary Pop Solo Vocal Performance (Paul McCartney)*
Revolver	*Best Album Cover Art (Klaus Voorman)*

1967

Sgt. Pepper's Lonely Hearts Club Band	*Album of the Year; Best Contemporary Album; Best Engineered Recording; Best Album Cover — Graphic Arts.*

Additional Recordings U.K.

The Beatles 1962–1966
Apple PCSP 717 (2 LPs)   April 1973

A Hard Day's Night
All My Loving
And I Love Her
Can't Buy Me Love
Day Tripper
Drive My Car
Eight Days A Week
Eleanor Rigby
From Me To You
Girl
Help
I Feel Fine
In My Life
I Want To Hold Your Hand
Love Me Do
Michelle
Norwegian Wood (This Bird Has Flown)
Nowhere Man
Paperback Writer
Please Please Me
She Loves You
Ticket To Ride
We Can Work It Out
Yellow Submarine
Yesterday
You've Got To Hide Your Love Away

The Beatles 1967–1970
Apple PSCP 718 (2 LPs)   April 1973

Across The Universe
All You Need Is Love
Back In The U.S.S.R.

The Ballad of John and Yoko
Come Together
A Day In The Life
Don't Let Me Down
The Fool On The Hill
Hello Goodbye
Here Comes The Sun
Hey Jude
I Am The Walrus
Lady Madonna
Let It Be
The Long and Winding Road
Lucy In The Sky With Diamonds
Magical Mystery Tour
Ob-La-Di, Ob-La-Da
Octopus's Garden
Old Brown Shoe
Penny Lane
Revolution
Sgt. Pepper's Lonely Hearts Club Band
Something
Strawberry Fields Forever
While My Guitar Gently Weeps
With A Little Help From My Friends

Rock and Roll Music
Parlophone PCSP 719 (2 LPs)   June 1976

Anytime At All
Back In the U.S.S.R.
Bad Boy
Birthday
Boys
Dizzy Miss Lizzie
Drive My Car
Everybody's Trying To Be My Baby
Get Back
Got To Get You Into My Life
Helter Skelter
Hey Bulldog
I Call Your Name
I Wanna Be Your Man
I Saw Her Standing There
I'm Down
Kansas City
Long Tall Sally
Matchbox
Money (That's What I Want)

The Night Before
Revolution
Rock and Roll Music
Roll Over Beethoven
Slow Down
Taxman
Twist and Shout
You Can't Do That

*Live! at the Star Club in Hamburg,
Germany 1962*
Lingasong LNL1 (2 LPs)   April 1977

Ain't Nobody Shaking Like The
Leaves On A Tree
Ask Me Why
Be-Bop-A-Lu-La
Besame Mucho
Everybody's Trying To Be My Baby
Falling In Love Again
Halleluja I Love Her So
Hippy Hippy Shake
I Remember You
I Saw Her Standing There
Kansas City
Lend Me Your Comb
Little Queenie
Long Tall Sally
Matchbox
Mr. Moonlight
Red Sails In The Sunset
Reminiscing
Roll Over Beethoven
Shimmy Shimmy
Sweet Little Sixteen
Talkin' 'Bout You
A Taste Of Honey
To Know Her Is To Love Her
Twist and Shout
Your Feet's Too Big

The Beatles at the Hollywood Bowl
Parlophone EMTV4   May 1977

All My Loving
Boys
Can't Buy Me Love

Dizzy Miss Lizzie
A Hard Day's Night
Help
Long Tall Sally
Roll Over Beethoven
She Loves You
She's A Woman
Things We Said Today
Ticket To Ride
Twist and Shout

Love Songs
Parlophone PCSP 721 (2 LPs) November 1977

And I Love Her
Every Little Thing
For No One
Here, There and Everywhere
I Need You
I Will
I'll Be Back
I'll Follow The Sun
If I Fell
In My Life
It's Only Love
The Long and Winding Road
Michelle
Norwegian Wood
P.S. I Love You
She's Leaving Home
Something
Tell Me What You See
This Boy
Words of Love
Yes It Is
Yesterday
You're Gonna Lose That Girl
You've Got To Hide Your Love Away

The Beatles First   EP
Polydor 236-201
June 1964 Reissue August 1967
(with additional material by Tony Sheridan)

Ain't She Sweet
Cry For A Shadow
If You Love Me, Baby
My Bonnie
Nobody's Child
The Saints
Sweet Georgia Brown
Why?

A Collection of Beatle Oldies
Parlophone PCS 7016 December 1966

Bad Boy
Can't Buy Me Love
Day Tripper
Eleanor Rigby
From Me To You
A Hard Day's Night
Help
I Feel Fine
I Want To Hold Your Hand
Michelle
Paperback Writer
She Loves You
Ticket To Ride
We Can Work It Out
Yellow Submarine
Yesterday

Rarities
Parlophone PCM 1001
November 1979

Across the Universe
Bad Boy
I Call Your Name

I'll Get You
I'm Down
The Inner Light
Komm, Gib Mir Deine Hand
Long Tall Sally
Matchbox
Rain
She's A Woman
Sie Liebt Dich
Slow Down
Thank You Girl
This Boy
Yes It Is
You Know My Name (Look Up My Number)

Additional Recordings U.S.A.

EP

The Beatles With Tony Sheridan and Their Guests

MGM SE 4215 February 1964
(other artists provide additional material)

Cry For A Shadow
My Bonnie
The Saints
Why

Also released as:
This Is Where It Started
Metro MS 563 August 1966

EP

Jolly What! The Beatles and Frank Ilfield on Stage

VeeJay VJLP 1085 February 1964
(with additional material by Frank Ilfield)

Ask Me Why
From Me To You
Please Please Me
Thank You Girl

EP

Ain't She Sweet

Atco SD 33-169 October 1969
(Tony Sheridan and the Beatles with additional material provided by The Swallows)

Ain't She Sweet
Baby
Nobody's Child
Sweet Georgia Brown
Take Out Some Insurance On Me, Baby

Also released as:
The Amazing Beatles
Clanon 601 October 1966

The Beatles vs. The Four Seasons
VeeJay VJDX 30 October 1964
2 LPs

Also released as:
Songs, Pictures and Stories of the Fabulous Beatles
VeeJay VJLP 1092 October 1964

Anna (Go To Him)
Ask Me Why
Baby, It's You
Boys
Chains
Do You Want To Know A Secret

I Saw Her Standing There
It's You
Misery
Please Please Me
A Taste of Honey
There's A Place
Twist and Shout

The Beatles 1962-1966

Apple SKBO 3403 April 1973
2 LPs

(same as British release)

A Hard Day's Night
All My Loving
And I Love Her
Can't Buy Me Love
Day Tripper
Drive My Car
Eight Days A Week
Eleanor Rigby
From Me To You
Girl
Help
I Feel Fine
In My Life
I Want To Hold Your Hand
Love Me Do
Michelle
Norwegian Wood (This Bird Has Flown)
Nowhere Man
Paperback Writer
Please Please Me
She Loves You
Ticket To Ride
We Can Work It Out
Yellow Submarine
Yesterday
You've Got To Hide Your Love Away

The Beatles 1967-1970

Apple SKBO 3404 April 1973
2 LPs
(same as British release)

Across The Universe
All You Need Is Love
Back In The U.S.S.R.
The Ballad of John and Yoko
Come Together
A Day In The Life
Don't Let Me Down
The Fool On The Hill
Hello Goodbye
Here Comes The Sun
Hey Jude
I Am The Walrus
Lady Madonna
Let It Be
The Long and Winding Road
Lucy In The Sky With Diamonds
Magical Mystery Tour
Ob-La-Di, Ob-La-Da
Octopus's Garden
Old Brown Shoe
Penny Lane
Revolution
Sgt. Pepper's Lonely Hearts Club Band
Something
Strawberry Fields Forever
While My Guitar Gently Weeps
With A Little Help From My Friends

Rock and Roll Music

Capitol SKBO 11537   June 1976
2 LPs
(same as British release)

Anytime At All
Back In The U.S.S.R.
Bad Boy
Birthday
Boys
Dizzy Miss Lizzie
Drive My Car
Everybody's Trying To Be My Baby
Get Back
Got To Get You Into My Life
Helter Skelter
Hey Bulldog
I Call Your Name
I Wanna Be Your Man
I Saw Her Standing There
I'm Down
Kansas City
Long Tall Sally
Matchbox
Money (That's What I Want)
The Night Before
Revolution
Rock and Roll Music
Roll Over Beethoven
Slow Down
Taxman
Twist and Shout
You Can't Do That

The Beatles at the Hollywood Bowl

Capitol SMAS 11638   May 1977
(same as British release)

All My Loving
Boys Can
Can't Buy Me Love
Dizzy Miss Lizzie
A Hard Day's Night
Help
Long Tall Sally

Roll Over Beethoven
She Loves You
She's A Woman
Things We Said Today
Ticket To Ride
Twist and Shout

*Live! at the Star Club in Hamburg,
Germany, 1962*

Lingasong/Atlantic LS-2-7001   June 1977
2 LPs

Ain't Nothing
Be-Bop-A-Lu-La
Besame Mucho
Everybody's Trying To Be My Baby
Falling In Love Again
Hallelujah I Just Love Her So
Hippy Hippy Shake
I Remember You
I'm Gonna Sit Right Down and Cry Over
  You
Kansas City/Hey Hey Hey Hey
Lend Me Your Comb
Little Queenie
Long Tall Sally
Matchbox
Mr. Moonlight
Red Sails in the Sunset
Roll Over Beethoven
Shaking Like A Leaf on a Tree
Sheila
Shimmy Shake
Sweet Little 16
Talkin' 'Bout You
A Taste of Honey
Till There Was You
To Know Her Is To Love Her
Where Have You Been All My Life
Your Feet's Too Big

Love Songs

Capitol SKBL 11711   October 1977
2 LPs
(Same as British release)

And I Love Her
Every Little Thing
For No One
Here, There and Everywhere
I Need You
I Will
I'll Be Back
I'll Follow The Sun
If I Fell
In My Life
It's Only Love
The Long and Winding Road
Michelle
Norwegian Wood
P.S. I Love You
She's Leaving Home
Something
Tell Me What You See
This Boy
Words of Love
Yes It Is
Yesterday
You're Gonna Lose That Girl
You've Got To Hide Your Love Away

Rarities

Capitol SHAL 12060
March 1980

Across the Universe
And I Love Her
Don't Pass Me By
Help!
Helter Skelter
I Am The Walrus
I'm Only Sleeping
The Inner Light
Love Me Do
Misery
Penny Lane
Sie Liebt Dich
There's a Place
You Know My Name (Look Up My Number)

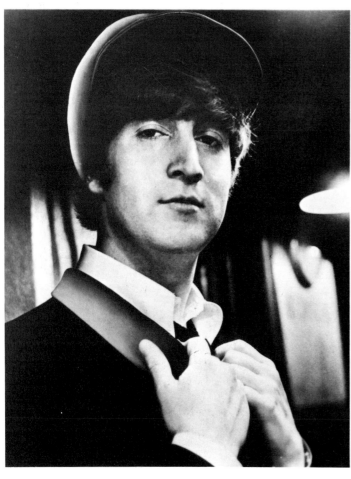
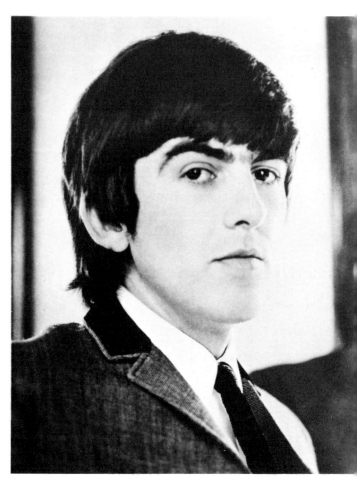

To (Be)atles Or Not To (Be)atles

And after that what changes what changes after that, after that what changes and what changes after that and after that and what changes and after that and what changes after that.

—Gertrude Stein

Composition as Explanation

There is no precedent in the history of popular music for the dazzling variety, versatility, innovation and relentless genius of the music composed and recorded by the Beatles, between 1962 and 1970. And we have to go back to Elizabethan England to find an adequate analogy to the profound, mysterious interpenetration of artistic genius and cultural milieu that illuminates the relationship of Beatles music to its era. While not even William Shakespeare's plays hit the streets with the phenomenal impact of a new Beatles album, the parallels between the two (or the one and the four) are engaging.

Both Shakespeare and the Beatles were the subjects of rumors, hoaxes and mad speculations centering around who really wrote their works, because some people just couldn't believe in the genius of either. The Shakespeare hoaxes and speculations are notorious. And the Beatles gags are equally ludicrous. Someone had it that a little old man in a basement wrote all the Beatles' material. Better to have speculated, in view of the variety of Beatles music, that 200 little old men in basements did it. Another had it that the Russians devised Beatles rhythms to tear American young people in two and start the revolution. The Russians are clever devils, all right, but their minds just don't run to the likes of "She's A Woman" or "Day Tripper." Only we could tear ourselves up that good. And as for McCartney having been replaced by an android, take a listen to the "Golden Slumbers" sequence on the *Abbey Road* album, and ask yourself if any android you know can sing like that?

Anyway, the silly-rumors-parallel flows from another: neither Shakespeare nor the Beatles had classical training in their particular fields. This makes them suspicious characters. Shakespeare never went to college. Of the Beatles, only George Harrison had a little formal music training. Paul McCartney once explained the Lennon-McCartney song-writing collaboration like this: "Neither of us can read or write music. John will whistle at me. And I'll whistle back at him." When they started using trumpets, violins, French horns, full orchestras, and other things fancier than two guitars, a bass and drums, George Martin functioned as a friendly negotiator between the Beatles' busy brains and the strings quartets and so on. He recorded their first single, "Love Me Do/P.S. I Love You", making an exception for the Beatles by allowing them to record their own compositions. As the Beatles musical ambitions and complexity grew, Martin's function as producer, his musical knowledge, and his flexibility became increasingly important. The Beatles sometimes disorderly methods, and wildly inventive genius, found in Martin both a steadying influence and sympathetic bemused cooperation. But he did not write Beatles music.

Both Shakespeare and the Beatles started off in a youngster's genre—passionate poetry of love and sex—and leapt effortlessly into the full human comedy, as understood in their respective eras. Both Shakespeare and the Beatles worked in media that required constant and intricate cooperation with other people. Both were part of a company. And both had about them a certain amount of social and sexual androgyny that yielded inspired posturings as well as deep and wide emotional range.

Both Shakespeare and the Beatles were absorbent geniuses, taking in and utilizing whatever was in the air, and in both cases, the air was vibrant with rich, new, colorful language, new ideas that pointed to the human being as "the grace of form", new influences of all sorts and a ferment of activity in all the arts, society, politics and the world. Finally, and very importantly, both Shakespeare and the Beatles took a raw art form not too well regarded by classicists and the high-fallutin', and turned low-level comedy and Spanish tragedies, in the case of Shakespeare, into the finest literature ever written; while the Beatles turned rock and roll, and popular music in general, into the finest of arts, breaking all the rules they didn't know, and some they did; and bringing to popular song both rich musical variety, thematic seriousness and compassion, and acute observation of the human mystery.

As the Theater was held in contempt by some people in the Sixteenth century, so rock and roll has taken its knocks in the Twentieth. Shakespeare and the Beatles changed all that, proving that artistic genius can, and often does, arise in the most unlikely places, transforming whatever it finds there into something for all time.

Well you can celebrate anything you want…
Yes you can penetrate any place you go.

The Beatles both reflected and created their era. And while it is impossible to know if Beatles music will weather 400 years of changing tastes and opinions, it is a good guess that the computer chips inside the starships of the future will hold not only *Hamlet* and Beethoven's Fifth Symphony, but also—well—which Beatles album would *you* most like to have with you on a starship?

All Together Now

The Beatles re-surfaced the mirror in which we see ourselves. We changed almost overnight from a society of lone cowboys into a society of communities. *All together now/Altogether-now/All Together now/Altogether-now*, sang the Beatles. To be together as a group, each contributing something to the artistic creation, was better than to be alone—much better. In fact, to be lonely seemed, to the generation of be-in's, sit-in's, love-in's, marches and happenings, an especially appalling fate.

All the lonely people/where do they all come from? sang the Beatles in "Eleanor Rigby". The high jump note for "do", copied exactly into the music from the spoken language, reflects a collective raised Beatle eyebrow, looking with compassion and sensitivity out from their warm friendly group to the lonely others. The song opens with a collective sigh, *A-a-a-ah, look at all the lonely people*. On the Beatles recording, the "n" of "lonely" is so lightly touched that it dissolves into "lovely". Since the Beatles, during this middle period, generally practiced meticulous enunciation of their words, one can construe this rare slur as meaningful— all the lovely, lonely people. The submerged passion reminds one of Puccini.

The song moves out of pathos by focussing our attention on beautifully drawn portraits of two specific characters—Eleanor Rigby and Father MacKenzie. In a melody remarkable for being composed of only two chords, the tonic E minor and VI major C, with no subdominant or dominant chords and no real cadence, a story is created by the juxtaposition of character description in the lyrics. And the lyrics are studded with gems such as the brilliant, *Waits at the window/wearing the face that she keeps in a jar by the door*. Who hasn't heard somebody's mother say, "I'm going to put on my face," meaning make-up? Whoever thought that she might literally be doing that, that she has no face but for the paint she puts on? "Let her paint an inch thick," says Hamlet, as he is looking at his old friend's skull in a graveyard, "To this Favor she must come." And finally, whoever thought a young rock and roll group would point this out, or choose to illuminate the tragic fates of an old maid and a failure of a priest, with *No one was saved?*

It was not all that surprising when an individual poet, such as Bob Dylan, got up and sang about the strange characters he knew or imagined ("Mr. Jones" et al). This is to be expected of a poet, once you accept a popular musician as a poet—an idea Dylan did something to further. But a group poet? A rock group that could act as one poet? A composing team that fed each other words, or lines, or bars of music, or half-completed songs, and came out with such works of genius as "Penny Lane" and "A Day In The Life"? And furthermore, a collaborative effort on material not only dealing with characters and events imagined in the third person, but a collaborative effort on material dealing directly with first person singular emotion, event, state of mind, love life and love loss?

Well, this is exactly what the Beatles appeared to do. They presented their private emotional experience as group material. And this had simply never been done before. John Lennon and Paul McCartney, who composed most of the Beatles songs, signed all their work Lennon-McCartney, and that double signature represents an interaction (with each other, and with the other Beatles) far more complex than the linked names of most other composing teams. Their lists of who did what—which they tried to sort out long after the Beatles disbanded—are riddled with such phrases as, "He wrote the middle eighth," or "I supplied the line …", or "I had the basic theme, but he helped me with the lyric." They certainly did compose separately at times, and developed distinguishable styles for certain genres. But for most of the Beatles career together, they were constantly tinkering with each other's work, or simply co-writing, sometimes writing every other phrase of a song.

For a time, the Beatles perceived themselves as one mind, or four parts of the same person. And, of equal importance, the Beatles were perceived by their audience this way, as: fire, air, water and earth; or mind, heart, soul and body; or lyric, melody, chord and beat; John, Paul, George and Ringo—one self-reflecting soul. As they put this new mirror up to us, we saw ourselves collectively for a while, or at least as collective members of Sgt. Pepper's *lovely audience*.

The Beatles did not effect this social transformation by themselves, but they certainly became its generally accepted apotheosis. Their influence in the music world was equally profound and definitive. They took rock music right to the outer limit of achievement, then went on to create a new music all their own. They changed the face of popular music completely, and reset all the precedents for just about everything in recording history and in entertainment. Their influence on society and on entertainment was paralleled by the exhilarating inventiveness of Beatles music itself.

They tore up all the rule books for songwriting, establishing, for instance, that you can change meter effortlessly in almost every bar of a song ("All You Need Is Love"—4/4 to 3/4 or 3/4 to 4/4), or that you can change bar patterns in the middle of a song and get away with it ("Day Tripper") without tripping over your feet, or losing your audience. They established that you can vary bar patterns (from the normal 32) in popular song, that you can spin a very witty yarn ("Drive My Car"), that you can create drama and first person narration in song ("Paperback Writer"), write a soap opera ("She's Leaving Home"), conduct a three-ring circus (*Sgt. Pepper's Lonely Hearts Club Band*), a tragic mini rock-opera (*Abbey Road*), make love in song ("I Want You [She's So Heavy]"; "Helter Skelter"), and do all of these things and many more with a whole new repertoire (for pop and rock) of chords, structures and instruments, including sitar, anvil, washtub, paper and comb, bubbles, and the recording machines themselves.

Their songs chronicled not only their good and bad emotional experiences ("She Loves You", "Good Day Sunshine"; "I'm A Loser", "I'm Down"), their experiences and fantasies as a group ("Yellow Submarine", "With A Little Help From My Friends"), their dizzying rise to fame and fortune ("Can't Buy Me Love", "Baby, You're A Rich Man", "Taxman"), but also the Beatles reflected the "tuned-in, turned-on" experiences of the whole '60's generation—and sometimes took the brunt of generational conflict. The BBC saw fit to ban the Beatles masterpiece, "A Day In The Life" for its line, "I'd love to turn you on." Most listeners, however, accepted the line, and admired the music, as a paradigmatic expression of their own desires.

The Beatles were very privileged artists, indeed. Their works appeared on some 545 million albums and singles throughout the world. Their creations dominated the radios and stereos of the world for seven solid gold years. Their records were anticipated and received with great joy by an audience of millions who instantly incorporated new Beatles creations into their lives. Many peoples' most vivid remembrances of the 1960's are laced with Beatles tunes.

This love-in began in a world that had grown rather suddenly cold. Into the post-Camelot malaise created by President John Kennedy's assassination in 1963, the Beatles poured their heartfelt "I Want To Hold Your Hand", breaking upon the world scene (in early 1964) like a refreshing and renewing ocean wave. They brought joy, wit, exuberance and optimism, not to mention great new rock and roll. When they belted out that first world-wide hit, the rock-out energy of the octave jump to the word "hand" told everybody with ears that although this gentlemanly request was tender and rather modest, the proposed touch would fire the whole being. The emotional level of the whole society went up an octave. The pure, high ecstasy of "hand" was kept on earth at the same time by the beat underneath "hand" coming straight from sexually and culturally rebellious rock and roll. The Beatles brought cool and wit, hope and fun, and something else.

It is interesting to note, and also significant to their later musical development, that while fans screamed in an orgy of sexual-religious idolatry, the Beatles themselves just stood there and sang and played. They seemed to be observing more than they were being observed. Taking a good look at other people was one of their most important, and interesting, qualities. They bounced a little, but they didn't shake, rattle and roll. They looked excited and pleased with themselves, but not in any sort of frenzy. Unlike hot Elvis Presley (whom they admired), the Beatles were cool.

But let there be no mistake. Along with the choir-boy look, and the relatively calm demeanor (for rockers), came music that electrified its listeners. The initial inspiration of Beatles music can be heard quite plainly in Paul McCartney's tear-up-the-house version of Johnson-Penniman-Blackwell's "Long Tall Sally", and John Lennon's raucous rendition of Berry-Gordy-Bradford's "Money". That this initial inspiration, and rootedness in raw rock and roll, metamorphosed in seven years

into the superb and sophisticated mini rock-opera of *Abbey Road* (Side Two) is truly a miracle of artistic growth. But the roots and the final result should be seen as one movement. The Beatles loved rock and roll, and returned to it again and again, in attempts to "get back" to their initial inspiration.

What a package they were—a marriage of lower class Liverpool, British polish, Elizabethan lust for life, and American soul, and just the right catalytic mix of radiant innocence and revolt against straight-laced restraint. Their music held just the right tension of love, sex, melody and drive to capitalize on the general social loosening that characterized the 1960's.

The first hints of the Beatles incredible creativity were there in this new ice and fire style, but very importantly, the hint of things to come was there from the beginning in their extraordinary melodies. "All My Loving", "And I Love Her", and "I Want To Hold Your Hand", are fine melodies by any historical standard. They hold up extremely well over the years, played by anyone. The melody of "All My Loving" (by McCartney) has the elegance of a Sixteenth century art song. And there were also hints of innovations to come in the almost painfully high harmonies of Lennon's "Please Please Me" and McCartney's "I Saw Her Standing There", and in the excellent orchestration of lyrics, lyric echoes, harmonies and instruments in Holland-Bateman-Gordy's "Please Mr. Postman", and in the puns and word-play in "Eight Days A Week" or "A Hard Day's Night".

The Beatles clean, soft, puffy mops of hair asked to be petted. Their straight suits said don't touch, while their music said do. This emotional tug-of-war was reflected in that same single, "I Want To Hold Your Hand", in the sweet, restrained, boyish line, *And when I touch you I feel happy inside*, sung with simplicity, one carefully enunciated word per note except for the second syllable of "happy" which is brought up fast. This touching restraint is then let loose at the end of the subsequent line, *It's such a feeling that my love I can't hide, I can't hide....* when on the third "I can't hide," there is an octave jump again, and a high howl of desperation in the height of the note and in the harmony.

In the early Beatles songs, a careful listener can hear also a variety of musical styles and points of view that foretell the Beatles later virtuosity, even though there is really only one topic in the early lyrics. From the surprising rhythms and dissonance of "Love Me Do" (the Beatles first recording, written by Paul at age 16), to the delightful opening bars of "I Saw Her Standing There" *Well she she was just seventeen / And you know what I mean...*—What a knowing wink there is in those lines!); from the quaint, joyous, quintessential "She Loves You (yeah, yeah, yeah)", to the agitated simplicity of "Hold Me Tight"; from the bright energy of "She's A Woman" and "Can't Buy Me Love", to the darker revelations of "I Call Your Name" and "A Hard Day's Night", and dozens of other songs, sexual experience and inexperience is laid open from every side. With ever-increasing musical and poetic sophistication, the Beatles explore every facet of youthful sexuality—desire, joy, frustration, pain, jealousy, ennui, comedy, boredom, ecstasy—you name it. This theme finally reaches maturity in the tender pathos of "Yesterday", the sweet irony of "Norwegian Wood", and the exquisite beauty of "Here, There and Everywhere" (to make a stunning comeback in later Beatles music, in the obsessive desire of "I Want You (She's So Heavy)", and the sexual devastation and recovery of "Hey Jude".)

But the Beatles, who were uniquely sensitive to the nuances of words, always called it, and meant it to be understood, as *love love love/love love love/love love love*. By the late 1960's, and largely through the artistic, emotional and intellectual growth of the Beatles, the word "love" came to mean peace for the whole world.

Clearly they believed there was a connection between their early insistence on romantic love and desire as pervasive themes and their later placarding of love as a political act and as a political philosophy. While John Lennon was the most vocal and visible of the four Beatles in making the connection overt, Paul McCartney probably made the larger artistic contribution to this particular thematic connection in Beatles music, by the highly developed Romantic sensibility reflected in his songs, and by his crucial role in the production of *Sgt. Pepper's Lonely Hearts Club Band*. But the four Beatles were of one mind about it. The connection is there in the music, linking songs together, in the words, in the collaboration, and in the performance by all of the Beatles.

Their ultimate vision of a world community united in love and peace is problematic now, and was probably problematic then. The difference is that it was believed in then. The Beatles became personally synonymous with the era in which Hippies stuck flowers into the death end of soldiers' rifles. And when the Beatles disbanded in 1970, the passionate yearning by many fans for the Beatles to reunite (the price for one concert of reunited Beatles got up to more than fifty million dollars), and the Beatles' adamant refusal, perfectly mirrored the post-coital sadness of the love generation as it pushed sometimes despairingly toward middle age. The break-up of the Beatles went on and on, like a messy divorce (along with the rumors of the never-to-be reunion). And it paralleled, and seemed to mirror, the social conflict and disintegration in the rest of the world in 1970. If the Beatles couldn't keep it together, who could? That's how magnetic they seemed to be.

And yet, for one brief shining moment that had also held on and on, like the codas to "A Day In The Life" and "Hey Jude", the Beatles provided their insatiable listeners with a rapturous glissando of album after album—*Rubber Soul, Revolver, Sgt. Pepper's Lonely Hearts Club Band, Magical Mystery Tour, The White Album, Abbey Road, Let It Be*—and the world had indeed seemed to be a better place. The mirror they re-surfaced showed a fuller, richer, more creative and more fertile human community than anybody had dreamed before. For that long lovely moment, it truly seemed, *There's nothin' you can do that can't be done./There's nothin' you can sing that can't be sung … It's easy.*

Innocence and Experience: The Magical Collaboration

The Beatles musical collaboration is an intriguing mystery. What remarkable chemistry lay behind the Lennon-McCartney song-writing partnership to produce such a spectacle of creativity? How in fact did the collective persona of the Beatles work to create a body of songs that is at once so musically diverse and so thematically coherent?

A lot of nonsense, including some nonsense by Beatles themselves, has been spoken and written about the musical collaboration since the Beatles disbanded in 1970. John Lennon, for instance, who had claimed after the heat of the break-up that he and Paul McCartney had stopped any real collaboration very early, later admitted in a *Playboy* interview that, "I was lying," and that, in fact, a large portion of the Lennon-McCartney songs were composed "eyeball to eyeball." In the wake of Lennon's tragic death in 1980, a great many misinformed obituarists perpetrated the seriously unfair and misleading notion that Lennon was the "leader" of the Beatles—hardly a fitting epitaph for a man whose sense of justice had led him to admit his misstatements in public, and who had tried to correct them.

Among both major and lesser Beatles songs that are largely attributable either to Lennon or to McCartney, the numbers are about equal, balanced as well by a good many jointly composed songs, and a huge percentage of songs in which one helped the other with some portion of the composition. Further, it becomes overwhelmingly clear from a wide variety of sources on the Beatles history (including Lennon himself), that, but for McCartney, we might not have any Beatles music from 1967 to 1970. 1967 is the year in which McCartney began to act in some senses as both manager and orchestrator.

However, Beatles music is best understood as the jointly composed expression of a group of artists. While the emergence of McCartney as production leader in the middle Beatles period did quite a lot to further the coherent presentation of Beatles music, and may indeed have been instrumental in its creation, his leadership is stressed here because it has not been given due credit in the popular press. Lennon and McCartney traded off leadership roles and duties from the very beginning, while George Harrison and Ringo Starr made their own unique contributions to the group and to the music. In fact, a proper understanding of the Beatles group dynamics is very important to a proper understanding of the music itself. When people identify Lennon as the "leader" of the Beatles, they betray not only of the facts, but also of a very important Beatles quality, message and theme: unity.

The Beatles' togetherness, and their creativity, got its initial impetus from the kids "gangs," and the little skiffle bands, in Liverpool in the 1950's. Their special creativity evidenced itself as soon as they became active members of the Liverpool rock and roll scene. Paul McCartney and John Lennon wrote one hundred songs together in their early days, between 1956 and 1959. That was just their warm-up, for of these only "Love Me Do" was ever recorded. During that time, and later, they were also becoming rather completely versed in all the pop, rock and roll, country and western, and rhythm and blues music around them, so that they and the other Beatles could go through a repertoire of hundreds of others' songs as they warmed up for their own later performances and recordings. Beatles original composition prior to *Rubber Soul*, then, is an outgrowth of the several pop musical traditions in which the Beatles grew up as a performing group, enriched by their own considerable powers of invention.

However, the Beatles created their own distinct sound from very early on, both in their interpretation of others' work, and in their own compositions. There is some little imitation in their early songs. "Baby's In Black," and "Eight Days Of The Week," for instance, are variations of the over-ripe metaphor to be found in songs like Drapkin's "Devil In Her Heart," and Johnson's "Mr. Moonlight" (both recorded by the Beatles). While "Help!" seems to be a musical imitation of Gerry Goffin and Carole King's "Chains" (which the Beatles also recorded; Lennon and McCartney at one time aspired to be the new Goffin and King, a popular song-writing team of the 1950's).

But the Beatles own early recorded compositions were distinguished largely by the directness and honesty of emotion in the lyrics ("I Need You"; "Tell Me What You See"), by the stark simplicity of the lyrics ("Love Me Do"; "Please Please Me"; "And I Love Her"), by the startlingly inventive and beautiful melodies (often by McCartney), by the rich harmonies, by the wide range of chords, and in performance, by the sheer rock and roll energy of their interpretations.

In energetic rock songs like "Ticket To Ride" and "Day Tripper," Lennon early demonstrated an ability to turn the odd metaphor to good use, as his interest in playful, punny and funny language began to surface in Beatles lyrics. Simultaneously, Lennon showed an increasing depth of emotion, in such songs as the painful "You've Got To Hide Your Love Away" and "It's Only Love."

McCartney had wider musical interests and talents, and in fact (according to Lennon) encouraged Lennon to introduce a larger variety of notes and chords into his compositions. And Lennon had a way with words, published two books of witty fables, and concentrated on lyrics. But it is incorrect to characterize this song-writing team as music by McCartney and lyrics by Lennon. They both did both, and very well indeed.

As the Beatles mythology began to emerge—that the four lads were four personae of one unified whole—the function of the quiet, lovable drummer, Ringo Starr, became clearer, starting with his rendition of Russell-Morrison's "Act Naturally"—a perfect Ringo song. Certain Beatles songs were written by the Lennon-McCartney team just for Starr's low-range,

common-man voice. Because of who he was, and how he interacted with the others in the group, "Yellow Submarine" and "With A Little Help From My Friends" were eventually created—the two most important songs in Beatles mythology (beside the song, "Sgt. Pepper's Lonely Hearts Club Band"). This is a very important point in understanding how Beatles music was created. It mattered *who* you were in connection with the others, as well as what instrument you played.

Certainly the most memorable and popular song from this period in Beatles music is Paul McCartney's ballad, "Yesterday", one of the earliest in a long line of beautiful McCartney ballads, and one of the Beatles songs most covered by other artists. McCartney went into the studio to record it with George Martin, a string quartet, and without the other Beatles—marking another set of firsts in Beatles history.

The Lennon-McCartney musical collaboration is a mystery that may be, and should be, and will be (herein) explored, but it can never be fully sorted out. Some songs are assignable—and "Yesterday" is one—but this usually means that the credited man was the *primary* composer. (This is also true of early Harrison songs.)

McCartney woke up one morning with the tune for "Yesterday" in his head, but he didn't yet have the lyrics. He sat down to breakfast singing, "scrambled eggs" to himself, and so it remained for some time. It is an instructive little picture. As the tune spun around in his head, "scrambled eggs" stuck to it, because the syllables fit the notes, and maybe because the composer was hungry—food being a matter of more urgency at the moment than love or its loss. The rest of the story is not known. Perhaps he fiddled with it for a while, then forgot about it until he ran into his friend John: "Hey, Paul, what was that little ditty you were humming yesterday?"

Something like that happened, and "Yesterday" was born. In any case, that is how most of the other Lennon-McCartney songs were written—because the two of them were there. Very often songs were written on the spot in a guitar jam session, with both of them singing out any old words (as they did to their German audiences in Hamburg) until the right phrases emerged.

"Yesterday," with its richly textured harmonies, and its more mature and experienced view of love, served as a sort of prelude to the next development in Beatles music, the soulful album, *Rubber Soul* (1965). Suddenly, the simplicity of Beatles lyrics had made a quantum leap to profundity.

I'm looking through you/Where did you go?/I thought I knew you/What did I know?, sang McCartney in his philosophical "I'm Looking Through You". And in his witty "Norwegian Wood", Lennon sang *I once had a girl/or should I say/she once had me.* The boy-meets-girl convention went into the background in other songs. Friendship and nostalgia came forward as themes for "In My Life" (co-written by Lennon and McCartney).

And in Harrison's song, "Think For Yourself", love is altogether dropped as a theme, in favor of admonition. In addition, the arrangements of melody, echoes and harmonies had matured into elegant integrations of sound, such as, "You Won't See Me," and "Wait". The ecstatic harmony of "I Want To Hold Your Hand" became the indistinguishable blend of harmony and melody in "The Word". "The Word" (by John and Paul) also announced the single most significant development in Beatles philosophy: Romantic love had grown into universal love.

Everywhere I go I hear it said
In the good and the bad books that I have read
Say the word and you'll be free
Say the word and be like me
Say the word I'm thinking of
Have you heard the word is love?

In *Rubber Soul*, this already fabulously successful rock group was taking a good look at itself, was asking itself adult questions, and was distilling its own finest musical and lyrical qualities. *Rubber Soul* is mellow wine indeed. And the rich blend of the different maturing talents and personalities makes the album all of a piece. The Beatles were making a group statement: "We are growing up."

Revolver, the next year's album (1966), made another quantum leap. The Beatles had already established themselves as the finest popular composers and musicians of their age. With *Revolver*, they became the finest of contemporary poets. There are so many brilliant songs on *Revolver* that it is difficult to be selective. To begin with, *Revolver* introduced that all-time favorite, "Yellow Submarine," a combination of McCartney's catchy chorus and Lennon's blunderbuss, sung by Ringo in (what is now) his famous Billy Shears style. "Yellow Submarine" is the Beatles tune that is best loved and most sung by children; and the one by which the Beatles first demonstrated their wonderful enjoyment of each other's company. It instantly became a metaphor for the Beatles themselves.

Certainly "Eleanor Rigby" (largely by McCartney) well deserves its fame. "The Word" on *Rubber Soul* was "love", and "Eleanor Rigby" on *Revolver* is a devastating expression of love's absence, as well as a passionate expression of universal sympathy—*Ah! Look at all the lonely people!*

"Eleanor Rigby" is made all the more affecting by the creation of real, named characters, a practice that was to become one hallmark of Beatles music. Another song, "For No One"—notice the whine effected by the music on the words, *cried for no one*—is a perfect expression of intimate loss observed in the ordinary events of the day: *She wakes up, she makes up / She takes her time and doesn't feel she has to hurry / She no longer needs you.*

Wedded to these two songs of unhappiness, like yin and yang, are the songs of ecstasy, "Good Day Sun-

shine" and "Here, There and Everywhere", in which love of another takes on the power to flood the whole world with tenderness. It was after the release of *Revolver* that critics began rightly to talk about English Romantic poets Wordsworth and Blake in connection with Beatles music.

As Colin Campbell and Allan Murphy point out in their excellent Preface, "From Romance to Romanticism" (*Things We Said Today*, The Complete Lyrics and a Concordance to the Beatles' Songs, 1962-1970), it is difficult to find artistic analogies for the Beatles. They have been compared to all sorts of composers—Beethoven, Schumann, Schubert, Puccini, Mozart, Gilbert and Sullivan, Rogers and Hart, Goffin and King—and none of these analogies work very precisely, except for particular similarities. But very often, interestingly, it is the literary analogy that works best.

Middle and later Beatles music is very much concerned with words and ideas, and the lyrics reveal solutions to various life problems that are decidedly reminiscent of the English Romantic poets, particularly William Blake, whose mystical and magical view of nature, volatile emotional sensibility, innocence, primitivism, and anti-establishmentarianism, made him rather a pop hero to literary rebels in the 1960's. The Beatles inherited the Romantic philosophy, whether consciously ("...in the good and the bad books that I have read") or unconsciously (the unconscious being the favored psychic realm of the Romantics, in any case). Paul McCartney's rapturous Blakean songs to the beauty of nature and love, and John Lennon's rebelliousness and interest in heightened states of awareness—reflected so fully in the darks and lights of *Revolver*—add up to a rather thorough statement of classic Romanticism.

Death, Escape and Ecstasy

While McCartney was composing those Blakean songs of innocence and experience, Lennon was addressing the different, but related, topics of death and escape. Death finally enters the Beatles self-exploratory dialogue, by way of Lennon's "She Said She Said": *She said I know what it's like to be dead*. The composer exhibits rather a lot of ambiguity about conversations on the topic of death: *It's making me feel like I've never been born*. And true to the Romantic philosophy, he aims the death-talker in the other direction, to the golden age of boyhood, when *everything was right*.

In "Tomorrow Never Knows", Lennon points toward the next Beatles phase: escape from the death of ordinary life (another similarity with the Romantics) by way of psychedelic drugs. His increasing inventiveness, irony and wit, were demonstrated in songs like "And Your Bird Can Sing", "Doctor Robert", and I'm Only Sleeping" (which appeared on the United Kingdom *Revolver*, and in the United States on *The Beatles: Yesterday and Today*). "And Your Bird Can Sing" could well be seen as an admonitory reply to someone's bragging about his girl ("bird" meant "girl" in those days; while it also has phallic connotations), as well as a plea for communication. If anyone had doubts that the Beatles were launched into uncharted waters, the doubts were disproven by the next Beatles release, the stunning double A sided single: "Penny Lane/Strawberry Fields Forever".

"Penny Lane" (by McCartney) prepared listeners for the rich variety and dazzle of the *Sgt. Pepper* album to come, with a song of child-like wonder, treating us to a rainbow of colorful characters, from *the barber showing photographs* to the *pretty nurse... selling poppies from a tray* who feels *she's in a play*. The song laughs, *She is anyway*. The mood of the song is enhanced on recording by a delightful trumpet solo (Paul whistled it to George Martin who quickly wrote it down; Phillip Jones plays it perfectly), and also by the interplay of trumpet, clanging fire bell, and Paul's voice. On the final, heightened chorus, *Penny Lane is in my ears and in my eyes / There beneath the blue suburban skies*, McCartney's voice imitates the trumpet, creating a metallic ring of aural pleasure like no other Beatles performance.

While McCartney's "Penny Lane" seems decidedly upbeat compared to "Strawberry Fields Forever" (by Lennon), there is something a little whacky about the hallucinatory ecstasy in "Penny Lane". Studying the lyrics, one begins to wonder what exactly is going on *in the pouring rain...beneath the blue suburban skies*. "Penny Lane" takes the world in with the wide-eyed magical vision of a child, giving equal weight to all things "strange". Nothing adults do makes sense anyway. *...the banker never wears a mack / In the pouring rain — very strange*.

The song opens abruptly, as if by conjuring: *Penny Lane: There is a barber showing photographs*, and immediately becomes playful, *...of every head he's had the pleasure to know*. And although the playfulness has an undertone of sexual precocity, created by the words "head" and "pleasure", we are whisked away just in time by the friendly, *And all the people that come and go / Stop and say hello*. This ingenious and ingenuous peep show effect makes us want to laugh — *meanwhile back* — we have the chorus in our ears and our eyes, a clanging bell, a flash of sunlight, and we yield to the bright but elusive fairy tale images. We don't care what they mean. We are stripped of rational defenses against fantasy with the force of a potent magic wand, and opened forcefully, but pleasingly, to all-out sensual nostalgia.

"Strawberry Fields Forever", by Lennon, has exactly the opposite effect of its companion, "Penny Lane". Even discounting the electronic recording distortions on the Beatles version that add to its weird underwater sound, "Strawberry Fields Forever" is a strange and disturbing song. Its effect is to shut the listener out, or else to draw the listener unwillingly down in circles through its lyrics, its affectless thoughts looping back on themselves: *I think I know, I mean, er, yes / But it's all wrong / That is, I think I disagree*. There is a certain exhilaration and grandness in the opening of the music, *Let me take you down / 'cause I'm going to / Strawberry Fields*, and there is an attractive fairy tale flavor to the very title of the place. (Both Penny Lane and Strawberry Fields are real places in Liverpool, the scene of the Beatles' childhoods.) But quickly, the lyricist adds, *Nothing is real / and nothing to get hungabout*. This traps us into "misunderstanding" all we see (hear), for the lyric compresses the phrase "hung up about" — a phrase that in the 1960's often referred to sexual inhibitions or difficulties — into "hungabout" which has connotations of death by hanging, and poses the unsettling question: *What is nothing to get hung up about?*

The lyricist winks, *But, you know, I know when it's a dream*, but we are not all that comforted, and the net result is a sense of traumatic loneliness and confusion from which we want to escape. Affectless though the words are, however, the song is affecting. While "Penny Lane" brilliantly employed the Romantic ecstasy of nostalgia, in tune with the positive side of '60's "flower power", "Strawberry Fields Forever" boldly demonstrated the underside of '60's rebellion, the disturbing and uprooting effect of "changes".

In addition to their inherent and contrasting beauty, "Penny Lane" and "Strawberry Fields Forever" broke ground for the most important event in the history of popular music, the Beatles operetta, *Sgt. Pepper's Lonely Hearts Club Band*, by which they attempted to draw their complementary styles together into one vision.

—Milton Okun

Sgt. Pepper's Lonely

In 1967, *Sgt. Pepper's Lonely Hearts Club Band* rocked the world. The album came out in what was to become known as "the summer of love"—the heady summer of peace demonstrations and Hippie happenings. *Sgt. Pepper's Lonely Hearts Club Band* was its anthem. The Beatles had done it again. They were not only completely in tune with their constituency, but also *Sgt. Pepper* was the first miracle of studio recording technique, as well as the first concept album, conceived as a continuous tapestry of sound, or rock opera, to express the Beatles exhilarating but increasingly perilous condition as magical trailblazers in the ferris wheels world of the mid-1960's, and to express a possible alternative to falling: *I get by with a little help from my friends / I get high with a little help from my friends.* The inevitability of the rhyme scheme exonerates them a little bit from seeming to advocate what they seem to be advocating. "I", "by" and "high" have a certain poetic license issued to poets and Beatles.

The album title song is a Beatles self-description (*We're Sgt. Pepper's Lonely Hearts Club Band...*) It seemed to say that the Beatles, who appeared to have everything anybody could want, were stuck up there at the top, and despite all the razzle-dazzle of fame, they were *lonely.*

Wilfred Mellers observes of *Sgt. Pepper,* in his excellent book on Beatles music, *The Twilight Of The Gods:* "None of the songs is a love song". Love songs had been the predominant mode of Beatles music up to this point. The complete absence of this genre on *Sgt. Pepper* is remarkable. Of the "Sgt. Pepper" title song, Mellers writes that, although this opening number is full of fanfare, "...the music is far from being what it superficially seems. In tonality it is curiously ambiguous....This public show-case hides beneath its zest a certain jitteriness". These comments could well apply to the album as a whole (as Mellers demonstrates).

The glittery array of sounds, songs and spectacles introduced by "Sgt. Pepper" is presented as a Music Hall show, put on by those good-hearted and nutty gurus, Sgt. Pepper's Lonely Hearts, John, Paul, George and Ringo, in their latest incarnations. But the album whirls up and down and around the emotional scale like the dizzy solo dance of "Henry The Horse" in "Being For The Benefit Of Mr. Kite" (an effect created by electronic distortion of organ music). The key question being asked is sung by Ringo, representing all the Beatles in "With A Little Help From My Friends": *What would you do if I sang out of tune / Would you stand up and walk out on me?* The Beatles, ever full of tricks and double-meanings (beware!) were being both silly and serious. (Their "lovely audience" walk out on the Beatles? How silly! Be serious.) But behind their comedy and confidence lurked a secret pain. The distorting effects of their intense desire to please are evident everywhere on *Sgt. Pepper,* along with the brilliant artistic results consequent upon such extraordinary effort.

The overt message of *Sgt. Pepper* then—a delight in the sheer fun of entertaining, a narcissistic joy in each other's tricks and talents, an amused and tolerant view of others, and a belief that *our love can save the world* (as expressed in George Harrison's "Within You / Without You"—the oriental snake charmer at this carnival)—is accompanied by a covert message, a sigh of existential ennui, rather like that of the classic sad clown, or the trained horse whose fate it is to jump endlessly through hoops. Locked away from the outside world (the Beatles had retired from touring), they had huddled in the electronic cave of the studio, and conjured up a vision both of their own utopian and mystical conception of themselves, and of the tremulous waste-land world on which it teetered.

After the introduction of the band and its themes of vulnerability and loneliness, the first song suggests that one solution is to shut out unpleasantness and instead enjoy a vibrant fantasy experience. "Lucy In The Sky With Diamonds" (by Lennon) takes us to a place where *Rocking horse people / eat marshmallow pies* and *The girl with kaleidoscope eyes* appears and disappears. The rocket-like chorus has the same magic wand, sense-stripping effect as the chorus of "Penny Lane".

"She's Leaving Home" (also co-written) refers back to "With A Little From My Friends": *(Do you need anybody?) / I need somebody to love. / (Could it be anybody?) / I want somebody to love.* The man from "the motor trade" that the young woman leaves home for could well be described as "anybody". In a miracle of co-authorship, our two composers relate the story of the departing daughter and her bewildered parents in intricately woven lyrics that resemble the best ensemble acting, not unlike a good episode of "All In the Family", and with just as much ironic intent, evenly distributed sympathies and pathos.

"When I'm Sixty-Four" and "Lovely Rita" (both by McCartney) serve to fill out the cast of "lonely hearts" characters. "When I'm Sixty-Four" is a charming piece, and a more genuinely affectionate song than it is usually given credit for. It is a fanciful extension into old age of the theme of the opening song, "With A Little Help From My Friends". It does, however, indicate love's limits, rather than its fulfillment. *I could be handy mending a fuse / when your lights have gone,* indeed. "Lovely Rita", on the other hand, is somewhat darker than it sounds. The mood is positively barrelhouse bouncy, but the lyrics describe the absurdity and comedy of love in stark and ironic contrast to earlier Beatles music which had been largely a celebration of love, or at least had taken love quite seriously.

The reprise of the "Sgt. Pepper" song then reveals the group once more, energetically singing, *It's getting very near the end.* Lennon's and McCartney's voices rise in steeply pitched harmonies while they repeatedly emphasize the word "lonely" and "Sgt. Pepper's Lonely..." The reprise can be considered the group's intervention between the rather pointless extroversion of "Good Morning" and the more pertinent and poignant attempt to connect with the outside world in "A Day In The Life".

"A Day In The Life" seems at first to be a quite curious conclusion to the overall album. It is distinctly different from the Circus and Music Hall wonders of the rest of *Sgt. Pepper*. But "A Day In The Life", too, is a wonder. It is as if the Circus decided to have a little side show of moon rocks, or laser beams, to amaze with the future. It has been called a sonic montage.

"A Day In The Life" is quite pointed, however. It is Lennon's and McCartney's counterpoint, or reaction, to the illusory and magical tapestry of amusements, i.e. the foregoing album. While McCartney conducted the 41 piece orchestra, and George Martin fiddled with the knobs of his sonic machine, Lennon *read the news today, oh boy*. In an ironically sweet tune, punctuated by some fine drum work from Starr, the horrors of the dark world outside the Music Hall are revealed.

"A Day In The Life" is full of implied questions and fragments of reality (what Lennon read in the paper today; how McCartney rushed to work that morning), laced together by two sirens that musically lead the mind away from trouble: *I'd love to tu-u-u-urn yo-o-o-ou o-o-o-o-on*, and the ululating, *A-a-a-a-a-a-a-a-a-a-a-ah!*. The entire piece is an expression of the complicated riptides of being a Beatle, or of being anyone in the 1960's with its opposing currents of insistent driven Romanticism and conflicted social conscience, or of being Lennon and McCartney, with their increasingly divergent styles, interests and personalities.

But "A Day In The Life" offers its listeners no relief, really, from the musical and lyrical tension it presents. This is perhaps its most remarkable quality as a piece of music. It ends on an apocalyptic question mark, created by what sounds like an orchestral temper tantrum. The tense sonic build-up, and the forty-two second, foot-on-the-pedal crescendo in E major, may bear some relationship musically to the *I'd love to turn you on* siren, and to the hallucinatory *A-a-a-a-ah!*, but none of the three codas truly answers any of the questions that have been raised—except to suggest that the Beatles found *temporarily* satisfying diversions from their central problems, as expressed in a pre-*Sgt. Pepper* song ("Got To Get You Into My Life"): *What can I do? What can I be?*

Sgt. Pepper's Lonely Hearts Club Band answers: Well, you can be an entertainer. Its last cut, "A Day In The Life" asks: But is that enough?

The sonic ending may also be somewhat prophetic, for the tensions between togetherness ("Sgt. Pepper") and individuality ("A Day In The Life"), between magical mystery and naked reality, and between McCartney and Lennon, which are so deftly presented by the two, would eventually (over the course of several more albums) propel Lennon right out of the group.

The Walrus and The Carpenter

The *Magical Mystery Tour* period reveals the Beatles to be in some disarray, and also to be in varying states of reaction to the Beatles myth itself as it had been orchestrated by Paul McCartney in *Sgt. Pepper Lonely Hearts Club Band*. "Blue Jay Way" (by Harrison) expresses a moody longing for the party to get going again, although the lyric is dominated by images of fog and sleep.

Lennon's "I Am The Walrus" and McCartney's "The Fool On The Hill" present sharply contrasting styles and viewpoints on the problems of Beatles togetherness, although the two songs (as with so many Lennon and McCartney songs) fit together like two sides of a coin, and complement each other much like the images and characters in Lewis Carroll's poem, "The Walrus and The Carpenter", from which Lennon borrows a number of ideas.

Carroll spins a varnished tale around the odd goings on in his poem, "The Walrus and The Carpenter"; while Lennon's lyric in "I Am The Walrus" seems at first to be gibberish, held in line only by the perilous structure of the music which is almost without melody. "I Am The Walrus" introduces both a new lyric-dominated song style which Lennon will continue to develop throughout his career, and also it introduces a quality quite rare in Beatles music—repression.

The most significant fact that emerges from a comparison of "I Am The Walrus" with "The Walrus and The Carpenter" is that the Carpenter is missing from the equation in Lennon's lyric, and thus the intricate, balanced duality of imagery, and the duality of identity, in Carroll's poem is almost completely lacking in "I Am The Walrus", which resembles a mad-song wherein the poor deranged one can speak only one side of the metaphor. Indeed, "I Am The Walrus" drives one a bit loony trying to figure it out.

There seems to be some sense in the opening lines. *I am he and you are he as you are me and we are all together*, either as a celebration of togetherness (recalling McCartney's "All Together Now"), or as a signal of acute confusion of identity, the latter being more probable in view of the rest of the song lyric's content. Also, the later verse, *Sitting in an English garden waiting for the sun / If the sun don't come you get a tan from standing in the English rain*, would seem to be a complete thought. But what on earth does it mean?

In Carroll's poem, the Walrus says it is time "to talk of many things", and then he goes on to substitute nonsense like "whether pigs have wings" for real meaning. Both the Walrus and the Carpenter end up eating the poor foolish oysters—the Walrus knowingly and the Carpenter unknowingly. The Walrus is a deceiver, while the Carpenter airily ignores reality. The important point of the tale is that their differing viewpoints make no difference. They are one and the same actor finally.

By taking up the viewpoint of the Walrus, and suppressing that of the Carpenter, however, Lennon allows up from the unconscious mind all the nasty slimy refuse that the deceiver is hiding (*yellow matter custard / dripping from a dead dog's eyes*, and so on), and dumps it on the song as a sort of purgative to the psyche.

It is perhaps no accident that McCartney had pictured himself as a carpenter in the earlier song (on *Sgt. Pepper*) "Fixing A Hole". He can be seen as the missing half of the persona, or psyche, or metaphor in Lennon's "I Am The Walrus". And it is certainly no accident that Lennon mentions McCartney (in the defusing, confusing, amusing line, *"The Walrus was Paul"*) in a much later song, "The Glass Onion" (on *The White Album*), referring to several of McCartney's compositions, but most interestingly employing carpenter's terminology (*trying to make ends meet / trying to make a dovetail joint*) in what Lennon said was a compliment to McCartney for trying to keep the group together. (Beware of Beatles talking about their own songs[1])

McCartney's "The Fool On The Hill" presents a perfect character description of Lewis Carroll's Carpenter. While the Walrus bleats *goo goo g'joob* from his psychic refuse heap of images, the "Fool" stands in pristine isolation, suffering the fools around him with gentle tolerance, reacting with an apparently rational description of his situation (*He never shows his feelings; They don't like him*) remarkable for its almost complete lack of disturbing images, or images of any kind. "The Fool On The Hill" is clear like glass (a glass onion). And the "Fool" is alone, like the Carpenterless Walrus. But rather than having too much matter to deal with, the "Fool" creates a spinning (*round 'n' round 'n' round*) world out of airy nothing. "The Fool On The Hill" is one of McCartney's simplest, most haunting, and most beautiful melodies, presenting a yin/yang, ego/id, air/fire, light/dark contrast with Lennon's "I Am The Walrus."

In the commonly held complimentary theory about Lennon and McCartney, McCartney is held to be essentially a sweet, easy personality, with a highly developed Romantic philosophy and with a genius for whipping nostalgic melodies into exquisite ballads, or into high, weepy or bouncy camp; while Lennon is held to be more of a rocker, interested in the wallop of a driving tune, out to teach the world a lesson with exploding metaphors and charged words. There is some truth in these descriptions. And yet, they tend to slip out of your grasp through the kaleidoscope of their interests and talents.

"Across the Universe", by Lennon, is one of the sweetest songs written. "Julia", which Lennon wrote about his mother, is one of the weepiest. Lennon had a hand in writing "Michelle". He had a finger or two in "Penny Lane". And there is not a friendlier nor more nostalgic lyric in Beatles music than "In My Life". Which composer is the softy?

On the other hand, McCartney could ape the Rolling Stones in a hard rock number like "Why Don't We Do It In The Road", could thrust out a wicked voice on occasion, as in his ironical "Oh! Darling", and could simply freak out in a tongue-in-cheek orgasm like "Helter Skelter". He was the one who caused the bloody fist fights, back when, with his wild rendition of "Long Tall Sally". Which one is the hard rocker?

Furthermore, one cannot always be sure when one of these two composers is mimicking, parodying, or commenting on the other's work or experiences. For instance, "The Fool On The Hill" and "I Am The Walrus" could be McCartney and Lennon looking at *each other's* experiences, through a glass onion darkly. Confusing? Well, it may have been equally confusing to them. For each of the Beatles felt an intense group identity, as well as individual identities, and their music is an expression of the interaction of the two.

We sometimes get the clearly distinguishable viewpoints of each composer in a co-written song, such as "I've Got A Feeling", "We Can Work It Out", and the previously mentioned "A Day In The Life". At other times, the influences and viewpoints are indistinguishably fused, as in "The Word", "Yellow Submarine", "With A Little Help From My Friends", and "Baby, You're A Rich Man". "Getting Better", "She Loves You", are good candidates to suggest that we may sometimes be getting Lennon's experience interpreted by McCartney, or vice versa.

Whether or not these under-currents and cross-currents can be sorted out, they certainly do add dimension to our understanding of the works themselves. One of the finest qualities of Beatles music is its direct, passionate and sometimes savagely honest emotionality. And the people the Beatles knew best, for a good part of their career, under the sometimes frightening pressure of their fame—the people the Beatles would most likely have had strong emotions toward, were each other. The strong bonds between the makers of this music have a great deal to do with its emotional strength and effectiveness.

How did this emotionality get translated so directly into the music? From late 1966 to the conclusion of their career together, the Beatles seldom performed music in front of anyone but each other, or others closely connected to the Beatles in a tightly closed circle. They were thus liberated, in terms of their musical development, to experiment freely, even wildly, and to express themselves freely, and even wildly. No one but their good buddies was there to censor. (And when others were introduced into their recording sessions, troubles very quickly arose.) They achieved the sort of spontaneous, free-wheeling style that is characteristic of Black, Blues and Jazz artists. Only these white Englishmen had to go into seclusion to achieve it. (They had been there once before, in their wild, anything goes, Hamburg performances—a formative experience, and one that they recalled with great relish.) Unfortunately, this same circumstance—the air-tightness of the group—led eventually to its demise.

The intensity of the Beatles identification with each other is certainly indicated in various ways by many songs. The miracle of the collaboration, both of Lennon and McCartney, and of all four Beatles, is that along with the symbiotic personae, they each achieved and maintained a strong personal and artistic identity.

"Hey Jude/ Revolution"

Despite the intricacies of the Lennon-McCartney collaboration, there are some songs that epitomize each

141

composer's strengths and virtues. "Hey Jude", by McCartney, and "Revolution", by Lennon, are two excellent examples of their individual, matured musical powers.

With "Hey Jude", McCartney brings to fruition all of his genius for creating plaintive song. And he brings the themes of love, sensitivity and compassion to bear on friendship itself. Or does he finally leap into adulthood by regarding *himself* with compassion—after all those love ballads to others? When he first played "Hey Jude" for Lennon, there was a perfectly beautiful mix-up about whose life situation the song was appropriately addressed to. (John said, "It's me! It's me!" Paul said, "No, it's me.") All agree that "Hey Jude" started its life as "Hey Jules", while McCartney was on his way to visit Lennon's son Julian. But the lyrics are so masterfully written that they can be applied with emotional validity to a great variety of lives and situations. *Hey Jude, don't make it bad./ Take a sad song and make it betta-a-ah.*

The Beatles recording of "Hey Jude" is one of the greatest single sellers in recording history. It is doubtful that anyone could record a better version. But one never knows. Perhaps the most remarkable thing about "Hey Jude" is its essential simplicity. It is a lovely and easily performable ballad.

While Lennon's "Revolution" presents quite a marked contrast to "Hey Jude" in theme and style, "Revolution" too is a great, performable song. Lennon himself recognized that his songs were sometimes more idiosyncratic and less singable than McCartney's. This was due in part to Lennon's practice of running too many words flat out over the melody (as in "I The Walrus"). "Revolution" is a notable exception, an excellent melody, and a very catchy, exuberant and singable song.

The music of "Revolution" has seductive simplicity, lifted right from the Beatles' own rock and roll tradition. And to emphasize the correspondence between non-violence and sexy music, Lennon brings in an outrageously funny chorus of *Oh Shoo-be-do-a, Oh shoo-be-do-a,* sung in affectionately mocking Beach Boys style. It is very difficult to listen to the song without rocking.

While "Revolution" may not qualify as Lennon's greatest song, it is certainly exemplary of his most heart-felt intention—to weld political action, non-violence, and music together in a personal demonstration of his beliefs. *You ask me for a contribution.... We-e-ell....You know....We're all doing what we can.* Quickly, in staccato fashion, he adds, *But if you want money for people with minds that hate/Don't you know that you can count me out.* And in the chorus he creates an insistent falsetto declaration: *Don't you know it's gonna...,* with an octave jump to *be,* and a reassuring descent to *al-right.* "Revolution" preaches and pets, sounds off and turns on, wags a finger and grasps a hand, admonishes and reassures, and thus draws us, by the very strength of his personality so perfectly expressed by this music, into sympathy and agreement with his compellingly non-violent message.

The Wit of White

With *The White Album* aka *The Beatles,* or *The Double Album,* the Beatles set out to create a work as unlike *Sgt. Pepper* as possible. (Its whiteness is significant in view of *Sgt. Pepper's* elaborate and expensive album jacket.) And they succeed. *The White Album* takes pop and rock music, and the Beatles own musical history, apart, piece by piece. Although this was an act of self-alienation—and almost, one might say, of aggression—their dismemberment of pop and rock, and of themselves, is quite brilliantly done. The album is rich in bemused and blatant self-parody and inter- and intra-group mockery.

McCartney's nutty "Ob-La-Di, Ob-La-Da" is a funny send-up of Lennon's social conscience at work upon the bourgeosie, and also it is a parallel parody (on the same album with) Harrison's "Piggies", a song that oink-oinks about the upper middle class, as "Piggies" itself may be a parody of political rock.

"Happiness Is A Warm Gun" is a gorgeous bit of self-mockery by Lennon, that works simultaneously as a serious song about sexual violence. It is one of the finest performances on the album (said to be McCartney's favorite), particularly in its use of falsetto, and of caesura, in the final phrases of the song.

"Helter Skelter" may be McCartney's answer to Harrison's "Savoy Truffle". Harrison's song—a gooey doodad about rich desserts and painful cavities—mentions McCartney's "Ob-La-Di, Ob-La-Da." "Helter Skelter" combines the child-like fun of a ride down a playground slide (called a "helter-skelter" in Great Britain) with the wild orgasmic cry, *Do you, don't you want me to make you?* by which McCartney may have been trying to fuse two separate characteristics of his music— guilelessness and frenzy; and he may have also been re-asserting his ability to do a "heavy" rock number. He also contributes a quite silly and moving love song to his dog, "Martha My Dear".

"Dear Prudence" seems very like Lennon mocking McCartney (as "Helter Skelter" may also be a comment on Lennon's music). "Rocky Racoon" and "The Continuing Story of Bungalow Bill", by McCartney and Lennon respectively, have obvious resemblances. Both shoot arrows at other, primarily American, targets.

"Back In The U.S.S.R." is McCartney doing in the Beach Boys, after which he turns his genius for mimickry on the Rolling Stones, in "Why Don't We Do It In The Road?" He laughs affectionately at folksingers in "Mother Nature's Son", creating a quite lovely little song in the process; while Lennon aims straight at the heart of commercialized rock and roll in "Everybody's Got Something To Hide Except Me and My Monkey". "Glass Onion", by Lennon, in addition to its other puzzling and revealing characteristics, may be a nod in the direction of Bob Dylan, whom the Beatles admired, and whose lyrical complexity, and meaningfulness—and occasional obscurity—influenced Beatles lyrics.

And so on. *The White Album* itself is a helter-skelter of cross-references, and a Monty Python's Flying Circus of bizarre inventiveness—brilliant, devastating, affectionate and weird, all at once.

The "Invisible Singer"

On *The White Album* (which is notorious for its eccentricities—"Birthday", "Revolution 9", and "Good-night", for some) one of the most musically idiosyncratic recordings is George Harrison's version of his own "Long, Long, Long". An extraordinarily soft voice (Harrison's) whispers and echoes the lyrical, *It's been a long, long, long time/How could I ever have lost you*, which is then punctuated—one should say punctured—by distinctly foreground bam-bam's from drummer Starr. The watery, almost invisible voice, and the instruments, in the end resolve into an eery, ghostly wail after the final line, *Oh I love you*, bammed one more time by one drum beat. The total effect of the recording is to stand one's hair on end.

George Harrison, who functioned in the vital spot of lead guitar throughout the Beatles career together, was responsible not only for introducing the Beatles to Transcendental Meditation (which followed their drug period, and may have helped them out of it), but also for introducing the sitar and other exotic instruments into Beatles production. He eventually had to teach himself Eastern notation so that he could communicate with the Indian musicians he brought into the studio. The sitar was first used to lace the ironic strains of Lennon's "Norwegian Wood". The influence of Raga on Beatles music reaches its apogee with "Within You/Without You", on the *Sgt. Pepper* album, and is largely absent from subsequent albums, in which Harrison returns to the basic instruments of old-fashioned rock and roll (albeit with fancy electronic equipment).

Harrison was known to the other Beatles as "the invisible singer", for in early Beatles music he frequently backed Lennon's and McCartney's vocals. He can also be described, for the early period of their career, as the almost invisible composer. With an incredibly feverish composing team like Lennon-McCartney spewing out songs every minute of the day, it is not surprising that Harrison caught the bug. As an apprentice writer, he was allotted one cut per album. As his skill and desire grew, so did his fight for album space—which struggle became one of the many overt issues in the Beatles break-up.

Harrison's first composition (pre-Indian influence) was "Don't Bother Me" (1963), one of the few early Beatles songs to throw a little cold water on the good fellowship. The lyrics are neatly put together. His girl has gone away, and he says, *So go away/Leave me alone/Don't bother me*—a nice roll of words—to any who would, or did, intrude on his broken heart. Many of Harrison's lyrics are curiously ambiguous. "If I Needed Someone", "I Want To Tell You", and "It's All Too Much", for instance, reflect a much more cautious attitude toward life than the exuberant and ambitious Lennon-McCartney songs. When Harrison decides to take a stand, however, he does so with no equivocation or subtlety ("Think For Yourself", "Taxman", and "Piggies").

"While My Guitar Gently Weeps" is probably the most popular Harrison work on *The White Album*. But it was not until the album *Abbey Road* that Harrison wrote his best, most popular, and most beautiful songs, "Something" and "Here Comes The Sun", in which he synthesizes what he has learned from the others, what he has taught himself, and truly takes off on his own as a composer. "Here Comes The Sun" is a lovely composition, providing a beautiful light/dark contrast with, and a morning for, the troubled evening and night of *Abbey Road* Side Two.

Harrison's most important contribution to Beatles music, besides his compositions, is that, when Lennon and McCartney sat down (or jumped up) to write songs, they knew they had one of the best guitarists in the world to back the performance of the song. This certainly influenced the innovations in their music writing. Harrison was the one who insisted that they all tune their guitars before concert tour performances, at which nobody could hear them anyway, for all the screaming.

The End of The Road

Interestingly, it is Harrison's song, "I Me Mine," which best expresses the negative feelings among the group's members during the difficult period in which they were recording *Let It Be*, the only Beatles album that the Beatles themselves literally gave up on. They walked out, leaving hundreds of recorded song versions in the hands of producer Phil Spector, who then put the album together without their help. It was finally released, even though McCartney objected strongly to the pop-kitsch treatment given his song "The Long and Winding Road", and Lennon was unhappy also with the *Let It Be* version of "Across the Universe". Even so, there is some great music on *Let It Be*, including the two aforementioned, and the title song, and also "Two Of Us", "I Dig A Pony", "Get Back", and others.

Despite the personal differences the Beatles were having with each other, the vocal harmonies and the instrumentation on many of the *Let It Be* tracks are genuine and not over-dubbed. Lennon and McCartney can be heard singing and joking together, and they composed yet another song together, "I've Got A Feeling", which comes close to sounding like straightforward Beatle autobiography, revealing, among other things, that *Everybody had a hard year, Everybody had a wet dream, Everbody saw the sun shine*, and *Everybody put the fool down* ("fool" perhaps being a code word for McCartney, i.e. "The Fool On The Hill" and "Glass Onion").

Some of the tracks on *Let It Be* (namely, "I've Got A Feeling", "I Dig A Pony", "One After 909", and "Get Back") were recorded in the freezing cold on the roof of Twickenham studios in the last Beatles performance together, which was broken up by the police after neighbors complained of the "noise". (Or was it a "merry pranksters" trick? Who knows?) The strength and precision of the singers' voices are extraordinary under the circumstances.

McCartney's theatrical and deeply moving songs "Let It Be" and "The Long and Winding Road"—the latter a very popular piece of music—express both the teetering hopefulness and the pervasive sadness that the "Let It Be" (or "Get Back") sessions caused in the members of the band. A doleful McCartney *finds himself in times of trouble*, and plays puns on the meanings of the words *let it be*, asking for *words of wisdom*. In "The Long And Winding Road", despair and a feeling of abandonment settle in, but still with a wistful, pleading *Lead me to your door*. Typical of the Beatles, "Let It Be" is followed on the album by a joking, and broadly Liverpudlian, half-completed "Maggie Mae," sung by Lennon who hams it up and breaks up the tragic mood.

The Beatles were in the middle of their break-ups as they recorded the album *Abbey Road*. And, curiously, they never worked better together. The guitar musicianship and the drumming on the album are nothing short of spectacular. Many people consider *Abbey Road* to be the Beatles finest hour. Be that as it may, the album is a wondrous creation in many respects. Besides the maturity and solidity of the Beatles own performances, it contains some of their best single compositions, as well as a mini rock-opera (Side Two) that opens with the golden dawn of one day, "Here Comes The Sun" (by Harrison), and closes with the dark, scary "Golden Slumbers" (by McCartney) the following night, and takes us into the night, exploring the nightmare of rejection, absurdity and despair that arose as the Beatles divorced each other.

On Side One of *Abbey Road* appears Lennon's sinister "Come Together", Harrison's beautiful, mature composition "Something", McCartney's rebellious "Maxwell's Silver Hammer" and his sharply hurtful "Oh! Darling", as well as Starr's second performance as a composer, "Octopus's Garden," which casts a wistful glance backwards at those happy mates on the "Yellow Submarine", and finally, Lennon's heavy number, "I Want You (She's So Heavy)", the lyrics of which consist in the title words plus approximately twelve repetitions of the lines *I want you/ I want you so bad/ It's driving me mad.*

Abbey Road reveals a group of wildly creative musicians and composers, tapping heretofore unknown wells of ecstasy, bitterness, aggression, and—miraculously, as if through a dark night of the soul back up to the day—resolution of the tension that had begun with the wordless crescendo of "A Day In The Life". The dangling question that was posed by "A Day In The Life"—What was our success *for?*—is finally answered on *Abbey Road*, by the little Beatles rune, written by Paul, called "The End": *And in the end the love you take/ Is equal to the love you make.*

The *way back homeward* seems to be to go to sleep, to go to dreamland (*Sleep pretty darling, do not cry/ And I will sing a lullaby*). Ah, but there's the rub. The lullaby is a pretty one, the lyric borrowed, with a few changes, from Thomas Dekker's sixteenth-century song, "Golden Slumbers Kiss Your Eyes", but McCartney fills it with daggers, employing his ferocious blues voice to mock, to hurt, to disturb sleep, to belt: *Golden slumbers fill your eyes/ Smiles await you when you rise.* When was a lullaby ever sung with so little intention to soothe?

The nightmare begins with a full-throated Beatles chorus of *Boy, you're gonna carry that weight/ Carry that weight/ A long time,* reminiscent of the Scottish regiment in "Tunes of Glory". A little later, a swift and angry bit of percussion leads into another McCartney eruption. As if waking from and refusing a nightmare, he renews and heightens his ferocity and yells with almost child-like anger, *Oh yeah! All Right! Are you gonna be/ In my dreams / Tonight?*

Beatles music, as the expression of a band of musicians and composers, had always been dominated by song. Arrangement and instrumentation had always been used to back song—lyric, melody and message. The Beatles did not record jam sessions. So this battle of the instruments on *Abbey Road* is significant, particularly as it drowns out the lyric chanting of *Love you.*

The Beatles were also noted for their fine integration of sound, frequently called "a wall of sound". So the separation of the four instruments—drums (Ringo), bass (McCartney), lead guitar (Harrison) and rhythm guitar (Lennon)—on this section of *Abbey Road* can be understood as a musical metaphor for the separation of the group members themselves, which seems to have been as painful and traumatic as a cutting of umbilical cords. After this, there would be no more Beatles music, song or otherwise, for after this, there would be no more group. The tittering piano, and the tremulous voices intoning "The End", with a lovely descent by Martin's orchestra on the word "equal", is thus made all the more poignant.

This little opera is assembled with great skill (by Paul McCartney and George Martin). It is beautiful, moving and very entertaining. Lennon's public response to the conclusion of *Abbey Road*, and to the end of the Beatles, was something the man *who blew his brains out in a car* might have said a few days before his suicide, *I'm bored.*

Sonic crescendo.

Nevertheless, Lennon returned to the theme of unity and togetherness a few years after the Beatles disbanded, and spun out a utopian vision in his haunting, sweet, McCartneyesque ballad, "Imagine", that came directly from the heart of Beatles mythology: *Imagine there's no countries/ It isn't hard to do/ Nothing to kill or die for/ and no religions too// Imagine no possessions/ I wonder if you can/ No need for greed or hunger/ Or brotherhood of man// You may say I'm a dreamer/ But*

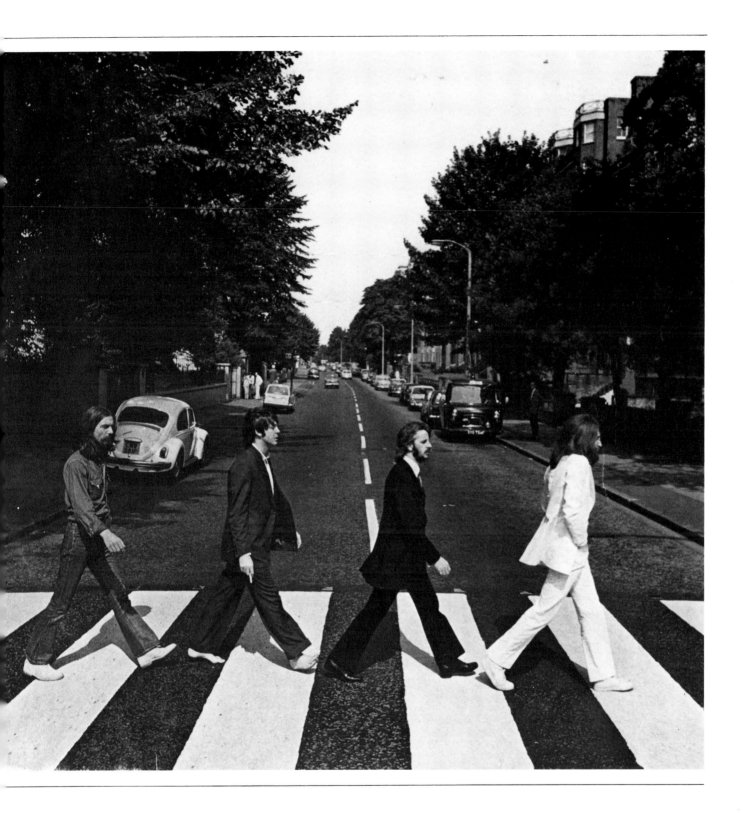

'm not the only one / I hope some day you'll join us / And he world will live as one.

John Lennon, that intense, angry young rebel rom Liverpool, certainly would not have been picked s a likely candidate to end up with such a lovely, lreamy vision. "Imagine" is more than reminiscent of he ending of another fairy tale, the animated film, "Yellow Submarine", in which all conflict is resolved in peace and love. The variety and color and illusion of *gt. Pepper*, or the virtuosity of *The White Album*, or the angry emotionalism of *Abbey Road* might be preferred to the erasures of differences in "Imagine". Still, "Imagine" is a beautiful song. Had Lennon not shared "the fellowship of the ring" with fellow Beatles Paul, George and Ringo, and had he not collaborated for fourteen years with the equally intense, Blakean rocker, Paul McCartney, could he have imagined "Imagine"?

And in the end / The love you take / Is equal to the love / You make. / A-a-a-ah!

—Milton Okun

Reminiscences of Merseyside

An Interview with Bill Harry

David M. Klein, a young journalist from Richmond, Virginia, tracked down Bill Harry at the end of 1980. This exclusive interview is the result.

A college classmate of John Lennon and Stuart Sutcliffe, Bill Harry established Mersey Beat *(Merseyside's Own Entertainments Paper) in Liverpool in 1961, as the Beatles were beginning their rise to fame. As editor of the paper during its four year existence, Bill Harry personally witnessed the birth of the "Mersey sound," the beat which was responsible for the British Invasion—England's worldwide takeover of the airwaves and record charts in the Sixties.*

Harry hasn't lost his thick Liverpudlian accent, though he now resides in London, where he's active in public relations in the music industry.

Klein: How did you first become involved with the Beatles? Was it before you put out *Mersey Beat?*

Harry: Oh yes, because I was at Liverpool Art College in the Fifties. I got to be very friendly with one of the new students —Stuart Sutcliffe. The two of us were on the Students' Union Committee. It was through Stuart that I became close to one of his friends, John Lennon.

Attached to the Liverpool Art College—the next-door building—is Liverpool Institute, the school where Paul and George were. And while we were at Art College, we used to get together all the time. Around the corner was a pub called Ye Cracke, and we used to go for drinks there and chat for hours.

What was happening at the time was a huge, fantastic craze called the skiffle boom, in which all young kids in every city in the whole of the British Isles were influenced by people like Lonnie Donegan, who did "Rock Island Line." They used to have what was called a tea chest bass, which is an old packing case with a rod and bass strings attached to it, and they used to play kazoos—the old penny whistles— and acoustic guitars. The skiffle groups started doing things like "Rock Island Line," old railroad songs, some spirituals, and the rest of it.

Paul went to see Lonnie Donegan at the Pavilion in Liverpool, and that inspired a lot of groups to start. There was a tremendous influence on the whole country—the skiffle boom was one of the first things that really got all kinds of British kids going with guitars. The feeling that they *needed* to do it. They developed into folk groups, country music groups, rock'n'roll groups, everything. And it survived in Liverpool while it seemed to have died everywhere else in Britain.

Groups started in Liverpool in what we called the "jive hives." They were town halls and ballrooms all over the city in which individual promoters would book for one or two nights a week. These were the places where the music really grew up, the places where the groups were able to play.

At the Art College, we had dances, and we knew that John and his friends had started a group. They didn't have any money, so we worked out a plan that the Students' Union would pay for the P.A. equipment, and the band would play for us. The basement, which was our cafeteria, was cleared out. It was full of old arches, and dark, almost a Cavern-like atmosphere prior to the Cavern. (When the Cavern first opened in 1957, it was purely a jazz club, and it wouldn't have any bands in there at all.)

Klein: How about the rise of the Beatles in Liverpool?

Harry: That happened after they returned from their trip to Hamburg. Previously, the Beatles had appeared in all these terrible little dives and small odd places like the Casbah, which was the cellar of Mona Best's house—she was Pete Best's mother—and that's where they got to know Pete.

Anyway, one of the promoters of the "jive hives" was Brian Kelly. He booked them in places like Litherland Town Hall and the Aintree Institute, and decided to go to town by putting up big posters all over the place. "Direct From Hamburg—The Beatles." A lot of kids thought they were a German group. The Beatles learned a lot in Germany—they got the black leath-

Cafe society in Paris, 1964.

er and started looking *different*, and of course they got all the girls going for them. This started their rise locally, because before that they weren't regarded as a top group. (The top groups were people like Cass and the Casanovas, and Rory Storm and the Hurricanes—one of my favorite bands at the time.) The Beatles, when they started, weren't anything. And when they started getting popular, I was starting *Mersey Beat.*

Klein: When was that?

Harry: It officially started in June 1961. I'd been working on it the year before gathering all the material and writing for other magazines.

Klein: When did the Beatles become the "top group" in Liverpool?

Harry: Officially, it was when we held the *Mersey Beat* Poll, and they came out the winners.

Klein: How close were you to the group by then? You knew them and saw them everyday I would imagine.

Harry: Oh, yes. When I started the paper I was still at Art College, Stuart had joined the group by then and he'd left and decided to go over and stay in Hamburg. Then John left school soon afterward, but I got my scholarship and stayed on. Virginia, who's my wife, now, was the only full-time staff member, and she worked in the office. So we used to get John and Paul and George dropping in to help out with the typing and writing and all the rest, and I used to meet them at lunch time at the coffee bar in Renshaw Street. I used to get John to write things, so I

Stu Sutcliffe

was in touch with them all the time, week after week.

Klein: What were they like then?

Harry: John, I'd say, was probably the most impressive in a straight way. He had a lot to offer in his sort of attitude and his writing.

Stuart, who was the most introverted and mysterious, was the most interesting in another way. He had this James Dean type image.

Pete Best was regarded as the most popular Beatle in Liverpool, especially with the girls. He looked like a young Jeff Chandler—he was very handsome. He didn't really have very much to say for himself, but the kids really loved him.

Paul has always been the same. A diplomat. Polite. Always courteous to everyone, always considerate to people. Just very pleasant to be around.

George never had much to say for himself. He was just sort of quiet and reserved, always in the background.

And Ringo was just a good mate. We'd go around to clubs together and he was very down to earth. He was the only member of the Beatles who came from what we call a working class background. The others didn't. They came from what we regarded as the posh part of Liverpool—the part with nice houses with gardens. People keep talking about the Beatles as "working class heroes," but Ringo was the only one who came from the *really* poor area.

Klein: How long did it take the Beatles to make it until they became the top cats in Liverpool?

Harry: When they were Number One in the *Mersey Beat* Poll, they were then acknowledged as the number one band. They'd been going in various forms since about 1957, but not really seriously. They'd never had a permanent drummer until they got Pete Best, and that was in August 1960. Pete stayed with them until August 1962. They were almost like a semi-pro group fooling around. So really, the period in which they really started as a stable group with a proper name, a proper background, proper professional music, being a professional band, was around August 1960. It was almost two years later when they started to get the real record acclaim and acknowledgement as the top band.

Klein: How did they feel when a fellow like Brian Epstein took interest in them and wanted to manage them?

Harry: They were completely amazed because there were no professional managers whatsoever in Liverpool. They groups never thought they'd ever be able to make a success. It was a *hobby*. All the groups in Liverpool—there was a great atmosphere between them—never really saw themselves as being successes because groups from the provinces had never really made it. The whole thing was tied up in London by what they called the "Tin Pan Alley Brigade." There were only amateur managers. Billy Kramer was managed by an old-age pensioner, and somebody else like the Searchers were managed by a lawyer, and so on. But of course these managers had no money. Their way of managing a group was just getting them a few bookings on the phone—or just the fact of having a phone made them a manager.

For Brian Epstein to take interest in them was incredible. Not only was he someone with "connections" in the record industry (from his record shop) but he was also someone who obviously had money. And the Beatles thought this was unbelievable.

The money paid to groups in Liverpool at the time was very, very low. And groups had to play up to three gigs a night to make any bit of headway, and end up with any money. Brian said that if he took the Beatles over he'd manage to get them the highest fees ever paid to a Liverpool group. And he actually managed to get them a gig for fifteen pounds and nobody on the scene could believe it. When he got that money, it was the highest money paid for a Liverpool group at any time.

—David M. Klein

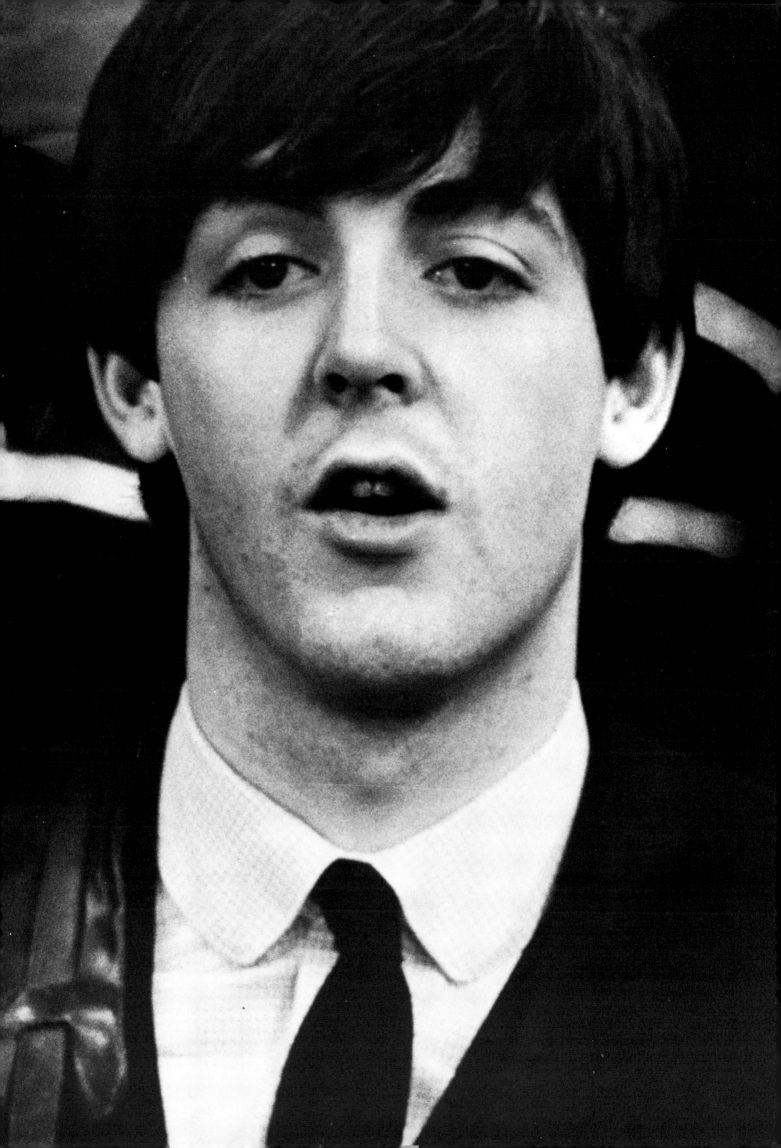

The Private Pleasures of a Beatles Collector:

At the time The Beatles' first album came out, I vowed never to grow taller than 5'11" because none of the Beatles had. Today, just over 6 feet; 19 years after the release of *Meet The Beatles*; my copy of the record with its dulled sheen and numerous scratches of age; the jacket re-glued, re-painted, resurrected from the pains of age; and "I love John and he's my favorite" still graffitied over the back photo; my Beatlemaniacal feelings have not lost any of their euphoric intensity.

Looking back over the years to 1962, it seems I was certainly destined to become a maniacal collector of The Beatles' music. Suddenly, 4 appallingly unique and blindingly charismatic men singing on a grainy film shown on *The Jack Parr Show* (The Bournemouth Concert, available on a bootleg album) assaulted my virginal mind and caused me to realize there was more to life than Mickey Mantle's homeruns and the exploits of super-heroes. Later they hit the charts with the 45 of "I Want to Hold Your Hand" (which I immediately bought) and Polly Mills nick-named me "The Bug" because I was a Beatlemaniac and a male (a rare combination at the time). Before my first girl I swooned for The Beatles—it was idolatry, it was obsessive love. That year I did two marvelous things that I'm still proud of though they were far from earthshattering: I formed a singing group and we lip-synched "I Want to Hold Your Hand"; and I wrote a song with my buddy, Felipe Bonilla. The song, for the class play, "Alice in Wonderland" was sung to the tune of "She Loves You". We sang "You're in Wonderland Yeah Yeah Yeah" twice for three days. All the girls I remember screamed.

Like many artists my creativity has been affected by the complicatedly intertwined with many stimuli; there is not a Beatles song that I've not listened to while engrossed in painting pictures over the years. For me Beatles records are muses to inspire my work; "great art inspires great art." Since I identify much of *my* life with *their* musical art, even a drab unproductive day in the studio can seem a little easier to take when I hear their songs. "Painter's block" can be alleviated by Beatles records; John's song, "Anytime At All" sung in its euphoric minor key, for example, always succeeds in easing anxieties. There is not one Beatles record of mine that doesn't sport smears of paint, often shaped like fingertips.

There are so many memories I have that are inseparable from The Beatles: the day in Woolworths when I bought *Rubber Soul*—looking at its cover—as impassioned as a little boy gazing at a thousand candy bars through a glass encasement—I simultaneously felt love, hero-worship, admiration, and anguish. And that same magical day when I played side two ten times straight before I played side one; I recall comparing my legs to George Harrison's on one of the back cover's photos. During these years I made up synopses of imaginary Beatles movies; I started writing a novel (with my own illustrations) where Paul loses his voice. I spent countless hours drawing the Beatles. In junior high one of my first oil paintings was of them godlike, engrossed in performing. I created record jackets for imaginary Beatles albums with new songs and time listings. I fought with my parents over the length of my hair and my records were confiscated as punishment when I was "bad".

For many collectors rare Beatle material is solely a venture for investment, but my reasons for collecting are intricately enmeshed in passions shared with my entire generation. The Beatles—as did my mother, my father, my friends, and my environment—affected my personality, stimulating my intellectual and artistic growth. There is a symbiotic relationship between me and my Beatles records; collecting (commercial and rare) is, for me, a vital necessity because in so many ways the Beatles and their music are extensions of myself and my past, and partially a key to my future. As I wouldn't trade in my mother for money I would never trade in my Beatles records.

For the many of us who were born in the fifties, growing up was growing up with the Fab Four, and with the other major bands that surfaced during the same period. My record collection that started with *Tubby The Tuba* when I was three years old has grown to such proportions that it would take approximately 35,000 minutes of listening time to get through them once.

In the same way that a person's shoes reflect their owner's personality and style, the records that I've procured over the years resemble me; brutalized and caressed, my Beatles records are visual attestations of endless years of enjoyment. Several of them, due to the wear and tear of my rugged passions, are wholly recovered with my own home-made jackets: *The Beatles Second Album* now opens up to a double spread with photos of screaming girls and one of The Beatles themselves running through an alley; *Yesterday and Today*, after I destroyed its original cover (ripping it up in order to see if I had the original "Butcher" shot), sports an elegant off-white jacket with only two small black and white photos the title done in "artsy" scribbled pencil.

"Brutalized and caressed"... In 1966, when *The Beatles Sixth Album* was released I immediately bought it and played it incessantly. But disaster interrupted my musical reveries, for the very next day I dropped the record on a hard parquet floor and it splintered, forever silencing 4 songs. One would have thought I'd touched napalm, for exploding into a cloudburst of sobs I stopped only when mother gave me money to buy a new copy. At that time I bought the records with my saved-up allowances. Today—whether I can afford to buy or not—I reach into my pocket. To this day I have both copies of *The Beatles Sixth Album*.

Because I collect out of an endless and frenzied enthusiasm and for the infinite pleasures I derive from Beatles music, ordinary facts and figures and certain questions allude and bewilder me. I am puzzled therefore when people asked simple questions such as the overall value of my entire Beatles inventory and "How many records of theirs do you have?" I laugh and —"Oh, I suppose 65 or 70!"

On the record that is commonly referred to as his "primal scream" album, John Lennon sang "the dream is over," I had to reluctantly agree with him that The Beatles were a finished chapter within Lennon's artistic development and within the annals of musical history. Yet even now it is hard for me not to want new and more Beatle music. Artists, by creating great works, provoke continual anticipation amongst their loyal public. So, with their breakup, (outside of John Lennon's solo career with and without Yoko Ono—I loved them as a band) I've come to understand this unyielding anticipation as a loyal fan and have found ways to provide my "new material" fix myself. John Lennon's five-year musical hiatus (1975–1980) was additional impetus for me to collect rare Beatles material. Clearly the closest solution to acquiring new music from the disbanded Fab Four was to find rejected out-takes, unreleased live recordings, "oldies" sung by them but never commercially released, and the Parlophone releases (their English label).

Way before their breakup, before they ceased public performance (San Francisco, August 29, 1966—

there is a crude bootleg of this last live concert) I, as numerous other Beatlemaniacs, inadvertently became a collector by buying Beatle Albums and singles the day they were issued. How many maniacal followers of The Fab Four can boast having the single "Ticket To Ride" with the credit line: "from the new Beatles film *Eight Arms To Hold You?*

If you've managed to keep many of the 45's you've got some interesting gems; "Lady Madonna's" vocals are higher in register and it's generally faster paced than on its subsequent album release. The same holds true for "Paperback Writer", where on the single, the guitar work sounds distinctly faster and more complex than it does on the *Apple* album. Other singles, rare for distinct musical differences or for their never having been released on albums are: "Help" (much faster on the single); "Strawberry Fields Forever" (different ending); "From Me To You" (recorded as a 45 on the Decca label before Capitol signed them—it has only recently been released on the Capitol LP, *Rarities*); "Ain't She Sweet," "My Bonnie" (these were also released on an anthology album of different bands of the early 60's).

The first album though that I bought knowingly aware of its "rarity" status was a first press issue of *The Savage Young Beatles*. I bought it only months after *The Beatles Second Album* came out—I was the envy of the entire P.S. 6, and a serious collector at twelve. In certain ways, it is a great album as it has Pete Best drumming and several songs are real rockers. But of the eight songs only four of them actually have The Beatles playing and in only one—"Why"—can you hear any of singing. Who sings? Tony Sheridan, whom they often backed up in the old days. I must add that the versions of "Ya Ya" and "If You Love Me Baby" are really "gear".

By far the easiest way for anyone to collect more Beatles material is to buy the English Parlophone releases, though there will seldom be many surprises (songs you've grown accustomed to group together on Capitol's albums were not necessarily planned that way in England). Occasionally you'll discover a song with a slightly different mix or instrumentation. These are relatively scarce. On the Parlophone version, though, of "She's A Woman", the piano is much more discernable, whereas Capitol's 1965 release is "heavy metal echoing in a deep tunnel;" the piano almost entirely drowned out by the emphasized cymbals. While John's harmonica sweetens the Capitol releases of "Thank You Girl," on Parlophone it is absent from the song after the initial opening. One of my favorite Beatle

Millions of record jackets ripped for this one!—the original butcher cover, now a collector's item.

songs, "I'm Only Sleeping", particularly illustrates the differences between the two labels. One finds the song on the Capitol album *Yesterday and Today* while in England it is on *Revolver*. Furthermore when *Yesterday and Today* was released the song simply "blew me away" but a good ten years later (in Rome, Italy) I bought the Parlophone *Revolver* and wow! the enclosed version of "I'm Only Sleeping" was fabulously different, its musical texture much more complex and similarly startling and arresting as Jimi Hendrix's guitar solo in his own song, "Are You Experienced?". And finally from the Apple period there are two George Harrison gems sadly overlooked by most people. The first called *Wonderwall Music* was an exquisite soundtrack for an obscure film of the same name, written around the time of *Revolver* when George was first getting involved with Indian instrumentation. The second record, *Electronic Sound* on "Zapple" records (The Beatles' intellectual and music-of-the-future label) contains two cuts: "Under The Mersey Wall" is interesting if not rather beautiful.

This is interesting because it's fun to compare the records. But the better rewards result from careful searching over long periods of time when you find non-commercially released material.

This material can either be discarded out-takes or early workings of Beatles' standards (ie.: "Sure To Fall," "Ask Me Why," "Dizzy Miss Lizzie"). In the so-called bootlegs you may hear your favorite song with a different vocalizing and harmony (ie.: "Mr. Moonlight," "Honey Don't"—John sings not Ringo, etc.) or without the standard guitar solo or instrumentation (i.e.: early versions of "I Saw Her Standing There" etc.).

What is so fascinating about these non-commercially released records is that you can't help but realize that they represent hard-working artists developing changing attitudes over a 15 year period.

More valuable than gold are famous songs re-recorded over a period of years. It is fascinating to listen to their fever-pitched, hard-pounding raw rock 'n' roll performance of "Matchbox" in Hamburg. Several years later, packaged by Capitol on *Something New*, it's a clean production, rock 'n' rolling but certainly not perspiration music. Again, on *The Beatles Broadcasts* (a non-commercially released album of many of the songs done live on BBC's *Pop Go The Beatles* there is an unbelievably arresting version of the song; Ringo's singing and percussion is hall-of-fame quality and the live orchestration is an improvement on the seemingly perfect Hamburg version.

Rare material ranges from 1971. (ie.: *The John Lennon Telecasts*—anyone doubting the "heaven-made" bond of John and Yoko should listen to their live duet of "The Luck of The Irish") to 1969 (The *Let It Be* out-takes), to 1963 (The Bournemouth Concert). These recordings either sound of stupendous quality or as if your record needle resembles a cat's claw. Yet the barometer is the material itself; I have songs that are recorded extremely poorly but are rare and wonderful. Though the sound on an album called *Yellow Matter Custard* is poor, "To Know Her Is To Love Her" still sounds as if it were sung by harmonizing angels.

The Beatles were together for so many years that eventually they could jam and play as if telepathic. In his *Playboy* interview John stated that this became a deterrent to their creative processes. Though quite tangible, this cohesive multiple creativity of theirs is one of the ingredients of the bootlegs that particularly shines out. The fabulous quality of these records is the Beatles' off-the-wall spontaneity and inherent understanding of each others' talents, musical leanings, and even comic sensibilities. Perfectly illustrative of the band's cohesive qualities is the "Back to The Commonwealth/White Power" jam from the *Sweet Apple Tracks*; clearly heard here is the tough raw rock 'n' rolling of the band, their spontaneous laughing, jesting, and joking, Paul and John's perfect interwoven singing harmonies, George's melodious guitar and Ringo's perfectly placed rhythmic percussion.

Sweet Apple Tracks is my personal favorite non-commercial release; these are two or four records (depending on which group of bootlegs you procure) documenting the Beatles' 28 days of work that are commonly known as the *Let It Be* sessions, and by the film of the same name. There are musicologists and critics who have dismissed this period as unproductive or only valuable for insights into The Beatles' squabbles. These pre-Spector recordings are fascinating audio-voyages into the last days of the Fab Four; the sessions are full of rare jewels, and the version of "Across The Universe" is one of the most perfect performances ever recorded by the band. John even sings one verse in a highly enunciated Irish accent.

It's truly wonderful collecting their music: their hamming-it-up; inserting wisecracks; singing in harmonies worthy of the Chipmunks; and ad-libbing lyrics. Above all, what makes these recordings so fascinating and precious are the tracks where the Beatles draw out scant phrases and isolated melodies (ie.: "I Me Mine") into full fledged songs; here are some priceless hints for

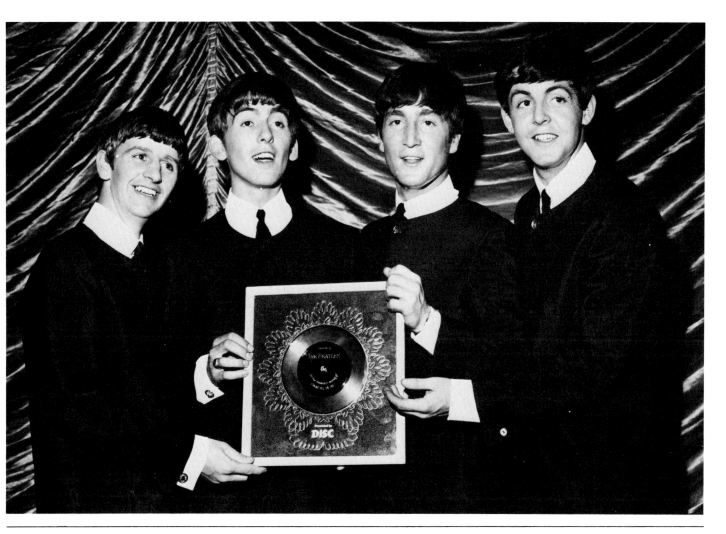

any person who has wondered how a song is born. Starting with several bars only partially resembling the well-known song, the Beatles (notwithstanding the *Hard Day's Night* tomfoolery of Latino and Bach fugue variations) gradually develop a song before your ears. Even after repeated playing, there is still no end in sight of my enjoyment listening to the Beatles originate and finalize "Let It Be," or "She Came in Through the Bathroom Window."

There are various publications that have listed out-takes and other material floating around, but they're unreliable; they list material chronologically and according to studio locations, but often when placed on records the material is juggled and packaged differently. Sometimes the records aren't titled or documented so that one often has to guess the origin and time slot. From personal experience I recommend using the blind approach; the incredible excitement of placing one of these records on the turntable, with bated breath, not knowing what you shall hear. If there's any dilemma it's the question: should I buy this one though I don't know what's inside? Experience teaches one to ignore this question, for there's no reward without taking a risk. One great song makes two albums worth all the money in the world.

Each collector has fantasies of finding some unique treasure for his collection. Regardless of whether it exists or not, even if it takes me a lifetime, I will someday find a live or out-take version of "Anytime At All." For me, it is quintessential Beatles and

John Lennon song, synonymous of all that the Beatles stand for and of all romance. Truly maniacal is my need to have every minute of every hour of every day of the "Let It Be" sessions—needless to say they probably are not all recorded, so be it.

Though I've bought records at garage sales and thrift shops from Manhattan to Philadelphia and in the oddest reclusive stores in Rome, Paris and London; I cannot really boast of any Beatles surprises from these haunts. My failures however, don't discourage continued "peekings." I've found that the most fruitful spots for the obsessed and knowledgable collector (like myself) are private record entrepreneurs who mainly sell commercially released records that are second hand and/or out-of-print. These shops cater to the general "commercial-record" buyer, although they place a high accent on their "collectors" inventory; the average person (fortunately, for me) would rather buy a record of avowed quality rather than a bootleg or non-commercial recording of any band's questionable material, or, better stated, "in the throes of artistic preparation." Though I have never been to the various Beatles' conventions, I'm sure one can find collectors selling their rare wares there. The big trick once you've found your "pot at the end of the rainbow" is to buy the record on the spot. Never say "tomorrow" because there's always someone behind you about to grab it. If you are collecting Beatles rarities, be a hog.

—Milo Reice

155

Power & Intimacy:

Like a lot of loud noises, it was extraordinarily difficult to hear. Yet, for me, at least, the arrival of the Beatles has always been their perfect moment, not only because of the screaming girls and the hyperthyroid journalism, the junk merchandising and the sudden importance of hair, the obnoxious disc jockeys and the pathetic adult attacks. As with any pop phenomenon, of course, the trappings were anything but beside the point. Yet they tended to obscure the most amazing fact of all: The Beatles had not only arrived, they had arrived complete. They would not get "better," in the six years left to them, because there simply wasn't much better to get. What they did, instead, and to their ever-lasting credit, was become more sophisticated, take the same idea and never shy away from its complexities. But *better?* You don't improve on "I Want to Hold Your Hand," "I Saw Her Standing There," "She Loves You," "Do You Want to Know A Secret," "Please Please Me," "Love Me Do," "This Boy," "Can't Buy Me Love," "You Can't Do That" and "From Me to You." You just elaborate.

When they hit America, the Beatles had already written and recorded all of those songs. And in that winter bursting into spring of 1964, all of them were thrown at us, in a rush, inside of six weeks: No wonder it created such an uproar; the sheer quantity of great songs was unignorable, as if Babe Ruth had hit sixty homers in his first season in the big leagues.

Note that we have not even considered such songs as "Money" and "Twist and Shout," "Chains" and "Devil in Her Heart," "Long Tall Sally" and "Boys." Those are six songs which represent about that many different approaches to rhythm and blues and rock and roll; the Beatles had mastered all of them, and a few more besides. But had they done only that, their achievement could never have had such scale. It was as writer-performers, not performers only, that the Beatles established themselves not only as merchandise but, from the very beginning, as artists.

There had been composer-performers before in rock and roll—Chuck Berry, Buddy Holly, Smokey Robinson, Curtis Mayfield. But all of those performers got away with writing because of the very singularity of their styles. No one could play guitar quite like Berry, sing quite like Smokey or Curtis. Holly's Crickets are the Beatles' archetype, of course (that's almost certainly where they got the idea for their name), but Buddy's career was truncated. And so it was left to the Beatles to continue the concept which he had established: great writer, great singer, great instrumentalist.

That greatness was years in the making, though one suspects after hearing their performances at Hamburg's Star Club and listening to reminiscences of their shows at the Cavern in Liverpool, that the spark of it was present from the day that Lennon and McCartney first met. But what's important is that America first knew them complete. The recognition came later, but only because in the initial explosion, it was hard to pay attention to details.

But the details are there. The Beatles were playing rock and roll with enormous power and great intimacy on those early records, and each song is elaborately constructed, from the propulsive percussion patterns that kick them along, to the simple but elegant guitar figures that give them their boost of excitement. They had mastered the most difficult aspect of rock craftsmanship, the ability to pre-plan spontaneity, so that the guitar solo in "I Saw Her Standing There," for instance, seems to erupt naturally, as a necessary adjunct of McCartney's desperate passion. "Love Me Do" is set up around a simple rhythm figure, so much so that it might have been as schematic as Bo Diddley if the group's harmonies were not so tightly pieced together, if McCartney and Lennon's vocal trade-offs were not so finely stitched, if the marvelous harmonica accompaniment had not confounded expectations. (That should have been a guitar!) And though the Beatles were still singing Meredith Willson's "Til There Was You," they had already surpassed it with the grandeur of "Do You Want to Know a Secret," a ballad of similar construction, but with a much greater emotional charge. Although the Beatles are supposed to be "primitives" at this stage, the construction of "Do You Want to Know A Secret," so simple and effortless, makes "A Taste of Honey," which follows it on their Vee-Jay album, seem cluttered and a bit strained in comparison.

For me, at least, they reached a peak with "I'll Get You" and "She Loves You," the two original songs which conclude *The Beatles Second Album* (and were originally coupled as a single). Listen to how effortlessly the voices modulate into the bridge of the former—the Beatles have already found a groove that most bands never reach. And "She Loves You," besides being some absolutely atomic rock and roll playing (those drums rumble like the Bomb), makes order out of chaos—patterned after the elementary R&B tunes they loved, this song has polish as great as its power.

But "She Loves You" was their most mocked song in those days: *Yeah, yeah, yeah* the TV hosts (and parents) mocked. Yet it is this song, more than any other, which convinces me that the Beatles did reach us as fullblown

artists. How far is *With a love like that / You know you should be glad / Yeah yeah yeah*, from the sentiments of "Hey Jude"? Both counsel acceptance of love as the greatest glory humanity can know, and both are correct. While it is true that Lennon, in particular, would grow more sophisticated in his use of language (a process already beginning with the brilliant *A Spaniard in the Works*), he would never state his basic message more succinctly. As scene-setting narratives, "She Loves You," "I Saw Her Standing There" and "Do You Want to Know A Secret" can hardly be improved upon, and as philosophical statements, "She Loves You," "Love Me Do" and "I Want to Hold Your Hand" make as much (or as little) sense as any of the latter work.

This leaves out magic and inspiration, but then, there is surely no one who would argue that they had less of that in 1964 than in 1967 or 1969. (They learned to use it more effectively, naturally.) Surely, they grew, and we with them, and who's to say where cause begins and effect leaves off on that score. Yet to this day, when people talk about the Beatles, it is not "Strawberry Fields Forever" or "A Day in the Life" which plays in the head, but something else: That incredible *One, two, three, FAH* count-off at the start of "I Saw Her Standing There," and yes, those *Yeah yeah yeahs* repeated forever, the ultimate Beatles' message. Yes to love, yes to joy, yes to the transforming power of what they did, from the very beginning.

—Dave Marsh

The Beatles Instrumentality:

A musician's instrument is the tool of his trade. Its physical ability to make noise, the type of tonal shapes that result, its body style and even color help to determine the music that results creatively. With a group of musicians gathered in a band such as the Beatles, the combined blend of their individual instrument choices often dictates the consequent sound, directions followed and influences generated.

The Beatles' success would ultimately lie in what they built on their basic interplay, but the foundation for that triumph was laid as early as the days in which they first chose what instruments to play.

There is little doubt that rock and roll wouldn't exist if not for the invention of the electric guitar. As an instrument, it is particularly suited to a style whose major hallmark is energy. Both percussive and melodic, able to rhythmically chord or single-note solo, it performs an amazing variety of functions. Easy to play (at least in its initial stages), its appeal is readily apparent for anyone who wants to get onstage within a week.

Given electricity to be able to compete with pounding, full-strength drums, mated with the bass

fiddle to provide a frequency link between drums and standard guitar (as an electric bass) this black-sheep descendent of ye olde Iberian lute formed the basis of a music molded in its image. Simple and passionate, it was most certainly pop (as in "ular"); volume-ized and attention-grabbing, it aimed at the active emotions, a total frenzy of involvement.

That music, rock and roll, was already well birthed and circling the globe when the Silver Beatles decided to make a go of it in the late fifties. Their direct model were the Crickets—in fact, a convenient inspiration for most white rock and roll bands then extant; yet in America where Buddy Holly's Fender Stratocaster (that most flashy of early electrics) had taken root in the developing surf instrumental bands of the west coast, in England, the guitar-playing figure of Eddie Cochran overshadowed all. Never as large an idol in America, Eddie's "Summertime Blues" and wide-bodied Gretsch created immeasurable impact, especially on one George Harrison, who is said to have followed Cochran town-to-town on his ill-fated last tour of the British Isles in early 1960.

The choice of a guitar make is, conscious or unconsciously, an emulation of style, whether embodied

in a particular musician or a guitar's reputation.

George's choice of a Gretsch showed his desire to be a player's player, the most musicianly of a band; and Eddie Cochran was as well-recognized for his guitar prowess as his voice. The Beatles' widespread use of such "jazzy" chords as sevenths and diminisheds within the confines of the previously inviolable I-IV-V progressions, not to mention their filigree melodic embellishment, would mean George's time on the big Country Gentlemen was not in vain.

The other guitar-playing Beatles also had their pick of the many brands available, but expecting to provide rhythmic backbone (Paul's bass and John's rhythm guitar respectively), they opted for practicality. Paul literally put the German-made Hofner bass on the map, using a light balsa wood violin-shaped left-handed model that allowed easy stage movement and added a bouncy snap to the proceedings. John's Rickenbacker played chords with a round prominence that would later give this California based company the king of electric twelve-strings in the sixties. Ever the songwriters, John and Paul would by instrumental design also be responsible for the basic song thrust as well. As for Ringo, he was always meant to be utilitarian, a drummer to provide a feisty beat; he did this directly, with wit, imagination, and the famous Ringo personality, and his spartan Ludwig kit (one snare, one rack tom, one floor tom, one bass drum, one hi-hat, two cymbals) showed his ability to cut economically to the heart of a rhythm.

One of the Beatles' greatest impacts, strangely enough, was simply that they were louder than most previous (i.e. rock-a-billy) standards of rock and roll. This came from their judicious choice of Vox amplifiers, an English company who rode the Beatles' whirlwind into complete (keyboards, guitars, and "Super-Beatle" amplifiers) instrumental dominance throughout the 1960's, reflected in the pop-op teardrop art of the Vox Phantom guitar.

During their early career, the Beatles stayed pretty close to home musically. Wanting to reproduce their live sound onto record, they layered their guitars as they would on stage, adding such easy-carryables as a harmonica if they wanted to sweeten their textural blend. They also concentrated on developing their voices, knowing that their use of strident vocal harmonies was unique. Previously, the only groups who really *sang* in the fifties were rhythm and blues or doo-wop vocal groups; instrumental bands were expected to stick to their instruments (as the Shadows and the Ventures) or party along.

The Beatles warbled in full throat, and it added to their appeal immeasurably. They all (even Ringo) sang, and their voices were so flexible and expressive that they could encompass an unusually wide range of music, from the broadly ribald ("Twist and Shout", "She Loves You") to the subtly poetic ("Til There Was You", "If I Fell").

It—the motion of their guitars, the driving drums, the glorious voices—sustained them through

George Martin with George and Paul in the studio. Note the antiquated (by modern standards) recording console.

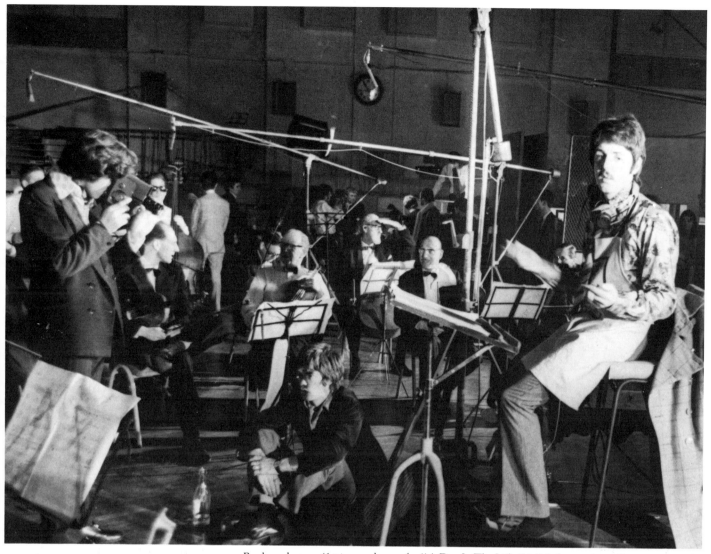

Paul conducts a 41-piece orchestra for "A Day In The Life." Mick Jagger, seated, waits patiently.

worldwide acclaim, a succession of gold records, Shea Stadium, and the stuff of *A Hard Day's Night*. But with "Yesterday" and the arrival of string arrangements on a Beatles record (the reaction at the time was one of disbelief), the band changed directions, expanded its awareness and began experimenting, using the studio as a broad palette in which to blend instrumental colors. Having left the live circuit, they were no longer dependent on the instruments they had to play on stage. By the time of *Rubber Soul*, they had become connoisseurs of a vast range of sound and technique. What they couldn't learn for themselves, they requested from others, and the Beatles' records opened up considerably.

George, for example, became fascinated with the intricacies of Indian music. Thus, on something like "Within You Without You", the haunting sound of the sitar, tamboura, and dilruba beckoned. When "Penny Lane" needed a baroque piccolo trumpet coda, Dave Mason of the London Symphony Orchestra came in to do the honors. Eric Clapton even guested a guitar (!) on "When My Guitar Gently Weeps". Paul sat increasingly more behind the piano, his knowledge of songwriting and pop sensibility expanding as horizontally as the keyboard itself; and John conceptualized, figured artistic directions, always called for more experimentation. Ringo drummed resolutely on, seemingly able to keep up with each one effortlessly.

In addition, they had one of the greatest instruments of all at their disposal: the modern recording studio itself. Though technology only granted them four tracks to work with as late as *Sgt. Pepper*, the Beatles mounted layers of overdubs to take their music in any direction desired. With a little help from their friend, producer George Martin, they were able to utilize abstract sound as musical components, such as the chicken cluckings that lead into "Sgt. Pepper", the hurdy-gurdy organs built into "Being For The Benefit of Mr. Kite", and most interestingly, the massive orchestral chord in "A Day In The Life" that took up two full symphony orchestras, several hands on the octaves of a piano, and a good deal of engineering expertise.

By the time of *Abbey Road*, the Beatles had explored nearly every musical nook, from the anarchy of "Revolution #9" and "I Am The Walrus" to the lush tin pan alley perfection of "Hey Jude" and "Let It Be", seemingly at home in any genre. Their last album would show them as accomplished musicians, the songs mature and confident, reprising a passage of learning stretched a decade or more. An ending as well as a new beginning, instrumental in changing the world.

— Lenny Kaye

Rubber Soul:

Wood and Smoke

I look on *Rubber Soul* as a masterpiece. I call it the Beatles' "wood and smoke" album. It generates for me a feeling of deep-colored, paneled rooms and warm fires, of wine and haze. There is a strong emphasis on acoustic instrumentation throughout, which makes me feel as if the Beatles are sitting around in my living room, unmiked and unamped, playing spontaneously and with sincerely friendly feeling. "I've Just Seen a Face" shows Paul in a happy, surprisingly witty mood. He stretches the lyric to fit his need, letting the rhymes fall in wonderfully unexpected places. The rapid guitar work matches his torrential, bouncy lyric line. Lennon lets us relax a little with the casual but intense classic, "Norwegian Wood." Again the emphasis is acoustic, but the introduction of George's now-famous sitar signals the beginning of an entirely new phase of musical culture.

The song is sad, told through a major chord which suddenly shifts to a minor one. Although McCartney's bass is disappointingly inappropriate, the group takes an essentially one-chord song and keeps it from ever becoming boring. It is surprisingly brief (exactly two minutes) yet laden with a yellow regret. The last image, a fade-out on the singer alone in the room staring at the fire, is highly visual, almost cinematic.

This mood is broken and a new one created when "You Won't See Me" crashes in. It is a trebly, bursting piece, easily hummable and invitingly sing-alongable. And I could swear the thing slows down before it reaches the end. Harrison's contribution, "Think for Yourself," continues his string of darker compositions. Its cautionary, bitter tone foreshadows Lennon's angry songs on Side Two. I believe that one of George's greatest contributions to the group's sound was his bold and creative use of harmony vocals. He consistently triple- and quadruple-tracked harmonies in his own voice, creating a rich texture in each of his recordings. He learned to develop his songwriting art through contact with John and Paul; they in turn enhanced their own songs by using his style of harmony technique.

"The Word" is an eerie little song, its chorus consisting of minor chords sung over major sevenths. The perky boom-chick rhythm is smoothed out by a layer of frosting from a tinny, insistent harmonium played by none other than George Martin, the Beatles' multitalented producer.

"Michelle" is a small miracle. It changes keys three times in as many bars yet never seems to wander. The tight backup vocals create a feeling of real support, almost as if the other Beatles are urging Paul on to tell his story. If they had been less careful, the Beatles might have resorted to a string section to enhance the piece, but they held to the acoustic-guitar format. It is McCartney's song all the way, as he lets his velvety bass take the solo bridge. The efforts of the singer to tell of his love to someone who can't understand his language is agonizingly complex and heartbreaking.

Side Two is really Lennon's, and it is a bittersweet delight. He is at his full literary power in "It's Only Love," where he jams the first verse with seventeen assonating or rhyming syllables. "Girl" has an almost Slavic feeling, especially in its refrain and instrumental passages. The "tit-tit" backup vocals are a subtle schoolboy joke, but Lennon's intense sigh on an intake of breath is quite moving. Ringo steps out for his debut on keyboards in "I'm Looking Through You," a swift-moving, rocking little number. "In My Life" is one of Lennon's best, one of those really personal songs of his which like "Help!" look back to his childhood. George Martin plays a baroque keyboard embellishment that adds a touch of class to an already sincere and beautiful song. "Wait" doesn't seem to me to be quite fully realized, stopping and starting as roughly as it does.

The album ends with a decidedly wicked tone, with Lennon no longer willing to take the pain given him by the women of "Norwegian Wood" and "Girl." Instead, in "Run For Your Life," he threatens death to a girl after catching her with another man. His lyric is sharp, but there is a deadly slur to the vocal, as if sung by a drunken, thick-tongued, and angry man.

It is a chilly note to finish on, but an effective one.

—Ron Schaumburg

Lennon-McCartney:
Who Wrote What

It's common knowledge that Paul wrote some alone and John wrote some alone. The royalties may be shared but sometimes not the workload on a particular piece.

We sat John Lennon down and went over the whole list of Lennon-McCartney material, that rich vein that changed the face of rock music almost overnight, going back to the first days of the Mersey-Liverpool Sound, up through Beatlemania to Sgt. Pepper, and the breakup.

LOVE ME DO: Paul wrote the main structure of this when he was about 16, or even earlier. I think I had something to do with the middle.

P.S. I LOVE YOU: Paul. But I think we helped him a bit. It was meant to be a Shirelles kind of song.

PLEASE PLEASE ME: I wrote all of this one. I was trying to do a Roy Orbison.

FROM ME TO YOU: Paul and me—we wrote this together in a van.

THANK YOU GIRL: Paul and me. This was just a silly song we knocked off.

SHE LOVES YOU: Both of us. We wrote it together on tour.

I CALL YOUR NAME: Me. I started it when I was about 15 and finished the middle eight years later, around *Help* or *Hard Day's Night* time.

BAD TO ME: Me. I wrote it for Billy J. Kramer.

IT WON'T BE LONG: Me. I wrote this on the second album. It was the song with the so-called Aeolian cadences, the same as in the Mahler symphony, at the end. I don't know what the hell it was about.

ALL MY LOVING: Paul. This was one of his first biggies.

LITTLE CHILD: Both of us. This was a knock-off between Paul and me for Ringo.

I WANNA BE YOUR MAN: Both of us, but mainly Paul . . . I helped him finish it.

I'LL KEEP YOU SATISFIED: Paul. This was for Billy J. Kramer.

CAN'T BUY ME LOVE: John and Paul, but mainly Paul.

AND I LOVE HER: Both of us. The first half was Paul's and the middle eight is mine.

I'LL BE BACK: Me. A nice tune, though the middle is a bit tatty.

WORLD WITHOUT LOVE: Paul. An early one he wrote when he was about 16 or 17. I think he changed the words later for the record by Peter and Garfunkel, or something.

ONE AND ONE IS TWO: Paul. That was a terrible one.

I FEEL FINE: Me. This was the first time feedback was used on a record. It's right at the beginning.

SHE'S A WOMAN: Paul. Though I helped with the middle. I think.

NO REPLY: Me. I remember Dick James coming to me after we did this one and saying, "You're getting much better now . . . that was a complete story." Apparently, before that he thought my songs tended to sort of wander off.

I'LL FOLLOW THE SUN: Paul. A nice one—one of his early compositions.

EIGHT DAYS A WEEK: Both of us. I think we wrote this when we were trying to write the title song for *Help*, because there was at one time the thought of calling the film, *Eight Arms To Hold You* or something. I think that's the story, I'm not sure.

IT'S ONLY LOVE: Me. That's the one song I really hate of mine. Terrible lyric.

YESTERDAY: Paul. Wow, that was a good 'un.

DAY TRIPPER: Me. But I think Paul helped with the verse.

WE CAN WORK IT OUT: Paul, but the middle was mine.

NORWEGIAN WOOD: Me, but Paul helped me on the lyric.

MICHELLE: Both of us. I wrote the middle with him.

WHAT GOES ON: Me. A very early song of mine. Ringo and Paul wrote a new middle eight together when we recorded it.

IN MY LIFE: Me. I think I was trying to write about Penny Lane when I wrote it. It was about places I remembered. A nice song. Jose Feliciano did a nice version of it.

RUN FOR YOUR LIFE: Me. Another one I never liked.

PAPERBACK WRITER: Paul. I think I might have helped with some of the lyrics. Yes, I did. But it was mainly Paul's tune.

ELEANOR RIGBY: Both of us. I write a good lot of the lyrics, about 70 per cent. Ray Charles did a great version of this. Fantastic.

HERE, THERE AND EVERYWHERE: Paul. This was a great one of his.

YELLOW SUBMARINE: Both of us. Paul wrote the catchy chorus. I helped with the blunderbuss bit.

SHE SAID, SHE SAID: I wrote it after meeting Peter Fonda, who said he knew what it was like to be dead.

GOOD DAY SUNSHINE: Paul. But I think maybe I helped him with some of the lyric.

FOR NO ONE: Paul. Another of his I really liked.

AND YOUR BIRD CAN SING: Me. Another horror.

GOT TO GET YOU INTO MY LIFE: Paul. I think George and I helped with some of the lyric. I'm not sure.

TOMORROW NEVER KNOWS: Me. This was my first psychedelic song.

PENNY LANE: Paul. I helped him with the lyric.

A LITTLE HELP FROM MY FRIENDS: Paul. It was Paul's idea. I think I helped with some of the words. In fact, I did. Hunter Davies was there when we did it and mentioned it in the book. "What do you see when you turn out the light. I can't tell you but I know it's mine." That was mine.

SHE'S LEAVING HOME: Both of us. Paul had the basic theme. But all those lines like "We sacrificed most of our life . . . We gave her everything that money could buy. Never a thought for ourselves"— those were the thing (Aunt) Mimi used to say. It was easy to write.

BEING FOR THE BENEFIT OF MR. KITE: Me. I got some of the words off an old circus poster. I have it in the billiard room. The story that Henry the Horse meant heroin was rubbish.

WHEN I'M SIXTY-FOUR: Paul. I think I helped Paul with some of the words, like "Vera, Chuck and Dave" and "Doing the garden, digging the weeds."

GOOD MORNING, GOOD MORNING: Me. A bit of gobbledygook one, but nice words.

DAY IN THE LIFE: Both of us. I wrote the bit on "woke up fell out of bed" and I think Paul wrote, "I'd love to turn you on." I got the idea from a news item in the British *Daily Mail* about 4,000 holes in Blackburn.

BABY YOU'RE A RICH MAN: Both of us. In fact we just stuck two songs together for this one—same as "A Day In The Life"

I AM THE WALRUS: Me—I like that one. That was the time when I was putting Hare Krishna and all that down. I hadn't taken it up then.

MAGICAL MYSTERY TOUR: Paul. I helped with some of the lyric.

HEY JUDE: Paul. That's his best song. It started off as a song about my son Julian because Paul was going to see him. Then he turned it into "Hey Jude." I always thought it was about me and Yoko, but he said it was about him and his.

REVOLUTION: Me. I should never have put that in about Chairman Mao. I was just finishing when I did that.

BACK IN THE U.S.S.R.: Paul. maybe I helped a bit, but I don't think so.

HAPPINESS IS A WARM GUN: Me. That's another one I like. They all said it was about drugs, but it was more about rock and roll than drugs. It's sort of a history of rock and roll. The title came from an American gun magazine. I don't know why people said it was about the needle in heroin. I've only seen somebody do something with a needle once, and I don't like to see it at all.

WHY DON'T WE DO IT IN THE ROAD: Paul—one of his best.

JULIA: Me. Yoko helped me with this one.

EVERYBODY'S GOT SOMETHING TO HIDE: Me. Fats Domino did a great version of this one.

SEXY SADIE: Me. That was about the Maharishi.

BECAUSE: Me. This is a terrible arrangement. A bit like Beethoven's Fifth backwards.

ACROSS THE UNIVERSE: Me. One of my best songs. Not one of the best recordings but I like the lyrics.

Originally appeared in *Hit Parader*
Charlton Publications

Richard Lester Remembers:

"**I**t was like being at the center of the universe!" Richard Lester recalls the exultation of that halcyon Spring of 1964 when he directed the Beatles in *A Hard Day's Night*. His expressive face achieves the tragi-comic contradictions of a Modigliani portrait as he thinks on the past in his offices at the very same Twickenham Studios just outside London where much of the film was shot.

"I still don't know how we did it," he marvels seventeen years later. "The normal schedule is about ten to fifteen weeks. We shot the film in seven, cut it in two and a half. All this with the attendant problem of trying to film the Beatles in the streets. In seconds there would be 10,000 children, popping out of traps like a pantomime.

"If we didn't get the focus right, we'd have to do it another day, at another location. There was no time for rehearsal or to make normal mistakes."

Somewhere, a mature Beatles fan has in his or her possession a can of original film footage from the train platform scene of *A Hard Day's Night*. The boy loading up the film cans was young and about the same height and wore his hair the same as the Beatles. "He was walking off the train with a pile of film and suddenly this screaming started and he looked and he was being attacked and he had to throw the film at them to escape with his skin."

Another moment of enthusiasm gone wild was at the Scala Theater in London. Fans had brought hacksaws and cut through the iron bars of the door and attacked the crew on the stairs. Lester still shivers as he tells how he and his people beat them off using their Arriflex with a tripod that had little spikes. "We held it up as a defensive weapon because, literally, we would have been swept off those iron stairs and would easily have been killed. It was genuinely frightening."

It's difficult to realize that the Beatles first movie was perceived by most industry people at the time as just another rock and roll exploitation quickie to be produced as cheaply as possible for the fastest and widest distribution before the madness of Beatlemania faded away.

"Beatlemania" was, in fact, one of the considered titles until John Lennon came up with "A Hard Day's Night."

The "Can't Buy Me Love" sequence has since become the subject of cinema seminars and rapt discussion groups whenever Beatles freaks gather. "It's

my feet, you know!" The director stops in mid-explanation of how the sequence was filmed in three different locations on three different days. "The fire escape was in one location with a little bit of field. The shot in slow motion and the messing about in the field was a second location. And the helicopter shot over that little cement square—if you look carefully, you'll see there's only three of them. Paul was out sick that day and I was wearing his shoes!"

What was so exuberant about that sequence was its contrast to the earlier sequences. Until that point in the script which merely says, "The boys play in a field," the film had a claustrophobic feeling to it, almost everything shot in enclosed spaces, a good part of it inspired by John's remarks on his return from Sweden.

"Did you like Sweden?" Lester had asked him.

"It was a room and a room and a car and a room and a room and a car..." Lennon had replied.

Lester had kept this feeling in mind during much of the filming until it was time for the Beatles to rebel. "We see them break out. We needed a visual example of that escape. Suddenly, the film opens up and that's really the point of 'Can't Buy Me Love'."

A case can be made for the genesis of that scene in the earlier Richard Lester (now) classic, *The Running, Jumping and Standing Still* film which was actually shot in one day in a field in North London. Every foot of film was used in the final edit and no scene was shot twice. Eleven minutes long with no discernible plot, the movie starred Peter Sellers and a number of his zany friends cavorting silent-movie style at breakneck speed with a vintage car and a two-handled saw until the earth opened and swallowed them up.

In fact, that movie is credited as the reason the Beatles movie producer Walter Shenson chose Richard Lester as director. An odd choice in retrospect. Philadelphia-born with no background of Liverpool or the culture that spawned the Beatles, known professionally for making over 350 television commercials, it was nevertheless one of those happy accidents that when Shenson asked him what he thought about the Beatles, "it turned out that I had worked with people who knew them and that Alun Owen and I had even gone to Paris to see them."

Retrospectively, was there anything Dick Lester would have done differently in terms of the music and the actual making of *A Hard Day's Night*?

The BEATLES "A HaRD DaY's NiGHT"

Lester considers this and then replies, "I wouldn't have thought so. It's interesting how films come about. We set a fairly strict set of parameters of what we did want to do, what we didn't want to do, what we didn't want to repeat. We made a fictionalized documentary examining their work and their life. We had to make them prisoners of their own story. Or, as John said, 'I'm an extra in my own film'.

"It was an extraordinary time for me. Later, *How I Won the War* was a reflection of the pessimism that had taken over the world in 1967 just as the two Beatles films and *The Knack* were an earlier reflection of that small moment of optimism, the sense of possibilities that people felt—certainly in Britain—that the class structure was once and for all destroyed. And, of course, it wasn't. It was a false dawn."

Often referred to during the mid-Sixties as "The Intellectual Beatle," Richard Lester mourns the death of that optimism in music as well as in film. "What the Beatles gave us was the sense that it didn't matter where you came from, how you spoke, whether you were educated. If you wanted to go out and do it, you could do it all on your own without any help from 'The Establishment,' from your elders...

"That sense of optimism was enormous. When it arrived in America, I suspect that it had so many Union Jacks planted on it that people thought everything was great if it's English. It certainly gave the young people in Britain a sense of false security. All that happened is that once that generation dissipated itself and became adult like everyone else, they moved along the comb of history."

Richard Lester's place in film history is secure. He made the rock and roll movie respectable and, to some critics, an art. "All I did was shift the camera in time with the music," he insists.

Living with his wife and two children in the English countryside, Richard Lester rarely visits London, and can't remember his last trip to America. He listens to almost no popular music. "Mine is now a totally traditional movement starting with the Impressionists and going into the 19th Century German romanticism and then to Beethoven and then back to Bach."

A saturnine smile and a glance at his watch point out that he must hurry to catch a plane for Oslo. "I will end up as an old man trying to swallow a bit of pate´and a glass of sauterne while listening to Mozart. After all," he pauses for effect, "the players are secondary to the music."

—Jeannie Sakol

A HARD DAY'S NIGHT

	B & W
Date filmed:	**March–April 1964 in England**
World Premiere:	**July 6, 1964 — London**
N.Y. Premiere:	**August 11, 1964**
Length:	**87 minutes**
Screen Play:	**Alun Owen**
Director:	**Richard Lester**
Producer:	**Walter Shenson**
Distributor:	**United Artists**
Stars:	**The Beatles, Wilfrid Brambell, Norman Rossington, Victor Spinetti**

A day in the life. The Beatles ham it up in their first full-length feature film with brilliant direction, sight gags and camera tricks (shifting the angle of the camera to the beat of the music) by Richard Lester. The title first appeared in Lennon's book of nonsense stories *In His Own Write*. Eight songs include: "I Should Have Known Better," "I Love Her," and the title tune. *A Hard Day's Night* has only the barest of plot lines: the Beatles prepare for a TV-concert while hampered by over-zealous fans and an off-the-wall grandfather. They travel by train; try to avoid mobs of screaming teenagers; pose and mug for photographers; give a tongue-in-cheek press conference; record in the studio and play a concert that ends the movie. Favorite moments: George refuses to wear shirts peddled by a hustler, saying, "They're dead *grotty*," and Ringo's riverside conversation with a hooky-playing schoolboy. *A Hard Day's Night* is a joyful and zany romp, fueled by the charm and engagingly innocent manner of the Fab Four.

HELP!

	Color
Date filmed:	February-May 1965 in London, the Bahamas, and Austria
World Premiere:	July 29, 1965 in London
N.Y. Premiere:	August 23, 1965
Length:	90 minutes
Screenplay:	Marc Behm & Charles Wood
Director:	Richard Lester
Producer:	Walter Shenson
Distributor:	United Artists
Stars:	The Beatles, Leo McKern, Eleanor Bruin, Victor Spinetti

The Beatles are chased by an Indian cult desperate to capture a sacrificial ring—which happens to be on Ringo's finger. More fun, more chase scenes, camera gimmickery, madcap ad-libbing, slapstick and infectious humor. The movie is enlivened by seven new songs, including "Ticket to Ride," "I Need You," "You're Gonna Lose That Girl," and of course, John's beautiful rendition of the title song. The fantasy adventure which takes them from the Caribbean to the Alps, casts the Beatles as "themselves." There are no concert scenes and by being cast as "players" in their own movie, the Beatles are at times overshadowed by the exotic backdrops, as John said, "It was like having clams in a movie about frogs." Favorite scene: The Beatles on skis for the first time in the Alps.

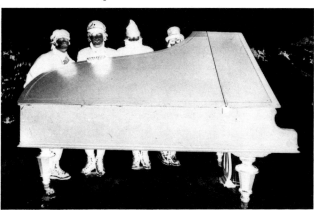

MAGICAL MYSTERY TOUR

	Color
Date filmed:	September-October 1967
World Premiere:	(Made for TV—b&w) December 26, 1967 (BBC-1 TV)
Length:	60 minutes
Screenplay:	—none—
Director:	The Beatles
Producer:	The Beatles
Distributor:	Apple Films 1967
Stars:	The Beatles, Bonzo Dog Doo Dah Band, Mal Evans (roadie), Mike McGear (Paul's brother), Beatles Fan Club secretaries, extras, and technical crew

The first and last all-and-only Beatles production, *Magical Mystery Tour* was mainly directed by Paul and Ringo, though each of the Beatles conceived and starred in different short (and often impromptu) segments. Their press release stated: "Away in the sky, beyond the clouds, live four or five magicians. By casting Wonderful Spells they turn the Most Ordinary Coach Trip in to a Magical Mystery Tour..." Paul's concept for an "improvised" movie chronicling the adventures of the Magical Mystery Tour bus is basically a fanciful and expensively-produced home movie. The film was not a critical success when first shown, partially because it was conceived for theatrical release, and the film was instead shown on tiny British TV screens, the first time in black and white. Songs on the Magical Mystery Tour album include: "Blue Jay Way," starring Ringo's dog Tiger; Paul's solo filmed in Nice, France; and John at the height of psychedelia in "I Am The Walrus." Magical Mystery Tour was never officially released in America and is rarely shown.

YELLOW SUBMARINE

	Color
Date filmed:	1968
World Premiere:	July 17, 1968 (London)
N.Y. Premiere:	November 13, 1968
Length:	85 minutes
Screenplay:	Lee Minoff, Al Brodax, Jack Mendelsohn, Erich Segal
Director:	George Dunning
Producer:	Al Brodax
Animation	Heinz Edelmann
Distributor:	United Artists
Stars:	starring the Fab Four in cartoons; The real Beatles make an appearance in the final sequence.

The Blue Meanies (who hate color, and everything for that matter) invade Pepperland where all is music, color and love. A host of fanciful animated figures (including of course the Beatles) appears in this lighthearted and witty pop fantasy. The Beatles had virtually no hand in the film's production or script. The voices were those of professional actors. The Beatles do appear in a scene at the end. The four new songs in the movie were actually leftovers from the time of *Magical Mystery Tour.* George Martin, the Beatles producer, orchestrated his own compositions for the soundtrack. The strength of the film lies in the dazzling technique of the visuals; over 5 million separate sketches were made. A pop version of *Fantasia.*

LET IT BE

	Color
Date filmed:	January 2-30, 1969
World Premiere:	May 20, 1970
N.Y. Premiere:	May 18, 1970
Length:	88 minutes
Screenplay:	———
Director:	Michael Lindsay-Hogg
Producer:	Neil Aspinal
Distributor:	United Artists
Stars:	The Beatles

An inside look at the making of the *Get Back — Let It Be* album, and documentary of the last days of the Beatles as a group, in the studio and their final concert. To fulfill their contract to United Artists for a third movie (the animated *Yellow Submarine* was not acceptable), the actual filming took only three weeks. The director, Michael Lindsay-Hogg, had previously worked with the Beatles on promotional films for "Paperback Writer," "Revolver," and "Hey Jude." The Beatles said *Let It Be* shows them with "all their warts." Tension among the four is sadly obvious, though the famous jam of "Get Back" on a rooftop in London's famed Savile Row stopped traffic and is a testament to the Beatles' enduring ability to make great music and move our hearts.

CONTRIBUTION—Music

THE FAMILY WAY

Music by:	Paul McCartney
World Premiere:	December 18, 1966 (London)
N.Y. Premiere:	June 28, 1967
Length:	115 minutes
Screenplay:	Bill Naughton
From:	Bill Naughton's play *All in Good Time*
Director:	John & Ray Boulting
Producer:	John & Ray Boulting
Distributor:	Warner Brothers

CONTRIBUTION—Music

WONDERWALL

Music by:	George Harrison
World Premiere:	May 17, 1968 (Cannes Film Festival)
London Premiere:	January 20, 1969
Length:	92 minutes
Screenplay:	G. Cain
From:	a story by Gerard Brach
Director:	Joe Massot
Producer:	Andrew Braunsberg
Distributor:	Cinecenta

CONTRIBUTION—Acting

HOW I WON THE WAR

Featuring:	John Lennon as Musketeer Gripweed
Date Filmed:	September-October 1966
World Premiere:	October 18, 1967 (London)
N.Y. Premiere:	November 8, 1967
Length:	109 minutes
Screenplay:	Charles Wood
From:	a novel by Patrick Ryan
Director:	Richard Lester
Producer:	Richard Lester
Distributor:	United Artists

CONTRIBUTION—Acting

CANDY

Featuring:	Ringo as Emmanuel the Gardener
Date Filmed:	November-December, 1967
World Premiere:	February 20, 1969
N.Y. Premiere:	December 17, 1968
Length:	119 minutes
Screenplay:	Buck Henry
From:	a novel by Terry Southern & Mason Hoffenberg
Director:	Christian Marquand
Producer:	Robert Hagglas
Distributor:	Cinerama Releasing Corp.

CONTRIBUTION—Acting

ROCK 'N' ROLL CIRCUS

Featuring:	John Lennon and Yoko Ono
Date Filmed:	December 11, 1968

Never Commercially released

Producer:	Michael Lindsay-Hogg

CONTRIBUTION—Acting

THE MAGIC CHRISTIAN

Featuring:	Ringo Starr as Youngman Grand
Date Filmed:	March-May, 1969
World Premiere:	December 12, 1969 (London)
N.Y. Premiere:	February 11, 1970
Length:	92 minutes
Screenplay:	Terry Southern, Joseph McGrath and Peter Sellers
From:	a novel by Terry Southern
Director:	Joseph McGrath
Producer:	Dennis O'Dell
Distributor:	Commonwealth United Films

PROMOTIONAL FILMS

1964:	*A Hard Day's Night* Featurette—Behind-the-scenes of the Beatles' first movies.
1967:	*Penny Lane*—A first view of the psychedelic Beatles.
1967:	*Strawberry Fields Forever*—Beginning the Sgt. Pepper era.
1968:	*A Mod Odyssey*—A colorful look at the making of *Yellow Submarine*.
1969:	*Cold Turkey*—TV spot put together by John & Yoko, with scenes of their Bed-ins for peace.

PERFORMANCES ON FILM

1962:	*Cavern Club*—A rare look at the Beatles' early days in Liverpool.
1963:	London Palladium, October 13, 1963—Birth of Beatlemania—broadcast live in the U.K. "*The Beatles Come to Town*".
1964:	*The Jack Paar Show*, January 3, 1964—Paar showed the very first film (taped from an English concert of the Beatles one month before the live Ed Sullivan concert.
1964:	Washington Coliseum, February 11, 1964—The first U.S. Beatle concert. It ends abruptly because the lone cameraman ran out of film.
1964:	*The Ed Sullivan Show,* February 9, 1964—Live from New York February 16, 1964—From Miami February 23, 1964 73 million viewers for the 1st segment. Sullivan was the first to present the Beatles "live" on national network TV.
1964:	*Around the Beatles*—Live English TV show. Includes the song "Shout," which was never released.
1965:	Beatles at Shea Stadium, August 15, 1965, 50 minutes—Produced by Sid Bernstein, with a chorus of 60,000 screaming fans. World Premiere: May 1, 1966 (BBC-TV)
1968:	"Hey Jude"—Rehearsal, Summer 1968—In the recording studio with George Martin
1968:	"Hey Jude," Fall 1968—Live on the *David Frost Show*. The finest hour of the Beatles singing the 60's most popular songs. Shown with "Hey Jude" in America on the *Smothers Brothers Show*.
1968:	"Revolution" (Live version)—Also from the "Hey Jude" *David Frost Show*.